Succeeding At Your YAHOO!® Business

Frank Fiore
Linh Tang

800 East 96th Street
Indianapolis, Indiana 46240

Succeeding At Your Yahoo! Business

Copyright © 2006 by Que Publishing

All rights reserved. No part of this book shall be reproduced, stored in a retrieval system, or transmitted by any means, electronic, mechanical, photocopying, recording, or otherwise, without written permission from the publisher. No patent liability is assumed with respect to the use of the information contained herein. Although every precaution has been taken in the preparation of this book, the publisher and author assume no responsibility for errors or omissions. Nor is any liability assumed for damages resulting from the use of the information contained herein.

International Standard Book Number: 0-7897-3534-2

Library of Congress Catalog Card Number: 2006923768

Printed in the United States of America

First Printing: June 2006

09 08 07 06   4 3 2

Trademarks

All terms mentioned in this book that are known to be trademarks or service marks have been appropriately capitalized. Que Publishing cannot attest to the accuracy of this information. Use of a term in this book should not be regarded as affecting the validity of any trademark or service mark.

Warning and Disclaimer

Every effort has been made to make this book as complete and as accurate as possible, but no warranty or fitness is implied. The information provided is on an "as is" basis. The authors and the publisher shall have neither liability nor responsibility to any person or entity with respect to any loss or damages arising from the information contained in this book.

Permission has been granted by Y-Times Publications, LLC for use of tips and tricks found in Chapter Seven.

Bulk Sales

Que Publishing offers excellent discounts on this book when ordered in quantity for bulk purchases or special sales. For more information, please contact

    U.S. Corporate and Government Sales

    1-800-382-3419

    corpsales@pearsontechgroup.com

For sales outside of the U.S., please contact

    International Sales

    international@pearsoned.com

Associate Publisher
Greg Wiegand

Acquisitions Editor
Stephanie J. McComb

Development Editor
Kevin Howard

Managing Editor
Gina Kanouse

Project Editors
Kristy Hart
Dan Knott

Copy Editor
Krista Hansing

Indexer
Lisa Stumpf

Proofreader
Sheri Cain

Technical Editor
Lon S. Safko

Publishing Coordinator
Sharry Lee Gregory

Multimedia Developer
Dan Scherf

Book Designer
Anne Jones

Page Layout
FastPages

Contents at a Glance

Introduction

Part I: Yahoo! Store to the Next Level
1. Can You Make a Living from Your Yahoo! Store?
2. Plan to Succeed
3. Architecting Your Online Storefront

Part II: Customizing the Yahoo! Store
4. Storyboarding Your E-Commerce Site
5. Customizing Your Yahoo! Store
6. Yahoo! Store Features and Advanced Techniques
7. Yahoo! Store Tips and Tricks
8. Designing Your Customized Yahoo! Store to Sell

Part III: Deconstructing a Yahoo! Store
9. Digital Product Store
10. Manufactured Product Store
11. High-Volume Product Store

Part IV: Growing Your Online Business
12. The Power of PARM: Positioning Your Business
13. Acquiring Customers (Part 1)
14. Acquiring Customers (Part 2)
15. Retaining Customers
16. Monetizing
17. Monitoring Site Sales and Performance
18. Public Relations

Part V: Operating Your Yahoo! Business
19. Customer Service
20. Warehousing and Inventory Control
21. Financial Planning

Part VI: Manning Your Yahoo! Business
22. Finding and Hiring

Appendixes
- A. Launching Your Yahoo! Business Quick Start Guide
- B. Business Plan Elements
- C. Important Resources on the Web

Index

Table of Contents

Introduction xvi

Part I: **Yahoo! Store to the Next Level** 1

1 **Can You Make a Living from Your Yahoo! Store?** 3
    What Does a Virtual Business Involve? 4
    Important Areas to Consider 5
        Do You Really *Want* to Have a Full-Time Business? 5
        Are You Prepared to Hire a Staff of People to Help? 6
        Do You Have the Capital to Grow Your Business? 7
        Are You Prepared to Write That Formal Business Plan? 7
    Building a Professional E-Commerce Site for Success 8
        Branding 8
        Promotion 9
        Management and Operations 9
        Legalities and Funding 10

2 **Plan to Succeed** 11
    Choosing a Business Identity: Who R U? 12
        Licenses and Permits 13
    Establishing a Legal Identity 14
        Sole Proprietorship 15
        Partnership 15
        Incorporation 16
    Your Marketing Plan 17
        Product or Service Description 17
    Defining Your Market Segment: Targeting the Customer 19
        Customer Types 19
        Customer Motivations 19
    Describing the Competition 20
    Managing Your Business 21
        Your Organizational Structure 22
        Your Implementation Plan 22
    Detailing Your Capital Requirements 23
        Getting the Dough 24

3 **Architecting Your Online Storefront** 27
    Website Development Versus E-Commerce Site Development 28

		The Three Cs 29

The Three Cs 29
    Content: Turn Your Site into a Learning Fountain 29
    Community: Building an Interactive Community 33
Commerce: Adding Multiple Revenue Streams 34
Your USP: Unique Selling Position 35
    The Four Ps and Your USP 36
Pulling It All Together 37

Part II: Customizing the Yahoo! Store 39

4 Storyboarding Your E-Commerce Site 41

Storyboarding for Fun and Profit 42
    Major Navigation Elements 42
    Web Page Elements 43
    Web Page Content 44
    Your Storyboard Plot? 45
    Your Copy: Writing for the Web 45

The Most Important Pages of an E-Commerce Site 46
    The Home Page: Get Them Shopping Right Away 47
    About Us Page: Let Them Know Who You Are 49
    FAQ Page: The First Place Your Customers Turn To 49
    Full Contact Information: Address, Phone, Fax, Email 51
    Privacy Policy: Get on the Right Side of the FTC 51
    Customer Service/Customer Policies: The Full Cost of Shipping and
        Handling 52
    Product or Services Catalog Pages 53
    Online Press Room 53
    Content Pages 54
    Community Pages 54
    Site Map 54

5 Customizing Your Yahoo! Store 57

Why You Should Customize Your Store 58
When to Customize Your Store 61
Different Options for Customizing Your Store 63
    Adjusting Variables and Inserting Custom HTML Headers and
        Footers 63
    Inserting Custom HTML Headers and Footers 64
    Using Web Hosting to Customize Your Store 65
    Using RTML to Customize Your Store 66
Customize: Design It Yourself or Hire an Expert 68

6	**Yahoo! Store Features and Advanced Techniques** 71
	Advanced Store-Layout Options and Ideas 72
	Advanced Store-Navigation Options and Ideas 77
	Advanced Promotional Options and Ideas 81
	Advanced Search Engine Options and Ideas 86
	Creating Product Pages Using Database Upload 87
	Uploading Multiple Images at Once 91
7	**Yahoo! Store Tips and Tricks** 93
	Enabling the Built-In Breadcrumbs 94
	Click to Enlarge 97
	Cascading Style Sheets 99
	Bestsellers 100
	Quantity Box 104
	Radio Button Options 106
	Free Forms (Email Form) 107
	List of On-Sale Items 109
	Related Items 110
	Text Page Titles 113
	Shipment Status Form 114
8	**Designing Your Customized Yahoo! Store to Sell** 117
	Eighteen Tips Every Yahoo! Store Owner Needs to Know 118
	Cross-Selling 118
	Up-selling: Offering Packaged Deals 118
	Using Colors to Make Your Important Information Stand Out 118
	Getting Visitors to Click the Buy Button 119
	Considering What Visitors See and Don't See 119
	Implementing Tell-a-Friend 119
	Adding Special Offers 120
	Designing Above the Fold 120
	Customizing the Shopping Cart Page 120
	Considering Product Positioning 121
	Getting Them to Return 121
	Creating the Page So It's Printable 122
	Formatting Your Content Copy 122
	Managing Content Flow 122
	Creating a Professional-Looking Website 122
	Performing Usability Testing 122

		Adding Product Guarantees 123
		Adding Credibility 123
		You're Not Done Designing Yet 124
		Eight Design Pitfalls You Need to Avoid 124
		Don't Make Your Visitors Think 124
		Don't Make Them Guess Where They're Going 125
		Avoid Shopping Cart Abandonment 125
		Avoid Content Overload 125
		Avoid Sending Your Visitors to Your Competitors 126
		Avoid Changing the Location of Your Main Navigation 126
		Avoid Graphic Overload 127
		Avoid Using Technology That Users Need Plug-Ins For 127
		Fifty-One Words That Sell 127
Part III:		**Deconstructing a Yahoo! Store** **129**
	9	**Digital Product Store** **131**
		General Company Information 133
		Product Information 133
		How Do Digital Products Work? 133
		How to Upload a Digital Product 134
		Pros and Cons of Selling Digital Products 136
		Selling Both Mac and PC Platform File Formats 136
		The Evolution of WriteExpress's Website Design 137
		Testing Your Site Design Effectiveness 140
		Marketing 141
		Additional Tips from WriteExpress 141
	10	**Manufactured Product Store** **143**
		General Company Information 145
		Product Information 145
		Website Layout and Advanced Features 145
		Product Package Deals 147
		Adding Credibility Banners 148
		Testimonials 149
		Website Development 150
		Outsourcing 151
		Outsourcing Your 1-800 Customer Service 151
		Back-End System 151

		Online and Offline Marketing Strategies 152
		Email Marketing—Newsletter 152
		Using eBay 153
		Pay-Per-Click Marketing 153
		Print Marketing 154
		Television Commercial Marketing 154
		Affiliate Marketing 154
		Tips and Recommendations from Owner Craig Abbey 155
	11	**High-Volume Product Store** **157**
		General Company Information 158
		Product Information 158
		Website Layout and Advanced Features 158
		Creating Multiple Website Niches with the Same Product Line 164
		Managing Multiple Websites 166
		Neeps Back-End System 166
		About OrderMotion 167
		Accounting 168
		Setting Up Your Warehouse and Bin Location System 168
		Shipping and Packaging 171
		Negotiating Shipping Cost 171
		Online and Offline Marketing Strategies 171
		Print Advertising 171
		Pay-Per-Click Advertising 172
		Affiliate Marketing 172
		Email Marketing 172
		Creating Repeat Customers 172
Part IV:		**Growing Your Online Business** **175**
	12	**The Power of PARM: Positioning Your Business** **177**
		The Power of PARM 178
		Positioning Your Business 179
		The Alphabet of Branding: USP, ESP, OSP, and BSD 180
		Underpromise and Overdeliver 182
		Tips for Online Branding 183
		Branding with the Big 5 185
	13	**Acquiring Customers (Part 1)** **187**
		Watering-Hole Marketing 188
		What's Your Marketing Goal? 189

	Advertising 190
	The Language of Net Advertising 191
	Common Advertising Vehicles 192
	Email Marketing. 194
	Best Practices of Permission Marketing 195
	Choosing a Proper Opt-In Email List 197
	Internal Marketing. 199
14	**Acquiring Customers (Part 2)** **203**
	Using Search Engines for Marketing 204
	Getting Listed at the Search Engines and Directories 205
	Search-Engine Optimization 207
	Make Your Site Spider-Friendly 208
	Top 10 Tips to Increase Link Popularity 209
	Search-Engine Marketing 210
	Choosing Appropriate Search Terms 212
	Writing Titles and Descriptions 214
	Ensuring Relevancy 215
	Microsites 217
15	**Retaining Customers** **219**
	The Importance of Retention 220
	Building a House List 221
	Registration Page Basics 223
	Subscribe and Unsubscribe Tips 226
	Steps to Email Marketing Success 227
	1. Test Your Subject Line 228
	2. Test Your "From" Lines 228
	3. Test Your Headlines 228
	4. Test Your Offer 229
	5. Test Your Response Options 229
	6. Test Text Versus HTML 230
	7. Test Your Links 230
	Additional Email Tips 230
	Succeeding with Email Newsletters 231
	News Versus Promotion 232
	Format Considerations 232
	Using Community as Retention 234
	Discussion Boards 235
	Chat Rooms 235
	Discussion Lists 236

16 Monetizing 239
- Creating Home Pages That Sell 240
  - Shoppus Interruptus: Losing the Sale 241
  - Other Ways to Increase Revenue 243
- Avoiding Fraud 244
  - Protecting Your Business from Credit Card Fraud 245

17 Monitoring Site Sales and Performance 249
- Mining Your Server Logs 250
  - Advertising and Promotion 251
  - Improving Your Value Proposition 251
  - Optimizing Your Navigation 251
  - Calculating Your Close Ratio 252
- Using Yahoo! Site Stats Resources 252
  - Viewing Web Hosting Site Statistics 254
  - Viewing Store Editor Statistics 256
  - Deconstructing a Statscounter Report 258

18 Public Relations 265
- What Is Public Relations? 266
  - The Importance of the Press Release 266
- The Online Press Room 267
  - Constructing Your Online Press Room 268
- Constructing the Press Release 269
  - Where to Send Your Press Release 272
- Outsourcing Your Public Relations 272

Part V: Operating Your Yahoo! Business 273

19 Customer Service 275
- Service Starts Before the Sale 276
- Service During the Sale 278
- Service After the Sale 280
- Follow-Up After the Sale 282
- Many Happy Returns 282
  - Handling Disgruntled Customers 283

20 Warehousing and Inventory Control 285
- Setting Up Your Warehouse 286
  - Getting Help 287
- Inventory Control 287
  - Setting Up Inventory Management 288

		Setting Inventory Levels 289

        Setting Inventory Levels 289
            Setting Inventory Levels for Product Options 290
        Just-in-Time Delivery: Saving Money on Storage 293
        Using UPS Online Tools to Streamline Your Shipping Process 293
        Packaging Tips 295

21 Financial Planning 297

        The Proforma 298
            Where to Start 299
        Organizing Your Financial Statements 301
            Creating Your Income Statement 302
            Creating Your Cash Flow Statement 302
            Creating Your Balance Sheet 304
        Quick Steps to Creating Your Financials 305

Part VI: Manning Your Yahoo! Business 309

22 Finding and Hiring 311

        Assigning and Understanding Staff Duties 312
        Outsourcing 313
        Independent Contractor Versus Employee 314
        The Hiring Process 314
        Hiring the Right Person 315
        Where to Find and Hire Employees 316
        Interviewing Candidates 316
        Screening Backgrounds and Checking References 317
        Hiring Family and Friends 318
        How Much Should I Pay?: Setting Pay Levels 319
        Getting Part-Time Help 320
        Getting Free Help 321
        Keeping Good Employees 321

Appendixes 323

A Launching Your Yahoo! Business Quick Start Guide 325

        Step 1: Register your domain name and sign up for a Yahoo!
            Merchant Solutions account. 325
        Step 2: Explore the Manage My Services control panel. 326

	Step 3: Set up the capability to accept payments online. Sign up for a merchant account or use your existing merchant account.	326
	Step 4: Organize and add products to your store.	326
	Step 5: Customize your store layout and navigation.	327
	Step 6: Configure your backend systems and operations.	327
	Step 7: Publish your site; open your store for business.	327
B	**Business Plan Elements**	**329**
	Who Is Your Business?	329
	What Does It Sell?	330
	Why Is It a Business? What Need Does It Solve?	330
	What Is the Implementation Plan?	331
	Where Is Your Business and What Markets/Customers Will It Service?	331
	How Will You Market Your Business and Your Product or Service?	331
	How Much Money Will You Need to Get Your Business Started and Running?	332
	Pulling It Together: The Business Plan Elements	332
C	**Important Resources on the Web**	**335**
	Yahoo! Store Resources	335
	Deconstructing Yahoo! Store Participants	337
	Email Discussion Lists	337
	E-Business Publications	339
	Employment Websites	341
	Press Release Distribution Services	342
	Mailing List Resources	342
	Financial Resources	343
	Web Analysis Tools and Services	343
	General Resources	344
	Index	**349**

About the Authors

Frank Fiore is an acknowledged e-business expert and accomplished author of six e-business books that have sold more than 50,000 copies. These include *2005 Online Shopping Directory For Dummies* (John Wiley & Sons, 2004), *Successful Affiliate Marketing for Merchants* (Pearson Education, 2001), *e-Marketing Strategies* (Pearson Education, 2000), *The Complete Idiot's Guide to Starting an Online Business* (Alpha, 2000), *Dr. Livingston's Online Shopping Safari Guidebook* (Maximum Press, 1996), *Tech TV's Starting an Online Business* (Pearson Education, 2001), and *How to Succeed in Sales Using Today's Technology* (Tom Hopkins International, 2003). His most recent book from Que Publishing is *Write a Business Plan in No Time* (2005). Frank was the online shopping guide for About.com and is a prolific writer of e-business features on InformIT.com. In addition to his writing endeavors, he has appeared on numerous TV and radio talk shows to discuss online shopping and the future of e-commerce, and he teaches college-level courses on e-business at Western International University. Frank lives in Paradise Valley, Arizona, with his wife and their Scottish sheepdog.

Linh Tang is an award-winning Web designer, a certified search engine optimizer, and an e-marketing expert. Linh has been designing websites since 1995 and developing Yahoo! stores since 2000. He is the founder of Beyond Ideas, LLC (www.beyondideas.com), an Internet development and marketing consulting company, and cofounder of Paper Models, Inc., both based in San Diego, California. Some of his clients include Fortune 100 companies and government organizations. Linh has a proven track record of increasing companies' Web traffic and online sales.

Dedication

To my wife, Lynne, who provides a loving environment of support for my writing endeavors.—F. F.

To my son, Tristan, and wife, Cathy. Thank you for your support and encouragements.—L. T.

Acknowledgments

We would like to acknowledge two very special people who helped make this book a success. We would like to personally thank Lon S. Safko, who was our technical editor for these two Yahoo! Success books with Que Publishing, whose insights and experience in business, Internet marketing, and e-commerce complimented our skill sets to produce the best book we could hope for. We also are in debt to the valuable contribution of Paul Boisvert, senior technical content producer at Yahoo!, for reviewing the manuscript for Yahoo! store accuracy.

Thanks, guys, you were a great help in keeping us on the technical straight and narrow.

Also, a big thank you to Joe Palko, CEO of Solid Cactus; Scott Sanfilippo, president of Neeps, Inc.; Craig Clark, owner of Pacific Pillows; and Robert Stevens, owner of WriteExpress for letting us deconstruct their websites. Your insight and experience will surely help our readers become successful Yahoo! store owners.

To Istvan Siposs and Michael Whitaker, with Y-Times Publications, for contributing Yahoo! store tips and tricks, and Melissa Sobel from Yahoo! who helped market this book and its companion, *Launching Your Yahoo! Business*. A special thanks to Stephanie McComb, our acquisitions editor at Que, who believed in this project and made sure that it saw the light of day, and Kevin Howard, whose help was invaluable in developing the book for sale.

We Want to Hear from You!

As the reader of this book, *you* are our most important critic and commentator. We value your opinion and want to know what we're doing right, what we could do better, what areas you'd like to see us publish in, and any other words of wisdom you're willing to pass our way.

As an associate publisher for Que Publishing, I welcome your comments. You can email or write me directly to let me know what you did or didn't like about this book—as well as what we can do to make our books better.

Please note that I cannot help you with technical problems related to the topic of this book. We do have a User Services group, however, where I will forward specific technical questions related to the book.

When you write, please be sure to include this book's title and author as well as your name, email address, and phone number. I will carefully review your comments and share them with the author and editors who worked on the book.

Email: feedback@quepublishing.com

Mail: Greg Wiegand
Associate Publisher
Que Publishing
800 East 96th Street
Indianapolis, IN 46240 USA

Reader Services

Visit our website and register this book at www.quepublishing.com/register for convenient access to any updates, downloads, or errata that might be available for this book.

Introduction

Back in the 1960s, it was said that opinions were like Volkswagens: Everybody had one. Fast-forward 40 years to today. When it comes to the future of e-commerce, it's no different. It seems everyone is trying to sell something on the Internet. But what about the facts?

Some day, in the early part of the twenty-first century, the e-commerce landscape will contain either hundreds of thousands of e-commerce sites or just a few Wal-Mart–type sites competing for the attention and dollars of online consumers. As attractive as it might be to think that Wal-Mart will rule the Internet, as it seems to rule any community where it sets up shop, it just ain't gonna happen. This includes current Goliaths like Amazon.

Consumers like choices. They enjoy their *personal freedom to choose*. To think that they would sheepishly allow one merchant to fill all their needs is whistling in the dark.

Okay, then. What will the future of shopping online look like?

What was it that Dennis Hopper said? "The '90s are gonna make the '60s look like the '50s"? We're past the '90s now, but the thinking still applies. We've had a resurgence of "retro" these last several years, and the Net is adding its own line to Hopper's quote. The Internet will make the recent turn of this century look more like the turn of the last. This will add up to a resurgence of the nineteenth century, but this time on a global scale.

In short, we're becoming a planet of shopkeepers. That will change the face of e-commerce. Fueling this change is Yahoo!, which is paving the way to the future of consumer choice with the Yahoo! store program.

Now, making money to augment your income using a part–time e-commerce business is not easy. Making an entire living from your online business is even more difficult. Making money on the Net is *not* easy. To paraphrase an old investment quote, if you want to make a small fortune in e-commerce, start with a large one. Just look at the many dot-bombs that have crashed and burned over the last four or five years.

Why is it so difficult to make a living online?

There are a variety of reasons, and they come in all sizes. There's the cost of building and maintaining a full-blown e-commerce site. Web servers, database servers, email servers, and a host of software applications are only the start of long laundry list of expense items. Then, there are the personnel—programmers, Web designers, IT specialists, businesses developers, marketers, and customer service and warehouse people. Finally, there's warehousing and shipping the products themselves. The money needed to run a successful online business flows like a river: You need money to create it, maintain it, and then advertise and promote it.

This is where the Yahoo! store program can help.

The Yahoo! stores have grown into one of the largest online shopping destinations on the Web today. The nearly 20,000 Yahoo! stores have a 71% reach among online consumers, the highest on the Web. In May 2005, there were 21,317 searches for the phrase "Yahoo! store," according to Yahoo! search marketing. Many of these stores have become so successful that they have grown from small "mom and pop" or part-time businesses to full-time businesses.

When a business becomes a full-time operation, a whole new set of skills and knowledge is needed to operate a Yahoo! store like a true e-commerce business. This book gives part-time business owners that advanced skill set and knowledge so they can customize their Yahoo! stores and move to the next level of making a living from a Yahoo! store.

A small to medium-size business can save thousands of dollars in programming and marketing costs by building on and customizing an existing Yahoo! store. Yahoo! provides a booklet with instructions on how to market a Yahoo! store, but it is very limited. The booklet also doesn't provide strategies, tips, or comprehensive marketing tools to grow a Yahoo! store into a full-time business. Although it offers basic customization instructions, it does not cover advanced features for turning more visitors into customers.

This book shows you how to take the standard Yahoo! store to the next level by customizing the Yahoo! storefront to take full advantage of the successful e-commerce strategies and tactics in use today. In short, this book shows you how to set up and run a true full-time business.

Who Should Buy This Book

Unlike our first book, *Launching Your Yahoo! Business*, which was for those who wanted to dip their toe into the e-commerce ocean, this book is for a small to medium-size part-time business or a current full-time business that needs the skills and knowledge to set up and run a true full-time business and take advantage of the successful e-commerce strategies and tactics in use today.

You might already have a standard Yahoo! store and want to customize it and evolve it into a full-time business. Or you might have an online business idea and want to leap into the e-commerce water with both feet and create a full-time online business. Either way, this book can steer you in the right direction to succeed at making a living with the Yahoo! store program.

What's in This Book

First, this book informs the reader how to customize a Yahoo! store using the basic elements of the Yahoo! store Catalog Manager, including how to architect an e-commerce website. It then deconstructs three different types of Yahoo! stores, showing how they are formed and how they sell the products or services they offer. An entire section covers how to position a Yahoo! store, acquire customers, retain those customers, and monetize the traffic to the store. Finally, this book shows how to set up the necessary accounting and operations systems to successfully run a business, and how to acquire and hire the necessary staff.

Sidebars

In addition to the basic information in the text, *Succeeding at Your Yahoo! Business* includes several sidebars that include defined terms, tips, warnings, and directions to Web resources.

The "Yahoo! Talk" sidebar describes the different terms Yahoo! uses when describing its store technology and procedures. Understanding these terms will help you better comprehend the instructions and concepts in the text.

The "Warnings" sidebar alerts you to mistakes you might make when setting up and launching your Yahoo! store. By avoiding these mistakes or misunderstandings, you will be able to establish your Yahoo! store without having to repeat steps or make time-consuming changes.

The "Tips" sidebar helps you set up, launch, and manage your Yahoo! store in a more efficient manner and helps you save time and money.

The "Web Resources" sidebar points you to valuable resources on the World Wide Web that will help you manage and market your Yahoo! store.

Finally, we have established a website at www.myecommercesuccess.com to inform you of the latest developments in the Yahoo! store. The Net moves fast; to stay ahead of the game, you need to keep up-to-date on not only the new developments with Yahoo! store but also the newest development in e-commerce. We suggest that you visit our website frequently. In addition, throughout this book, you will see sidebars labeled "Free Informative Article" that offer free valuable articles on the My E-Commerce Success website for you to download after you register on the website. You can register by visiting www.myecommercesuccess.com and using the ISBN 0-7897-3534-2 of this book. Besides the free articles referenced in the "Free Informative Article" sidebars, we offer a periodic *eCommerce Management Newsletter* on managing and marketing your e-commerce storefront to keep you abreast of the latest developments in e-commerce.

Let's get started and let a *thousand shopkeepers bloom!*

Part I

Yahoo! Store to the Next Level

1 Can You Make a Living from Your Yahoo! Store?
2 Plan to Succeed
3 Architecting Your Online Storefront

CHAPTER 1

Can You Make a Living from Your Yahoo! Store?

In This Chapter

- What a virtual business entails
- Important things to consider when deciding on a full-time business
- Building a professional e-commerce site for success

For a small entrepreneur, the true test of succeeding in the world of e-commerce is whether you can make a living at it. Some have done well with a small part-time Yahoo! Store (especially if they followed the advice in our first book, *Launching Your Yahoo! Business* [Que, 2006]). Others have a physical (brick-and-mortar) business that is already successful and provides a full-time living but does not have an online presence (clicks) to extend that success (bricks and clicks).

If you're in either one of these camps—and we assume that you are because you purchased this book—it's decision time. Are you ready to quit that full-time job and take the risks incurred in building a professional real-time business? If you have a storefront in the physical world, do you know what it takes to offer, market, and fulfill orders for merchandise and requests for services online?

What Does a Virtual Business Involve?

If you believe the hype of an Internet business on TV and in the print media, you think that all e-commerce entrepreneurs are multimillionaires. You've probably seen testimonials like this:

> It's like having my own "Internet vending machine" making money for me while I watch TV, play with my kids, vacation. . .even while I sleep!" —Alice Mitchell, satisfied customer of *Click & Grow Rich*

Well, folks, it's just not that easy. As in any business venture, succeeding in e-commerce takes work—lots of work, and lots of sweat, to boot. Creating a successful business online has about the same odds of succeeding at creating a business in the physical world. More often than not, those businesses fail. In addition, starting an e-commerce venture and being successful at it offers a whole new set of challenges. Running an online business is not easy. If you are operating a part-time business online, you are aware of this fact.

Free Info Download the free informative article "Flying Under the Radar" at www.myecommerce success.com.

True, if you are successful, many of the challenges of a physical business are not present in a virtual business. You don't need to spend money on expensive brick and mortar. Your store is open 24 hours a day and 7 days a week, internationally. The need for actual salespeople is dramatically reduced or eliminated. If you drop-ship your products from a distributor or manufacturer, you don't need a lot of warehouse space.

That doesn't mean a virtual business is all wine and roses. You might not pay rent for a physical storefront, but you need to pay someone to host your store's website. Those salespeople you don't need are replaced by customer service reps answering questions on the phone and responding to emails. As for customer service, that is even more important and will take up more of your time than a physical storefront.

It all comes down to this: You can make your online business succeed, but it takes work.

> **tip Sourcing Products**
>
> A great resource for products to buy at wholesale prices is Wholesale World (www.wholesale-world.us). You'll find an extensive list of wholesale-supply companies in many popular product categories. The company also offers helpful advice on how to buy goods wholesale at www.wholesale-world.us/retailers.php, and maintains a list of manufacturers that are willing to drop-ship products at www.wholesale-world.us/drop-ship.php.

Important Areas to Consider

It goes without saying that running a full-time online business will take more time, more money, and more energy than you are expending now in your current business endeavors. Perhaps you established a Yahoo! store for "fun" or as a hobby, or to earn a little extra cash. Maybe you have dreams of becoming a successful entrepreneur and just dipped your toe into the e-commerce ocean to see if you liked it and could succeed. Or perhaps you've heard how you can use the Internet to expand your physical-world business beyond the limitations of your local market.

In any case, if you truly want to run a full-time business on the Net and have decided to control your own destiny, you should ask yourself the following questions.

Do You Really *Want* to Have a Full-Time Business?

Are you willing to drop other time-consuming activities, such as your full-time job, to do it? Do you have a passion for the business idea that you chose? One reason new businesses fail is that the owner lacks passion for his or her company vision. Like a strong passion, what was done for "just fun" or as a hobby will now be all-consuming. Your long days as an employee will seem short compared to the time needed to run a full-time business.

You must also consider your goals. What are they? To create a small family business with a decent income that will be passed on to your heirs? Or perhaps to use your business as an investment in the future, hoping to sell it to much larger company and retire early on the proceeds? Or do you have dreams of an IPO and seeing your company name up in lights on NASDAQ?

> **Web Resource**
>
> **Are You Suited to Own a Business?**
>
> Fill out the Business Challenge Questionnaire at www.avantrex.com/business/bizquest.html to see if you are really suited to own your own business. The Avantrex people will analyze your responses and contact you with their suggestions. The questionnaire takes only a few minutes.

If you have a service business, can its expansion actually hurt the business? Expanding or increasing the products you sell offers the security that you have control over the quality and quantity of your merchandise. But if you have a service business, will you be able to hire additional people who can provide the same level of service that your service company is currently known for? You need to hire not just any people to sell and ship your merchandise, but hire the *right* people to maintain your high level of service.

Are You Prepared to Hire a Staff of People to Help?

Up to this point, you might have had family members or friends help you "on the side" with your part-time business. But a full-time business has *employees*, not family and friends. That means taking on an entirely new set of responsibilities, including hiring, payroll, and tax collecting. Don't forget the laundry list of local, state, and federal government rules and regulations that pertain to running a full-time business: withholding and unemployment taxes, Medicare and Social Security withholdings, and a host of government rules and safety regulations. Of course, if you have the budget for it, you can outsource many of these duties. For a small part-time and even full-time business, however, that option can get expensive.

Hiring people can have both a positive and negative effect on your business (see Chapter 22, "Finding and Hiring"): positive if you hire the right people, negative if you don't. Up to this point, you were probably the CEO, buyer, marketing manager, and customer service rep all rolled into one. But if you expand your business to full-time and it succeeds, you will need to hire people to replace you in those responsibilities. If you choose the wrong people, your business can suffer; worse yet, you could find yourself having to micro-manage every aspect of your company instead of doing your job of growing the business.

Do You Have the Capital to Grow Your Business?

Growing a business takes money. That little space in the corner of your house or basement that you used as your office will not do if you plan to go "big time." You'll need a real office away from the house and any and all distractions. You might consider, as a start, one of the many business centers available today where you can rent a separate office space but use the shared secretarial and receptionist services, have access to office machines, and even have the use of a conference room.

You'll also need to consider other overhead costs, such as warehouse space, advertising and marketing costs (marketing on the Internet is not free, although is can be lower in cost than in the brick-and-mortar world), and professional expenses if you plan to use an accounting service to track and manage your growing business. If you plan to take your existing small business online, you have a whole new set of cost considerations, such as creating a customized online store that reflects your current business, hosting your website, managing your database and inventory, and providing top-notch customer service in a virtual world. That's not even mentioning the challenges of search-engine marketing, email marketing, and a host of other promotional tools.

Are You Prepared to Write That Formal Business Plan?

Now that your business has a track record, it's time to dust off your original business idea and assumptions, and compare them to reality. Don't believe that just because you took the time to lay out a business plan at the start of your business that you don't need to revisit it now that you have a successful part-time business under your belt. A business plan is a living, breathing document that is always in transition. You should update it periodically, especially if you plan to take your part-time business full-time or if you plan to venture into the virtual world with your physical-world business. Plan your work and work your plan.

You might find that new factors have entered the equation and that you must modify and flesh out your business plan. Remember, a business plan is not a destination, but a roadmap to success; it's a way to monitor your business assumptions and make changes to it along the way.

If you decide that establishing a full-time business will require additional capital, a formal business plan is necessary to approach funding sources for money, whether those sources are investors or a bank loan. That means complete financials, including a proforma, cash-flow and income statements, and a balance sheet. Even if you are not seeking funds, a proforma and cash-flow statement that are well thought out will tell you the amount of money you will need to operate your business. Many part-time businesses are expanded using savings, second mortgages, lines of credit, and credit cards.

The point of answering these questions is not to throw a wet blanket on your enthusiasm, but to help you decide whether you are ready to jump feet first into what can become a time-consuming and capital-intensive situation. Normally, if you want to succeed in e-commerce, it takes money, time, more money, technical skills, more money, marketing and operational know-how, and still more money.

But there is good news—and it's not saving 15% on your auto insurance.

The Yahoo! store program can dramatically reduce the cost of creating a full-time customized online business—and help you succeed at it. Succeeding in a full-time online business has to do with professionalism. The chapters that follow will show you how to create a fully professional and customizable Yahoo! store and help you succeed in the world of e-commerce.

Building a Professional E-Commerce Site for Success

The saying goes that on the Internet, nobody knows you're a dog. That's fine only if your small business can project a professional-looking one—and that takes some work.

The basic Yahoo! store that you've built using Yahoo! Store Editor, or the free site you set up for your offline business through one of the free Web communities, such as Yahoo! GeoCities, can carry your full-time small business only so far. To succeed on a full-time basis using a Yahoo! business, you need to customize your online storefront to reinforce your company's brand.

Branding

The design of your e-commerce site holds the key to company branding. The importance of branding cannot be stressed enough. It's the starting point of any successful company, online or offline. Is your brand a description of your company? Or of you? Shoppers could care less about who you are; they want to know what you can do for them.

What we're describing here, of course, is a company's unique selling position (USP). The USP is the company brand, and the company brand is its USP. We spoke of the USP and its importance in our first book, *Launching Your Yahoo! Business*. Your company brand is your identity—who you are, what you can provide customers, and how you differentiate your business from the competition.

CHAPTER 1   Can You Make a Living from Your Yahoo! Store?

> **Web Resource**
>
> **What's Your Branding IQ?**
> Take the five-minute Branding Test at www.chadwickcommunications.com/brandiq to find out if you put your brand first at your company.

Good online branding encompasses a storefront that is customer-friendly in both design and content. Easy-to-understand site navigation has content and visitor interaction that promotes the sale of your product or service. The "look and feel" of your storefront should communicate the correct message about your company and your offerings to your target customers. This can be accomplished using the customizing features available through the Yahoo! store program and through carefully architecting your website.

Taking time to design, or architect, your website on paper and put your USP into your website from the start will go a long way in creating a professional and successful promotional vehicle for selling your goods or services.

Promotion

"Early to bed, early to rise. Work like a dog and advertise." Funny, but true. A good understanding of online marketing, and translating that understanding into a solid online marketing plan, is very important if you want to succeed with your full-time Yahoo! business.

A professional online business requires a professional marketing plan that describes how to position a business in the digital marketplace, acquire and retain customers, and, most important, make money from customers. Your comprehensive marketing plan is the vehicle that promotes your company's brand.

Management and Operations

Even if your business is termed "small," you are faced with the organizational challenges of any full-time business. These include your day-to-day operations of inventory control, customer service, employee relations, recruiting and hiring the proper people, payroll, benefits, and key personnel training.

> **Web Resource**
>
> **Do You Know How to Properly Manage a Company?**
> The ACOA website offers a detailed Business Management Questionnaire at www.acoa.ca/e/business/practices/page01.shtml that will help you shed light on your management practices and strategies.

Obviously, to run a full-time business, you need personnel other than yourself. You also need a management team to supervise your staff as it grows with your business. Employee relations and leadership qualities are just as important in a small business owner as they are in the CEO of a large company. In addition, how you recruit, hire, pay, and offer benefits to your employees will affect the success of your full-time business. Collecting and reporting city, state, and federal taxes also comes into play when you have employees.

As for customer relations, there is no face-to-face or real-time interaction with customers when running an online business. Current technology can help with some of this, but "pressing the flesh" of a customer is still many years off. That means your business must try doubly hard to create a solid relationship with customers and prospects.

Legalities and Funding

Capital drives business. If you are going to build a full-time professional business, acquiring capital will become a necessary component of your business plan. The formal business plan (see *Write a Business Plan in No Time* [Que, 2005] by Frank Fiore) that you will need to create for your professional business will require, at the very least, a three-year financial projection of revenue and expenses, called a proforma. The proforma helps you build a budget for your small business that you can use to manage your cash flow.

Your business plan should also describe not only what your funding needs are, but how and where you will acquire the funds. The exercise of writing a formal business plan will be a great help in not only raising capital for your business (even if you self-fund your business), but managing it as well.

When you become a small business, it's also time to rethink your business structure. Should you incorporate or remain a sole proprietor? If you do incorporate, what form of corporation is best?

The questions of branding, marketing, operations, funding, and more are covered in the upcoming chapters. In the next chapter, we look at the most important components of a formal plan.

CHAPTER 2

Plan to Succeed

In This Chapter

- How to choose a business identity
- How to establish a legal identity
- How to define your market in your business plan
- How to manage your business in your business plan
- How to detail your capital requirements

E-business "has become just business," said Louis Gerstner, the CEO of IBM. And he's right. If you think that doing business online is different from doing business offline, you're making a mistake. Planning a formal full-time business requires a formal business plan. In this chapter, we discuss the most important components of a formal plan and what they contain.

Your formal plan must include who you are and what you sell; how you'll market your product or service; how you'll manage your company's people, time, and events; an estimate of how much funding you will need to launch, grow, and run your business; and where you plan to find the funds to do it.

We do not have room in this book to show you how to write a complete business plan (we cover only the most essential parts of the formal plan in this chapter), so we refer you to another book by Que that is an excellent no-nonsense tool for writing business plans: *Write a Business Plan in No Time* (Que, 2005) by Frank Fiore.

Choosing a Business Identity: Who R U?

Naming a business can be both fun and frustrating. You might have a great name in mind for your company but find that it is already taken. If so, you'll need to be creative. A name that's catchy or cute could seem fine in the beginning, but these types of names can be misleading. Of course, there are exceptions—Amazon and eBay, for example.

Still, if chosen properly, your company name can be a powerful promotional tool in your marketing tool box. Or, if you're not careful, it can create a misleading or even unpleasant image in a potential customer's mind. Keep these things in mind when naming your business:

Free Info Download the free informative article titled "The RAF and ROI" at www.myecommercesuccess.com.

- Don't be tempted to make up some odd name. Sure, it worked for Amazon and eBay, but why take the chance of identifying your business with a *nom de plume* that butchers the English language or leaves consumers scratching their heads over what you sell? Amazon, eBay, and Cingular have names that do not reflect their business, but they have the marketing clout to create name recognition in the consumer's mind. Don't make potential customers see your name and ask, "What in the world does that mean?"

- Catchy is fine—cute is not. Remember, you want to project a professional image for your business. Boo.com might be a good name for a Halloween shop, but not an apparel store. (And yes, Boo.com was the name of very large online apparel store that imploded during the dot-com crash.) Be careful of your spelling, too. Is it easy to spell or easy to understand? Does it make sense? For example, Accompany.com was another dot-com business. Imagine this conversation between a sales rep at Accompany and a customer:

  "This is Accompany calling."

  "A company? What company?"

  "Accompany."

  Tricky spellings are also hard to look up online or in the phone book. This could harm your attempts at getting top placement in Net directories, such as Yahoo!. Don't make the mistake of placing *aaa* or any *As* in the front of your name. It might work for taxi companies, but not for consumers trying to remember the name of your online business. Finally, try to keep your name short; it's easier to remember. You're running an online business, not a law firm.

- Name yourself for growth. That unique selling position you have honed down to a very specific market and product might not make a very good business name. For example, the name Joe's Music Store would limit business. Some day, Joe might want to add videos, DVDs, and e-books to his product line. Joe's Entertainment Outlet might be a better name to start with. Make your business name open-ended and flexible for growth. Also, stay away from trendy names. Tie-dyed T-shirts might be making a comeback, but it would be better to name your T-shirt store Al's T-Shirts than Al's Groovy Sixties T-Shirts.

- Make sure your name is available. The best place to find out is through your state government. Find the department or agency that handles trade names, such as the (state) Corporate Commission, and do a search on the business name you want to see if it's available. The name will have to be available if you want to open a business account under it. Also, check the Internet. Do a search on Google.com using the name you chose, and see what search results come up.

Licenses and Permits

Your next step is to get legal. After you have chosen your name, it's time to look into permits and licensing. Find out if you can even have a business. If you will run your business from your home, do any rules or restrictions in your community will prevent it? These are called CC&Rs (covenants, conditions, and restrictions). You also need to find out about zoning laws.

Your city and state will probably require you to get a business license. You will need to fill out their forms detailing the type of business you are, where the business is located, who is running it, and more. If you plan to sell retail items, you'll also have to get a seller's permit, sometimes called a transaction privilege license. After all, the state, county, and city want their sales taxes, and you have to collect them.

Finally, set up your DBA, which stands for "doing business as." This is your official and public registration of a business name. It enables you to conduct business under a name other than or in addition to your company's legal name. The business can be a sole proprietorship, partnership, corporation, or limited liability company (LLC). If you have multiple businesses, you can also create multiple DBAs under the same entity. Banks will also require you to file a fictitious business name before you can open a bank account to deposit checks under that name.

> **warning**
>
> **Get That DBA**
>
> Getting a DBA (doing business as) is not a bad idea. Why? It protects the name of the business that you chose. Your business could be sailing along nicely without a DBA when some other businesses decide to use it. If you haven't filed for a DBA and they did, you could be forced to change your name. That can get expensive and become a detriment to the business you already have built.

Establishing a Legal Identity

After you've established your business name, it's time to consider the legal identity of your business. You have several choices, depending upon the type of company you want, tax considerations, and the necessity of outside funding. We take a look at each one here so you can review their advantages and disadvantages as they apply to your particular business situation.

Basically, five legal types of businesses exist:

- Sole proprietorship
- Partnership
- Subchapter S corporation
- C corporation
- LLC corporation

Sole Proprietorship

If you're starting and running a business all by yourself, a sole proprietorship is one you might choose. The advantage of establishing a sole proprietorship is that it's inexpensive and simple. There are no papers to sign or file with the government. Legally, by just being in business, your company is considered a sole proprietorship.

The sole proprietorship is not a legal entity. It simply refers to a person who owns the business and is personally responsible for its debts. A sole proprietorship can operate under the name of its owner, or it can do business under a fictitious name, such as Bob's Auto Repair. The fictitious name is simply a trade name; it does not create a legal entity separate from the sole proprietor owner.

To be ready for business, a sole proprietor needs only register his or her name and secure local licenses. A distinct disadvantage, however, is that the owner of a sole proprietorship remains personally liable for all the business's debts. So, if a sole proprietor business runs into financial trouble, creditors can bring lawsuits against the business owner personally. If such suits are successful, the owner must pay the business debts with his or her own money, automobile, savings, and home.

> **tip** **Tax Consequences of Your Choice**
>
> Keep in mind that your company type has tax and financial and legal liability consequences. Choose the one that best fits your personal situation.
>
> This book is in no way intended to provide or suggest legal or accounting advice, written or implied. Before you make any decisions regarding the type of corporation that is right for you, your type of business, and the state in which you operate, we strongly urge you to seek professional counsel.

Here's another thing to keep in mind. Whether or not you take the earnings out of the business for living expenses, you are personally taxed on the income. Of course, you can deduct your business expenses on your personal tax returns.

Partnership

Going it alone can be a scary endeavor. That's why many businesses are formed under a partnership. If you have a partner in your new business but don't want to incorporate, the partnership form of business might be the way to go. The advantage of a partnership is that it's simpler and less expensive to establish than setting up a corporation. You and your partner (or partners) retain personal liability for the actions of your business, and you are not shielded from a personal tax on the business earnings, although you can deduct your percentage of the business expenses.

Incorporation

The last form of business entity is the corporation, and it comes in three types:

- C corporation
- Subchapter S corporation
- LLC (limited liability corporation)

If personal liability and tax issues are of concern, then you should consider forming a corporation of some type. A corporation is considered a legal entity. In the vernacular of the field, a corporation creates a veil between you and the corporation that protects you personally from any of its *legal* activities. Notice the word *legal*: A corporation will not protect its members if the business performs an illegal act. If that happens, the members and/or executive team of the corporation can be sued or taken to court—and jailed. The recent ENRON, TYCO, and WorldCom debacles are a prime example. This is called piercing the corporate veil.

Let's look at the C corporation.

Forming a C corporation limits your personal liability for business debts, and the earnings of the corporation do not pass directly into your personal tax return. Being a legal entity, the C corporation pays salaries and taxes and deducts expenses like any other entity or "person." The shareholders pay personal income tax only on money that is paid to them as salary, bonuses, or dividends (income). But running a corporation is not cheap, and it takes work. Meetings must be held, minutes recorded, tax forms filed, and so on; it all takes time away from running your business. In addition, you must pay separate income taxes, both state and federal.

A lighter version of the C corporation is the Subchapter S corporation. The S corporation is a corporation and gives you the limited liability of a corporate shareholder. The difference is that as a corporate shareholder, you pay taxes in the same way a sole proprietor or a partner does.

Finally, there's the LLC (limited liability corporation).

Since the establishment of the LLC as an alternative C corporate entity, the S corporation has lost much of its appeal and has been replaced in most cases by the LLC.

The LLC is a combination of the best parts of a C corporation, a sole proprietorship, and a partnership. What makes it so desirable is that it includes limited personal liability, as with a C corporation, but, as with partnerships and sole proprietorships, the LLC is not a separate taxable entity. The tax situation for an LLC is the same as for a partnership or sole proprietorship: Business earnings and losses are reported on the owner's personal income tax return.

> **Web Resource**
>
> **Learn More About Legal Entities**
> There is little space in this book to go further into the forms of legal entities for companies. The Nolo website (www.nolo.com) is a great resource for information on the different forms of business entities and how to form them.

Your Marketing Plan

An important part of a formal business plan is the section that describes how you plan to market your business. All of your promotion, advertising, and marketing plans are contained in this section. This section also describes your USP (unique selling position) and how you plan to position your company in the marketplace.

The business of business is selling something. That something is the product or service that you plan to offer to the marketplace. This is the prime objective of your plan. You might say that this is where the rubber meets the road in your business plan.

Product or Service Description

In your plan, you will want to state not only what you plan to sell, but also why consumers will buy it. Look at this section as your chance to clearly explain what you sell, along with its features and benefits, and discuss what needs or problems they address in the marketplace.

One important thing to remember is that your reader might not be nearly as versed in your product or service or the industry you are in. That means you have to describe your product simply and in detail. That includes not only a description of the product or service, but what industry you will sell within and the average cost of the product. It also includes the sourcing of your product. Who will you buy it from? If you are writing an internal plan, this is an opportunity to review your sourcing strategy and whether you can get earn a better profit by improving the sourcing of your product. Also, detail in your plan whether the product you sell requires any additional support and how you will provide it. (All products do.)

On the other hand, if you're providing a service, tell the reader what the service is and why you can provide it. Professional service companies, such as law or medical offices, consulting firms, accountants, and design companies, provide services by employing people. A computer-networking company that offers access to the Internet or a telephone company provides a service by owning and maintaining a network infrastructure.

Don't omit the specific problem your product or service addresses and how that problem is solved. Keep your answers specific and measurable, and show a benefit to the buyer. Here's the hard part: Answer these questions in just one sentence that anyone can understand it. Test it on your spouse, family, friends, and neighbors; ask them what they think it means.

Above all else, remember that your unique selling position is not about you or about your business—it's about your customers' problems and how you solve them. You need to speak to the needs of the consumer you are targeting.

tip Product or Service Fundamentals

Consider these fundamental characteristics of your product or service when creating your unique selling position. How many of them does your product or service meet?

- Does it save time or money?
- Does it offer large savings?
- Is it exclusive?
- Does it provide convenience?
- Can you deliver it faster?
- Will you provide better service?
- Is it easier, economical, or simpler to use?
- Does it reduce upkeep, or is it easy to keep up?
- Will it have long life?

tip Buying Motivations

Consider these buying motivations of your product or service when creating your unique selling position. How many of them does your product or service meet?

- Pride of appearance
- Pride of ownership
- Desire for prestige
- Desire for recognition
- Desire to imitate
- Desire for variety
- Desire for safety
- Desire to create
- Desire for security
- Desire for convenience
- Desire to be unique

Defining Your Market Segment: Targeting the Customer

A target market is a group of prospective customers with a set of common characteristics that are distinguishable from other types of customers. Your job is to understand and describe these common characteristics in your plan and tell how you will make those potential customers your own. You might have more than one target customer. For instance, maybe you are an accountant who has both business and individual clients. Or perhaps you manufacture computers for the home, business, and educational markets. You need to explain these customers in their own unique way.

Keep this in mind: Don't explain *why* your target market needs you. Explain *how* you plan to meet their needs.

Customer Types

The type of customer you sell to, especially if you plan to sell online, is one way to categorize your target market.

Some customers are looking for convenience, want to save time, and are primarily impulse shoppers. For these customer types, convenience is prized over price. That's the target market of convenience stores, such as 7/11 and Circle K. Then, there are the window-shoppers. They're willing to take their time when making a purchase. They like to have as much information as possible before making a purchase.

Other types of customers are those who are drawn only to brand names and who are very brand conscious. Selling off-brand products will not fly with this group of customers. Finally, there are bargain shoppers who are interested only in a good deal. They are looking to buy products and services at a discount or they are keen comparison-shoppers looking for the lowest price.

Customer Motivations

Describing the buying motivations of your customer is another way to define your target market.

First, of course, is the product or service motivator—the need to satisfy with merchandise and services. Your unique selling position is designed to meet a specific product or service motivational need. Second is the information motivation—the need to know. Your target market might be customers who are information addicts and who need to know the latest financial, celebrity, or sports news. Third is the entertainment motivator—the need to be entertained.

For an online business, there is one other motivation: the need to connect with others. The Internet is well suited to meeting this motivational need of community, and many businesses have developed along those lines. One example is iVillage, at www.ivillage.com, a website for women. Another is ePinions, at www.epions.com, a consumer opinion site on products and services from A to Z.

Describing the Competition

There's no escaping competition in life. That goes double for business. The business environment is very competitive, more so now than ever before. A reader of your plan will want to know who your competitors are, how they compete with you, and how your business is positioned to compete with them.

Pick a dozen or so of your nearest competitors and start a file on them. Find examples of their advertising and promotion materials and their pricing strategy, and toss them in a file folder. Check current and back issues of the Yellow Pages to see if your competitors are increasing, decreasing, or maintaining their promotional exposure. Also, check their websites; search Yahoo! news, website ads, and specials; and sign up for a competitor's newsletter.

> **Web Resource**
>
> **Competitive Research Resources**
>
> The Internet is filled with resources that can help you find your competition and provide you with the necessary information to evaluate them. You can draw on media sources, Web directories, and competitive intelligence services.
>
> Here are just a few:
>
> - The U.S. Web100, www.metamoney.com/usIndustryListIndex.html.
>
>   This site lists the top 100 companies in the U.S., in more than 50 industry categories cataloging more than 400 of the Fortune 500 U.S. corporations with websites.
>
> - Hoover's Business Links, www.hoovers.com/free/.
>
>   This is a directory of more than 15,000 business-related websites, divided into seven major categories. Hoover's editors select the links based on timeliness, quality, and ease of use.
>
> - CI Seek, www.bidigital.com/ci/.
>
>   This site offers the Competitive Intelligence Resource Index, a search engine and categorical listing of sites related to competitive intelligence. Categories range from associations to software, with books, companies, documentation, education, jobs, and publications in between.

- Business.com, www.business.com/.

  This is a business search engine and directory, including company and industry profiles, news, financials, statistics, and, most important, competitive analysis.

- Dun & Bradstreet, www.dnb.com/.

  This is the granddaddy of all company information.

This is not the place in your plan to toot your own horn. In other words, describe your competition from an objective and *unbiased* perspective. Analyzing and describing your competition is a double-edged sword. At first, it might seem a dubious addition to your business plan. Why tell the reader you have competition at all?

Here's why: Many first-time business-plan writers don't realize that investors want to know whether there are other profitable and successful businesses in your marketplace. It could help convince an investor to fund you, and you will have a proven market. If your technology, distribution, or USP is better, you've built a good case for success.

Managing Your Business

It's not just what you do in your business, but also who is going to do it and when you plan to have it done. That is, what are your plans to manage the people, time, and events of your business?

For example, what kind of organizational structure will your company have? Who does what in your company, what various responsibilities does each have, and what tasks are assigned to each of them? Within the divisions of your company, how many of your team are executives, managers, and key personnel? This is often *more* important to someone who is considering investing large sums of high-risk money into your venture. The first thing they ask is, "Will it work?" Then, it's "Can *you* (and the team you assembled), actually do it?"

> **warning**
>
> **Think Twice About Employing Family and Friends**
>
> Don't make the mistake of placing unqualified friends or family in key management positions. You're running a professional business, and your management team should reflect that professionalism.

Your Organizational Structure

When deciding your organizational structure, keep these tips in mind:

- List all the tasks that need to be done in your company. Keep the description as broad as possible: administration, sales, marketing, operations, customer service, public relations, production, research and development, and so on.
- Organize these tasks into departments.
- Detail the roles and responsibilities of each of these departments.
- Include the names of those who will fill these positions. If you don't have specific people yet, describe the position's responsibilities and the type of expertise and experience necessary.

Finally, the organizational form of your business affects your organizational structure and the human resource requirements of your company. There are differences in how you describe your personnel team based on whether your company is a sole proprietorship, partnership, or corporation.

If you're a sole proprietorship, *you* are the management team. This section should describe the abilities and expertise you bring to the new business, the areas in which you will need help, and how you'll get that help.

For example, if you're lacking in marketing, will you bring on a consultant to help you with your advertising plan? Will you hire a bookkeeper or use an outside accounting service to keep your books? Will you store and ship your products, or will you use a third-party fulfillment service?

On the other hand, if your business is a partnership, be prepared to discuss who the partners are and what experience and skills they bring to the business (include full resumes). You should explain how the different abilities of the partners complement the others' and add to the success of the business.

If your business form is a corporation, you should list the offices of the corporation—president, vice president, secretary/treasurer—and the board of directors. In the directors' bios, include information on their expertise, why they were chosen, their current stock distribution (ownership), and what they will contribute to the business.

Your Implementation Plan

How you implement your business venture is as important as the venture itself. This is done by conveying to the reader what your implementation plan will be. The value of a plan is measured in its implementation.

An implementation plan sets out the logical steps, or phases, you will need to go through to turn your business idea into reality. In other words, it converts your business plan into action.

Besides conveying your plan to a reader, an implementation plan provides a way of managing your people, time, and events to be completed within a given timescale. It also describes what future plans you will have for your business after initial success—a continued growth or exit strategy. Among other reasons, identifying future plans is one way of telling how you will stay competitive and one step ahead of the competition. In other words, it provides a snapshot of how you intend to set up your business and implement your plan over time.

Detailing Your Capital Requirements

The old saying goes, "It takes money to make money." That doesn't necessarily mean that it takes a lot of money, but it does take some. Some entrepreneurs believe that revenue and sales can handle all their money requirements and that they can fund the growth of their company out of profits. This is rarely the case. It *always* takes longer and costs more.

Substantial start-up costs can be involved when starting or expanding a new venture. Then, there are the cash flow considerations. If you're selling a product, you will most likely have to pay for your inventory or the manufacturer of the product before you can generate enough sales to cover the costs of the product and your normal overhead. Same goes for a service company: You'll have overhead and personnel costs to cover before you make your first sale.

In most cases, this means you will need money or investment capital right off the bat. So if you're writing a business plan to raise investment capital (actually, even if you don't), you'll need to do the following:

- Decide how much money you'll need in general and how you will use it (proforma).
- Decide on where you will acquire the funds you will need.
- If you have investors or are looking for a loan (through family, friends, or a 401[k], for example), decide how you plan to repay the loan or compensate the investors.

In addition, you should have a rough idea of how much money you will need for the following:

- Advertising and marketing
- Salaries and wages
- Office equipment
- Manufacturing equipment
- Physical plant expenses
- General operating expenses

A complete listing of *all* anticipated expenses is important. One line item can mean a huge unexpected expense. For a complete list of typical expenditures, see *Write a Business Plan in No Time* (Que, 2005) by Frank Fiore.

In your plan, describe these uses (and others) of the funds.

Getting the Dough

When it comes financing your business, you have to ask yourself a few important questions. How much do you need? What kind of financing is right for your business? Where will the funds come from? What will you be willing to give up for an investment in your company? Basically, start by asking yourself what kinds of financing you're likely to need and what you'd be willing to accept in exchange.

Are you willing to give up a piece of your company for the money you need? How much? And are you willing to give up control? If you want to maintain control of your company, you'll have to either give away less for less money, dip into your own pocket, or borrow the cash. If you borrow the money, how much can you afford? You'll have to make payments on any loans. Your budget (proforma) can tell you what you can afford and how much you can pay back over a time.

Web Resource

What Kind of Financing Is Right for You?

The Business Owners Idea Café is an easy-to-understand source of information on company financing. At its website, you can educate yourself on the different kinds of financing a business. You can also test your own attitudes toward the consequences of using various funding sources. You can find the information on financing options and the quick attitude test at www.businessownersideacafe.com/financing/kind_of_financing.php.

Personal Funding Sources

The most obvious source of capital is your own pocket. Many a small company was started on personal savings, home equity loans, personal credit cards, and 401(k)s. Your credit cards are a ready source of unsecured loans. If your credit limit is $5,000 to $20,000 or more, you already have at your disposal a preapproved loan. Okay, so the interest rate is not great. But if you shop around (or just look in your mailbox), you'll find many credit cards offering short-term introductory interest rates at a fraction of the rates credit cards normally charge.

You can also bank your home and get a home equity loan line of credit or a loan from the Small Business Administration (SBA). This is much easier than trying to get a business loan because your home is the collateral. Then, use the funds from the line of credit to invest in your business.

Money Borrowed from a Bank

Bankers are a nervous bunch. Unlike venture capitalists or individual investors, they avoid risk whenever possible. Including a well-thought-out business plan with your loan application considerably increases your chances of getting a loan. A formal business plan shows that you are serious enough to do formal planning. That's a message bankers like to see.

Funding Through Equity Investors

Two types of equity investors exist: the angel investor and the venture capitalist. If you choose the venture capitalist, you need to decide the amount of control that you'll surrender and the time spent finding the money rather than starting your business. Venture capitalists will most likely demand equal control of your business and input into managing your company.

Show Me the Money
The Web has many good sources of information on venture capital. For example, Capital Resource Library at www.vfinance.com has links to everything from how to locate a venture capital firm to details of security law and articles related to getting investors.

Angel investors, on the other hand, most often stay out of your business and act as guides and counselors. That's why they're called angels.

In the next chapter, we discuss why you should customize your Yahoo! store and whether you should do it yourself or hire an expert.

CHAPTER

3

Architecting Your Online Storefront

In This Chapter

- The difference between website development and e-commerce site development
- The three Cs of e-commerce
- The elements of a unique selling position

Long before carpenters assemble the framework, the plumbers lay the pipes, the electricians run the wires, and the dry-wallers and painters finish the job, the architect designed the plans for a retail storefront. It's the same for an online store. In this case, however, the programmers and graphic designers build the store, and *you* must first architect your e-commerce site.

Architecting your e-commerce site is the first step of customization (and improving the performance of your Yahoo! store), and it happens long before you put mouse to pad and program your storefront. In this chapter, we discuss the basic elements that should be designed into your e-commerce website; in the next chapter, we show you how to "storyboard" your website pages.

Website Development Versus E-Commerce Site Development

There's a big difference between developing a standard website and developing an e-commerce website. Not every Web developer is an e-commerce site developer. The difference between developing a standard website such as a personal home page and a corporate information site (what's known in the trade as brochureware) is that the unique selling position (USP) of a business is designed *into* the e-commerce site while it's being created.

Let's explain. When creating a normal, noncommerce website, the developer works from a standard set of pages, such as a home page, an about page, a contact page, and content pages. When this same type of Web-development process is applied to an e-commerce site, the Web developer throws in the product or service pages and a shopping cart to store and process orders. How the e-commerce site will be marketed is an afterthought, examined after the e-commerce site is developed. The selling position is not built directly into the design of the site.

Free Info   Download the free informative article titled "Seven Sins Virtues of eCommerce" at www.easy-yahoo-commerceMyEcommerceSuccess.com.

In many cases, unless the Web developer has knowledge of selling, the site isn't put together from an e-commerce standpoint: The home page is just a description of the company and its products. The product or service pages are not written with an eye to closing a sale. The copy of the different Web pages themselves is not optimized for search engines to find the site. Content and community pages are not used much outside the product or service pages to promote the products or services. Little attempt is made to exploit external marketing, and no internal marketing is used.

The Three Cs

Maintaining an e-commerce website is more than just selling a product or service. That is, there's more than commerce in a well-thought-out e-commerce site.

A good e-commerce website contains the three Cs of e-commerce:

- **Content**—Selling products and services in a context relevant to your customers
- **Community**—Creating an online environment in which visitors and customers can interact
- **Commerce**—Creating revenue-generating streams for your storefront

That's the e-commerce site equation. Content builds community, which establishes credibility, which generates sales.

Content: Turn Your Site into a Learning Fountain

Content is king on the Net. People use the Net to learn. That's what drives visitors to a website. Content can consist of information and community participation—and even your e-commerce offers are considered content. Your site's content—whether it is information, community participation, or a product or service offer—must be interesting enough to make visitors come to your site, stay, and keep coming back for more.

Keep in mind that your content does not have to be closely related to your product, but it should meet your prospective customers' needs and desires. You need to make your Web store not only a place to buy things, but also a "Learning Fountain."

That's what Paul Siegel recommends. Siegel is an author, Internet marketing consultant, trainer, and speaker. He is the originator of the Learning Fountain, at www.learningfountain.com (see Figure 3.1),

> **tip Encourage Contributions**
>
> Offer a way for visitors to submit articles, to include their experiences on your site or in your newsletter. Not only do you get free help in building your site content, but you also gain long-term repeat visits from people whose content is included on your site.

a website that influences visitors by helping them learn. He is known for saying, "A Learning Fountain is a website that attracts prospects—not merely visitors—by helping them learn. While learning, they linger and buy."

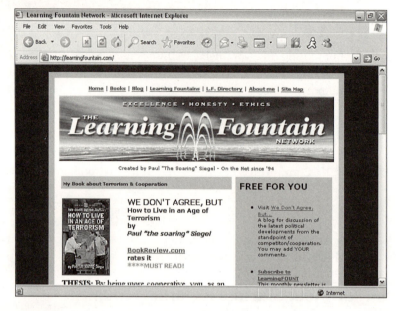

FIGURE 3.1
Paul Siegel's site is a great resource if you want to turn your site into a Learning Fountain.

Siegel divides content Learning Fountains into four types:

- Referrer
- Informer
- Advisor
- Context provider

The Referrer

No one knows the product or service you're selling better than you do. So use this knowledge to help your visitors understand all aspects of the product or service you sell. You might not have all the information they need, but with a little research, you can create a directory of sites on the Net that can provide the information visitors need and refer them to it.

For example, suppose you sell computer products. You could provide on your site a long list of product reviews comparing one product you sell to another. That would be a very time-consuming task. So instead, you could refer visitors to sites that specialize in these reviews, such as ZDNet, at www.reviews-zdnet.com.com (see Figure 3.2).

FIGURE 3.2

ZDNet is chock full of reviews on personal electronics and computer gear.

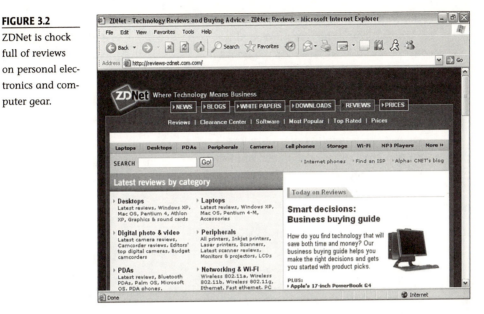

But keep this caveat in mind: Be careful about where those sites send their customers. Many sites have reviews but also have links to preferred providers or AdWords ads to competitor sites with those products. Once someone goes off your site, you have no control over that person's experience. One way around this potential problem is to get permission from the content site to "Reprint with Permission." This way, your shoppers stay on your site.

Or suppose you sell tools for the do-it-yourself home improvement. You can refer visitors to ImproveNet, at www.improvenet.com, which then will direct customers to design ideas and project estimators.

The Informer

Providing regular updated information on your site that is of practical use to visitors will bring them to your site and generate repeat visits. Include access to the latest news and articles. YellowBrix, at www.yellowbrix.com, aggregates content from hundreds of different providers in categories such as top news and weather, sports news, business and finance, entertainment, and lifestyles.

The Advisor

To make a buying decision, many shoppers need advice. By making product advice available to your shoppers, you increase the possibility of making a sale. For advice to work, it must be trusted and credible.

A good example of this kind of advice is at Amazon.com. This site pioneered the concept of reader reviews for the books it sells. Anyone who has purchased and read the book being offered for sale can write a review. A peer review looks more objective to a potential customer and increases the possibility of a purchase. Shoppers trust other consumers' opinions more than they trust the advertisers.

> **tip Consumer Opinions on Your Site Pay Off**
>
> According to Forester Research, 65% of community users rate the opinions of other consumers as important or somewhat important influences on their buying decision.

The Context Provider

Providing informational tools to shoppers to help them make a buying decision is another important content feature for your Web store. Consider giving the shopper the capability to solve a problem or determine a need in the context of your site using online tools, such as checklists, calculators, evaluators, and simulators.

Context-specific information can be either product specific or shopping specific.

First, let's look at the product-specific tools. Suppose you had a mortgage brokerage service on the Web. To help shoppers of your service make a buying decision, you might offer them a mortgage calculator on your site. They could calculate their monthly mortgage payment based on the type of mortgage they want, the interest rate, and any other options that would be available with the service.

Your context-specific information need not be product specific. You could offer several shopping tools at your site to make the shopping experience for consumers more

> **tip Let Your Shoppers Find the Exact Time Around the World**
>
> If shoppers need to contact a merchant or order by phone, they should know which time zone you are in. Place a link to world times on your site and offer this service. Find it at www.worldtimeserver.com/current_time_in_DZ.aspx.

> **tip Free Currency Converter**
>
> A great little service to add to your site is an international currency converter. This way, shoppers from anywhere in the world can determine the price of your products in their currency. Find it at www.xe.com/ucc/.

helpful. You could offer some useful general tools at your Web store, such as links to currency exchanges, international holiday listings, and a world time calculator.

Community: Building an Interactive Community

Siegel had one more important Learning Fountain: the Learning Community. People go online not just to be informed, but also to interact with other people. Filling this need at your Web store will help you turn shoppers into customers, and customers into repeat buyers.

Content can attract shoppers to your site. But to generate a continuous flow of repeat visitors, you need to provide access to an interactive community. Community is just as important as content when planning an e-commerce site. If done right, community features on your site will increase the number of page views per visit, giving you opportunities to offer more merchandise to your shoppers.

Establishing a Learning Community can help shoppers develop expertise by interacting with other shoppers who visit your site. Asking questions, discussing problems, raising issues, and enjoying the general camaraderie that develops in an interactive community breeds a kind of loyalty that is beneficial to the success of your Web store. And loyalty breeds repeat visits.

Another benefit of an interactive community is that it can add content to your site. Discussion boards and forums, chat rooms, and discussion lists can provide content by their very nature of generating information. For example, each day, you might post a short quote from one of your forums or discussion lists as fresh content to generate interest in a product or offer. This type of content can act as a traffic magnet, bringing continuous visitors to your site. Community-interaction devices, such as discussion boards and forums, chat rooms, and discussion lists, are also a great source for new product ideas and can improve your customer service, packaging, instructions, download process, and shipping methods.

You should include as many interactive community tools as possible on your website. The major tools of the interactive community are discussion boards or forums, chat rooms, discussion lists, newsletters, and, the new kid on the block, blogs. Yahoo! Small Business has integrated with two of the top blogging tools: Moveable Type and Word Press. Blogs focus on short bits of frequently updated topics, but they also foster community through comments. The blog owner also has some control by moderating comments before they're posted, so this could be better than a wide-open forum or chat.

To choose a blogging tool and create a blog, follow these steps:

1. From the Business Control Panel, click the Web Hosting Control Panel link.
2. Scroll down and click the Start a Blog link.
3. Here, you can choose either Moveable Type or Word Press as your blogging tool (see Figure 3.3).

FIGURE 3.3
Yahoo! Small Business has integrated with two of the top blogging tools: Moveable Type and Word Press.

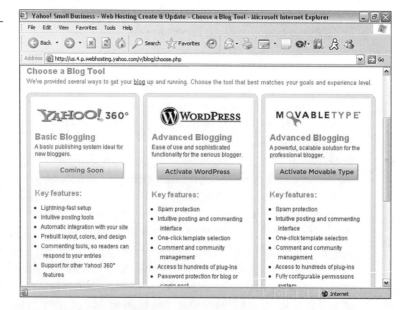

> **Yahoo! Talk**
>
> **Business Control Panel**
>
> The Business Control Panel is another name for the Manage My Services page. It's the hub where you can access your Store Manager, Web Hosting Control Panel, Domain Control Panel, and Email Control Panel.

Commerce: Adding Multiple Revenue Streams

The Net not only evolves quickly, but it also quickly evolves those that are on it. Take Yahoo!, for example. Only a short decade ago, it was a simple search engine. Then, it added email, games, investment information, white pages, and other services, and became a portal. In its latest incantation, it has added online store hosting and has evolved into a world-class e-commerce site.

Even e-commerce sites themselves have evolved. Amazon.com sold only books. Now, it's chasing the e-commerce dream, selling movies, CDs, electronics, toys, games, and a variety of other products. And what dream is Amazon.com chasing? Multiple revenue streams, which go beyond simple product sales. Adding many of these streams to your site will leverage your site traffic and generate additional income.

Here are some possibilities for multiple revenue streams:

- **Product or service sales income**—This is the main revenue stream of your Web store. It's what you built your e-business around, and it should be your prime focus. It's the bread and butter of your business and should be your top priority.

- **Advertising income**—When you've built up traffic to your site, you can consider turning some of that traffic into revenue. Advertisers are always looking for ways to get their product or service message out to potential customers. They know that placing ads on websites that cater to shoppers who might buy their products is a wise way to spend their advertising dollars. Banner advertising can generate $5 to $75 CPM (cost per thousand per impression). That means you could earn anywhere from .005¢ to .075¢ each time an advertiser's banner ad appears to your site visitors. It might not sound like much at first, but if thousands and thousands of your site visitors view an ad, the dollars add up fast.

- **Referral income**—Another income source is to refer your shoppers to another company's website. These are the affiliate programs that we discussed earlier. You might consider referring your shoppers to a non-competitive merchant in exchange for a paid click-through or a percentage of the sale. Income can vary from 5¢ to $1 per click-through, or from 5% to 20% of sales.

If you develop several of these income streams simultaneously, you can grow your site revenue beyond your product or service offers.

There's a bonus attached to building community interactions on your e-commerce site: free refreshed content. And refreshed content attracts both shoppers and the eye of search engines that list you.

Your USP: Unique Selling Position

As explained before, what separates a standard website from an e-commerce website is that the USP is deliberately designed during the creation of the site. The USP takes into effect the three Cs and immediately tells the following to a shopper at your website:

- Portrays in consumers' minds a compelling image of what your business will do for them that others cannot
- Gives consumers a distinct *reason* to buy from your company
- Gives your company a unique *advantage* over your competition

Advantage, *reason*, and *image* are your goals in creating a USP. Your USP creates the framework and lays the foundation for your compelling offer. Here's another reason to have a good USP: It keeps your business pointed in the right direction by helping identify your target audience for marketing. An effective and distinctive USP is specific and measurable, and conveys a customer benefit.

In a way, every organization's website is "selling" something: a product or service, information, membership for profit or nonprofit, or perhaps a political or social position.

So, put your mouse down, take out a pad and pencil, and answer the following questions as *simply* as you can. You're not creating a corporate mission statement here, so keep your responses simple:

- Why is your business special?
- Why would someone buy from me instead of my competition?
- What can my business provide a consumer that no one else can?
- What's the benefit to the consumer that I can deliver on?

Keep your answers specific and measurable, and show a benefit to the buyer. If you're confused by what you offer your customers, visitors will be, too. FedEx and Dominoes Pizza are great examples: "When it absolutely, positively has to be there overnight" and "Hot, fresh pizza delivered in 30 minutes or less, guaranteed—or it's free!"

The Four Ps and Your USP

You need to consider some additional aspects when fleshing out a USP. They're called the four Ps:

- **Pricing**—If you're going to compete on price, don't just say you're the lowest: Say why. For instance, perhaps you can sell at such a low price because of your ability to source product from the closeout industry, and you buy products at pennies on the dollar. Play up this uniqueness in your USP.

- **Positioning**—The Marines are looking for just a few good men—not all men, just a few. This is a great positioning statement because it makes the "business" of the Marines unique and differentiates them among the armed forces. Look for a similar positioning with your business. Perhaps your focus is gender based. Perhaps it's age based. Sell to a unique segment of the population, not to all of it.

- **Packaging**—Consider repackaging a common product that others sell. For instance, consider the iMac. It's just a PC, but look at the packaging. Not only did it sell, but it sold at a premium price! It also had two positioning statements with it: Get on the Internet in 20 minutes! and Think Different!

- **Promotion**—Look at the promotional possibilities of your product or service. Can you tie your product or service with a season or holiday? If so, you can benefit from the promotional activities and mind-share of consumers that already exist at that time of year.

Pulling It All Together

A marketable USP involves properly integrating the three Cs and four Ps, and communicating to customers what you will do for them. All the elements we've discussed, if done well, support each other and deliver a whole greater than the sum of the parts.

The content pages speak to your prospective customers' needs and desires, providing grist for the conversational mill for your site community. There's a bonus to this constantly refreshed content: Search engines find this type of content desirable when listing your website in search results. Content is one of the main criteria that search-engine spiders look for when ranking your site. Content generated especially from the community tends to have fresh text rich in keywords. The community interaction that you provide visitors to your site can help shoppers by allowing them to ask questions, discuss problems, and raise issues that can help you understand the needs of your target audience. This then breeds a kind of loyalty that is beneficial to the success of your business.

If *promotion* is one of the four Ps that you will use to identify your USP, the content pages of your site should reflect this. Similarly, the market niche you pick should enable shoppers to discuss with other shoppers the pluses and minuses of the product or service that fills that niche.

Above all else, remember that your USP is not about you or your business: It's about your customer. One final thought: Whatever you promise in your USP, be sure you deliver on it. Don't make the mistake of adopting a USP that you can't fulfill.

In the next chapter, we discuss how to storyboard your e-commerce website.

Part II

Customizing the Yahoo! Store

4 Storyboarding Your e-Commerce Site

5 Customizing Your Yahoo! Store

6 Yahoo! Store Features and Advanced Techniques

7 Yahoo! Store Tips and Tricks

8 Designing Your Customized Yahoo! Store to Sell

CHAPTER
4

Storyboarding Your E-Commerce Site

In This Chapter

- Using storyboarding
- Writing for the Web
- Identifying the most important pages of your e-commerce site

Although storyboards go back to the very beginnings of cinema with Sergei Eisenstein (1898–1948), Walt Disney and his staff developed a formal storyboard system in 1928 with Disney's first animated feature, starring Mickey Mouse in *Tug Boat Willie*. He used the storyboard concept to lay out visually the original plot and action of the story. Since then, storyboarding has become a staple in Hollywood when producing a motion picture.

Just as a storyboard is used in film production, it can be used as a guide for creating a website. When shoppers visit your online storefront, you are really telling them a story—who you are, what you sell, and why they should buy from you. A properly constructed storyboard tells that story long before you actually create your e-commerce website and lay out a logical order of the buying process.

So, let's get started on yours.

Storyboarding for Fun and Profit

Think of your storyboard as a flow chart that leads a visitor to your site through the process of shopping and buying. A storyboard consists of a series of paper pages; each page represents a Web page of your site. Each Web page consists of the following:

- The major navigation of your website and internal links within the pages of your site
- The important elements of the Web page
- The content of the Web page

Let's take a look at each one.

Major Navigation Elements

These are the top or side links to major sections of your storefront. Your major navigation should be no more than seven links. You can add navigation under those links as sublinks when the visitor arrives on those pages. This makes for clean, easy-to-understand use of your storefront. You should also repeat your major navigation as text links at the bottom of each page. You can add important text links beyond the shopping navigation of your site as well, such as links to your privacy policy, newsletter sign-up, and affiliate program sign-up.

Web Page Elements

Decide on the purpose of each page, and write those objectives into the pages of your storyboard. For example, lay out your checkout process screen by screen for your shopping cart programmer to create. Lay out all sign-up pages for newsletters or promotional emails. If you'll have a links page to strategic partners, lay out those pages also. Finally, create the layout for your community elements like discussion boards or chat rooms.

Consider developing a flowchart (see Figure 4.1) when planning your site, to help you lay out your Web pages visually. The flowchart will not only help you develop the top-level navigation menu, but it also will help you visually see how you can cross-link between subpages. Microsoft Word and PowerPoint have built-in tools to help you draw and organize your flowchart. If you are planning to outsource your Web design and development, creating a flowchart will help the contractor develop the Web pages in the appropriate category and give you a more accurate bid on your project.

> **tip** **Miller's Magic 7**
>
> In 1956, George Miller wrote a paper titled "The Magical Number Seven, Plus or Minus Two: Some Limits on Our Capacity for Processing Information." In it, Miller stated that a person's working memory can hold up to seven bits of information, plus or minus two, at one time. This "Miller's Magic 7" has become the basis of many Web page design decisions. Here's what his research found:
>
> - Give users only seven links (choices) in the active window.
> - Give users only seven items on the menu bar.
> - Give users only seven tabs at the top of a website page.
> - Give users only seven items in a pull-down menu.
> - Give users only seven items on a bulleted list.
>
> Keep Miller's Magic 7 in mind when designing your e-commerce website.

FIGURE 4.1

Developing a flowchart will help you visually lay out your content flow. This will also help your team if you are collaborating to build your website.

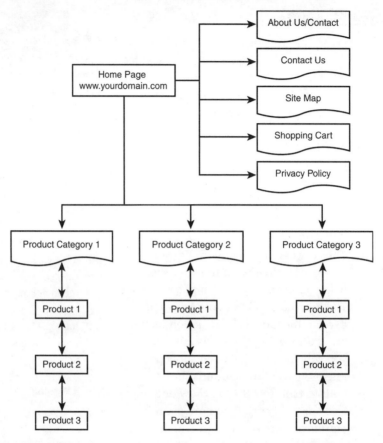

Web Page Content

Finally, you must write every bit of content that exists on each Web page of your site. This includes copy for the product or service pages, pages that describe your company, the press room, the privacy policy pages, the contact page, customer service pages, and more. We cover these more in depth later in this chapter.

> **warning**
>
> **Sell, Don't Entertain**
>
> Remember, the purpose of your e-commerce website is to sell shoppers, not entertain them. Keep the fancy graphics and animation to a minimum—or don't use them at all. Don't dazzle, sell!

Your Storyboard Plot?

Bryan Eisenberg of Future Now talks about the website storyboard. The most important question he asks is, "What is your plot?" Eisenberg suggests that each element of your storyboard address these critical questions:

- What do I want my visitors to know here?
- What do I want my visitors to do at this point?
- What do I want my visitors to feel right now?
- Where do I want my visitors to go next?
- How do I make it easy for them to do that?

He points out that you should also consider different options. For example, suppose that a shopper arrives not on your home page, but somewhere in the middle of your site. That can easily happen if someone searches for your product or service, or even a piece of content, and is directed to your internal Web page by search engine search results. Can visitors to your website easily find their way around your storefront and eventually buy something from you? Your site should be designed for shoppers to enter anywhere in your site, know where they are, and understand how they can get to where they want to be. Your site navigation should be intuitive, not ambiguous.

Free Info Download the free informative article titled "10 Keys to Home Pages That Sell" at www.myecommercesuccess.com.

Eisenberg points out that "for every day you spend planning and getting all the details right, you save yourself the cost and time of three days of remedial tinkering and development."

Good advice.

Your Copy: Writing for the Web

Writing style for the Web is not normally used for other type of documents. This is because Internet users do not really read a Web page—they scan it, picking out individual words and thoughts. Your writing style must reflect the way users read. The material you might have already written for your business, such as brochures, flyers, or advertisements, might not translate well for the Web.

Users do not necessarily read a page from start to finish, or even top to bottom. Their eyes are drawn to information that jumps out at them: bullet points, colored text, and one idea per paragraph. Users also shy away from Web pages that are cluttered with copy and confront visitors with a gray mass of verbiage instated of readable information.

Dartmouth College provides its faculty and students with these general guidelines when writing for the Web:

- **Summarize first**—Put the main points of your document in the first paragraph so that readers scanning your pages will not miss your point.
- **Be concise**—Use lists rather than paragraphs, but only when your prose lends itself to such treatment. Readers can pick out information more easily from a list than from within a paragraph.
- **Write for scanning**—Most Web readers scan pages for relevant materials rather than reading through a document word by word. Guide the reader by highlighting the salient points in your document using headings, lists, and typographical emphasis.

Keep these writing tips in mind when creating the content for your Web pages.

> **Web Resource**
>
> **Writing for the Web**
>
> Here are some good writing references on the Web to use when writing your Web pages:
>
> www.dartmouth.edu/~webteach/articles/text.html
>
> www.useit.com/papers/webwriting/writing.html
>
> www.useit.com/alertbox/9710a.html

The Most Important Pages of an E-Commerce Site

Now let's now look at the most important pages of your e-commerce website and what they entail.

Creative and catchy copy, good graphics, perfect coding—all these are necessary for a well-designed e-commerce site. But some important fundamental pages must be on your Web store to ensure that your customers quickly know your product offers, have their questions answered, and feel comfortable buying from your site. Essentially, your Web pages must turn window shoppers into customers.

Here are the most important pages you must have on your Web store:

- Home page
- About Us page
- Contact Us page
- Product or services catalog pages
- Customer service/customer policies page
- Privacy policy page
- FAQ page
- Press room
- Content pages
- Community pages
- Email recruiting page
- Site map

Let's look at each one in turn.

The Home Page: Get Them Shopping Right Away

Your home page is the most important page of your website because it tells your story. It has three very important purposes.

Sure, it's a colorful and enticing entry to your site and should look professional. But these are design elements. What's important are the business elements of your copy and the objectives of the home page:

- A tagline that quickly describes the benefits of the product, service, or organization
- A "What's in it for me?" description of the product, service, or organization with a *call to action*
- A way to acquire a visitor's email address to build a house list for future promotional mailings

The first thing your home page copy should convey is your USP. This should be done with a catchphrase of a few words and should be no longer than a sentence or two. For example:

- Avis: "We're second, so we try harder."
- FedEx: "When you absolutely, positively have to have it the next day."
- 7 Up: "The Un-Cola"
- Dominoes: "Fresh, hot pizza delivered in 30 minutes or less, guaranteed."

Second, ask for the sale immediately by sending visitors to your product or service pages, as seen at www.outpost.com (see Figure 4.2). Place your best products in the front of your store—on your home page—and then direct visitors right to the product page to buy.

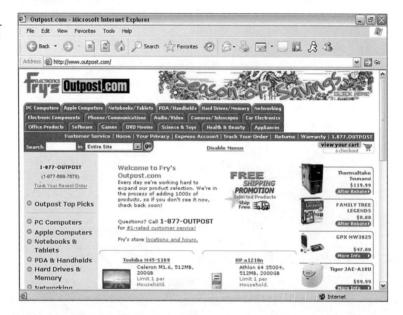

FIGURE 4.2
Outpost.com lets visitors shop immediately by offering specials on its home page with Buy Now buttons.

The Outpost.com home page is a good example: It offers impulse buys right on the home page.

Create that impulse buy on your home page with a button or icon that says "Buy Now!". That's an important element of sales. Any salesperson worth his salt will tell you to always "ask for the sale." Also, change the offers on your home page frequently. Just as news sites offer fresh content each day, you should offer fresh "content" in the form of "Today's Special" or seasonal items promoted on your home page.

At the very least, you should integrate and link to holiday products and timely gift guides from your home page to reflect these occasions:

- The Christmas holiday season
- Winter fun: skiing, skating, and clothing
- Mother's Day
- Father's Day
- Graduation
- Summer fun: beach, BBQs, and vacations

- Back to school
- Halloween
- Thanksgiving
- Special events: births, birthdays, anniversaries, and weddings

You should also have an email recruiting mechanism on your home page. For example, you might promote your electronic newsletter and ask visitors to sign up for it. Or perhaps you want to offer a free download, such as trial software, a music clip, or a report or tip sheet. If you can't get visitors to buy, then at the very least attempt to obtain their email addresses so you can market to them later.

About Us Page: Let Them Know Who You Are

Shoppers would like to know whom they're buying from. So tell them. Have a section linked from your home page to tell them whom they're buying from. Include a history of your business, who's involved, and your business philosophy and vision. Here's a chance to tell them more of your USP, beyond the catchphrase you used on your home page; you get to sell the customer on why he or she should buy from you and tell how you're different from your competition.

Inform the shopper on how you do business, what values you hold, and what's important to the customer. Remember, selling on the Net is not about you: It's about the customer. The customer is interested only in what your company will do for him or her.

> **tip** It's also a great idea to add your company mailing address (physical, not just the P.O. box), phone number, and email address on the About Us page. Some customers will confuse an About Us page for the contact page.

Finally, you might consider adding a picture of you and your staff, along with some brief bios on your About page. Online or off, people still want to do business with other people.

FAQ Page: The First Place Your Customers Turn To

FAQs, or Frequently Asked Questions, are the first place shoppers will go to if they want quick and easy answers to their questions. A FAQ on your Web store is essential and will save both you and your customers a lot of time. Logitech, at www.buylogitech.com/service.asp, has a good example of an FAQ page (see Figure 4.3).

The object of a FAQ is to list as many questions and answers as possible that a shopper might have, such as:

- Who are you?
- Where are you located?
- How can I contact you?
- What's the cost of shipping?
- Do you ship overseas?
- What are your return policies?
- How do I return something?
- What are your product warrantees?
- What are your payment methods?

If you're selling certain categories of products that need a technical explanation, you can include those in your FAQs, too.

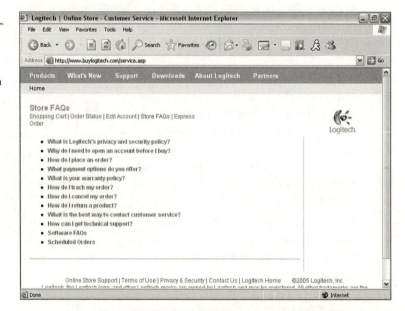

FIGURE 4.3
Logitech anticipates what customers might want to ask with its FAQ page.

When organizing your FAQ page, list the questions at the top of the page and link them to the answers on the same page (anchor). This way, shoppers can read all the questions up front, find what they are looking for, and jump right down the page to the answer with the question included. If you have many questions, you might consider breaking the questions into categories and then creating a menu page of these categories as the main page of the FAQ.

Make sure that you link to your FAQs from your home page. A well-written FAQ will be one of your most popular pages, so make it easy to find.

Finally, link the answers to your questions to other pages on your site, where appropriate, such as a map to your offices or links to products mentioned in your answers.

Full Contact Information: Address, Phone, Fax, Email

Shoppers want to know that you have a real business. One of the best ways to show that is to give them a variety of ways to contact you. An email address is not enough—in fact, it could be suspect. Here's the minimum amount of contact information you should have on your contact page:

- **Company address**—Display your full company mailing address. If you run your business out of your home and don't want to use that address, get a private mailbox at one of the commercial pack-and-ship business, such as the UPS Store or the U.S.P.S.

- **Phone numbers**—Provide your business phone and fax numbers. If you work from your home, install a second line or business line. Connect an answering machine to it with a professional-sounding message, or hire an answering service for after hours or when your line is busy. Also list your fax number on your site.

- **Email addresses**—Provide different email addresses for each department or function of your business. At the very least, have a different email address for customer service, even if all email is forwarded directly to you.

- **Toll-free customer service number**—Your credibility as a business increases dramatically when shoppers see that you can be reached through a toll-free customer service number. A toll-free number is affordable and is worth the small investment. Publish the number on your contact page. If you'd rather not staff a customer service phone line, then outsource your 800-number to a service company that will answer your calls on a cost-per-call basis.

A good contact page can help build a level of trust in your business.

Privacy Policy: Get on the Right Side of the FTC

Next to credit card security, privacy issues are second on the list of customer concerns. It's becoming vital that e-businesses post their privacy policy on their site. Your customers want to know what you intend to do with the personal information you collect when they place an order on your site. Yahoo! Merchant Solutions guidelines require that all store owners post and adhere to a privacy policy. Yahoo! also adds a default privacy policy statement that summarizes Yahoo!'s relationship with your company and privacy practices in relation to Yahoo! shopping. Your own privacy policy will need to be added after Yahoo!'s default privacy policy statement.

You can find sample privacy policies on the Better Business Bureau's website at http://bbbonline.com/privacy/sample_privacy.asp.

> **warning**
> **FTC Is on the Prowl**
>
> The FTC has made it known that if websites do not take the initiative in creating good privacy policies, it might intervene. If that happens, be prepared to follow government rules and pay the fines when you break them.

In a survey of 1,400 websites examining the privacy practices of commercial sites on the World Wide Web, the FTC found the vast majority of privacy policies on websites to be woefully inadequate.

What does this mean to you?

The FTC will be scrutinizing websites to see how they adhere to protecting consumer privacy, so it's important that you have a privacy policy on your site. And there's an easy way to do it.

The Direct Marketing Association has a section on its website (http://www.the-dma.org/privacy/creating.shtml) that has an easy-to-use privacy policy page creation form. Simply answer the questions and click the Submit button; the DMA will send you a privacy policy Web page to post on your site. The Generate HTML Page button enables you to see a copy of your statement on the screen as soon as you submit the form.

When you get your page, edit the page as needed. You might want to clarify some aspects, add your company name to the title of the page, or make other modifications to make the policy fit your site.

That's all there is to it. One last thing: Make sure your company abides by your stated policy—the FTC might be checking.

Customer Service/Customer Policies: The Full Cost of Shipping and Handling

Currently up to 70% of all online shopping carts are abandoned by shoppers before they reach the final checkout page. This number is appalling. Picture going to your local grocery store and seeing that 70% of the people fill their shopping carts with food and then just leave the store! That's what's happening to many online merchants today.

There are a number of reasons for this. Either the customers didn't feel they had enough information about the product to make a buying decision or they still had questions about the credibility of the merchant. But another reason for abandoned online shopping carts is that customers don't like surprises. And one of the worst is being surprised with the true cost of a shipped product at the very end of the transaction.

Before they complete their transactions, your customers need to know the total amount of their order, including shipping, handling, and applicable taxes. Customers should have the opportunity to see the changes made to the total transaction cost, such as changes to shipping methods and gift-wrapping charges, before they check out.

To avoid surprises, consider adding a shipping policy and rate pop-up chart on all your product pages. This lets visitors know what your shipping rates are before adding the product to the shopping cart.

If you want to surprise your customers, surprise them with good offers and great service.

Product or Services Catalog Pages

These pages represent the catalog of products or services that you sell. How you describe your offerings is just as important as the offerings themselves. You should sell not only the "steak," but also the "sizzle." Take some time to describe how the particular product or service meets a customer's needs; don't offer just a dry tome of features and specifications.

Online Press Room

A site press room is a source of publicity about your company and an important resource for journalists who want to do stories on your business. We talk more about a press room and press releases as a customer-acquisition device in Chapter 18, "Public Relations." But for now, keep this in mind when creating your press room copy for your storyboard.

A good e-commerce press room should do the following:

- Describe your company and what makes its products or services unique
- Provide images, photos, or downloadable information for your product or service

- List the key people in management and detail each person's professional and business backgrounds
- Provide a press contact, someone who can tell the company story consistently
- Ask if a visiting journalist wants to receive future press releases, and provide a choice of contact method
- List all your latest press releases and media mentions

Content Pages

As we stated in Chapter 3, "Architecting Your Online Storefront," your site's content must be interesting enough to make visitors come to your site, stay, and keep coming back for more. And that doesn't include the content on your product or services catalog pages.

Keep in mind that your content does not have to be closely related to your product, but it does have to meet your prospective customers' needs and desires. You need to make your Web store not only a place to buy things, but also a place visitors can become informed and educated in their buying decision.

Community Pages

In Chapter 3, we said that content can attract shoppers to your site. But to generate a continuous flow of repeat visitors, you need to provide access to an interactive community. So create any and all content for the community interaction pages of your website, including, perhaps, discussion board threads and chat room instructions. Community features will increase the number of visits, giving you opportunities to sell your products or services to shoppers.

Site Map

You might also consider a separate page on your online storefront for a site map. Like the table of contents of a book, it's a list of hyperlinks to each page of your site. A site map serves as an orientation for site visitors and shows them the scope of the site (see Figure 4.4). Site maps are important for another reason, too. Search engines use them to spider your site and catalog all the pages of your Web store. You can also create a Google site map to increase visibility of all your product pages on Google.com. Google Sitemaps is any easy way to submit all your URLs and get detailed reports on how Google directs traffic to your site and how the Googlebot sees your pages. For additional

CHAPTER 4 Storyboarding Your E-Commerce Site 55

information on Google Sitemap, visit www.google.com/webmasters/sitemaps/. Also make sure you add a link to your site map on the home page of your website.

FIGURE 4.4

Site maps help search engines catalog all the Web pages of your store; they contain links to all your product pages.

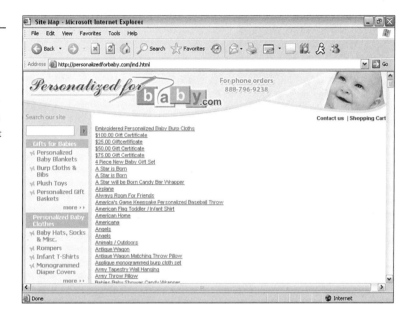

When you have your storyboard written, you're ready to create or customize your e-commerce storefront. In the next chapter, we discuss why you should customize your Yahoo! store, what the different options are when customizing your store, and whether you should customize the site yourself or have a professional do it.

CHAPTER

5

Customizing Your Yahoo! Store

In This Chapter

- Why you should customize your store
- The different options when customizing your store
- Whether you should customize the site yourself or have a professional do it

You're cruising along with your current Yahoo! store, and it's generating a decent amount of income. But you know you can generate more traffic and more revenue, and convert more visitors into buyers by taking your site to the next level. Looking at your competitor websites or other Yahoo! stores, you would like to implement some of the features, functionality, and design elements they have.

Whether you are taking your current Yahoo! store to the next level or you want to leap into the e-commerce water with both feet and start creating a full-time online business, you will need to know what's available to you.

If you are starting a new e-commerce website, you will want to keep these ideas and features in mind when designing and developing your store. If you haven't established a Yahoo! store, look at the quick-startup checklist we provide in Appendix A, "Daily, Weekly, and Monthly E-Business To-Do Lists." You might also want to pick up our first book, *Launching Your Yahoo! Business* (Que, 2006), for more thorough instructions on setting up a Yahoo! store.

Why You Should Customize Your Store

Customizing your store doesn't necessarily mean doing a complete redesign of your site and spending a lot of time and money. Although you can do a complete redesign, you might just want to improve your store by adding advanced features, such as a Recently Viewed Items section like the one on Amazon.com (seen Figure 5.1) or a Tell a Friend email component (see Figure 5.2).

Let's take a look at some of the reasons you might want to customize your store. Knowing why you should do it will help you determine whether you should do it:

- **Branding**—You want your website "look and feel" to be unique and consistent with your collateral material, such as your logo, business cards, brochures, and flyers. The out-of-the-box Yahoo! store template might not give you the brand recognition you desire, and you don't want your site to look like other Yahoo! stores.

- **New look**—You want your site to look new and fresh. A newly redesigned website can create excitement and a new experience, especially if you have a lot of recurring customers.

CHAPTER 5 Customizing Your Yahoo! Store   59

FIGURE 5.1
Amazon.com offers a Recently Viewed Items section. Visitors can easily navigate back to products they were interested in.

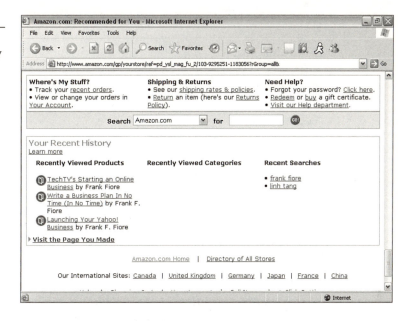

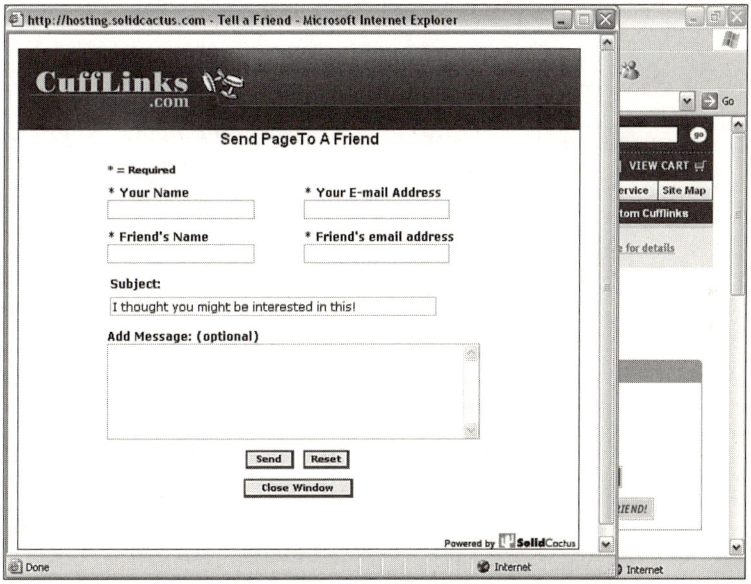

FIGURE 5.2
The Tell a Friend email feature is a great tool for spreading the news about your website and products. Visitors can send an email to friends and family about your site without having to use their email account. They can send an email with a personalized message with an online Web form from your site.

- **New features**—You want to implement new features, such as multiple product-image views, a shipping policy pop-up chart, discussion boards, subscription pages, shopping and customer service tools to help customers, or a "Send this page to a friend" component. You research other competitor websites and see features that are working for them that you would also like to implement. We discuss specific advanced features in this chapter.

- **New technology**—You want to add new technologies, such as Flash video, to describe your products; or integrate other payment options, such as PayPal, to increase sales. Keeping up with and implementing new technologies can make your website more efficient and create a better buying experience, which results in more customers.

- **Expansion**—You started out with only a few products, and now your product line has increased so much that it's impossible to maintain. You need a solution for updating and uploading products quickly and as easily as possible.

- **Search engine optimization**—Search engine traffic has become an important part of your marketing strategy. You want dynamically generated features that will help your site achieve higher search engine ranking. Search engine traffic can help reduce cost of per-customer acquisition.

- **Navigation and flow**—The way you thought your customers will navigate through your store isn't the way they actually move through it. You discover that they don't see or pay attention to your main navigation bar. You need to add other navigation options, such as breadcrumbs, to help them navigate your site.

- **Maintenance**—Adding new products, updating images, and editing descriptions has become time consuming and more difficult with the volume of orders that is coming in. You need a better solution to manage your products.

- **Ease of use**—You want to improve your website's ease of use. You don't want to have the customer click five times before getting to certain products. You're getting more customer service calls and emails because the site isn't user-friendly and the customer is confused about how to order a product. Your site must be intuitive, not ambiguous.

- **Retention and acquisition**—Why are customers abandoning the site when they get to the checkout page? Are you losing customers because of the way your site is set up or the way it looks? A professional layout and design will help improve customer acquisition.

- **Cross-selling**—If customers are going to purchase from you, why not introduce them to other products that relate to or complement the product they are purchasing? Displaying cross-selling items in the right place will help increase sales.

- **Complex buying choices**—You need a new solution for the complex buying options for particular products. Products such as computers have many features that can be upgraded and customized during the purchasing process. You want a customized solution that will allow your customers to easily choose which features they want.

- **Competition**—Your competitor(s) have a better website with advanced features and a better design. You're afraid that customers would rather purchase or do business with them. You want to at least be equivalent or superior to their websites.

- **Reduced support phone calls and emails**—Confusing and unfriendly product layout, ordering process, and site navigation can cause unnecessary support calls and emails. Solving these issues could reduce or even eliminate these tasks.

On the other hand, the old saying goes, "If it ain't broke, don't fix it." There are plenty of reasons to customize your store, as we just mentioned, and there are many reasons not to—or, at least, to be aware of. Just because you can doesn't always mean you should.

Before you dive into any major website modifications, be sure you've done your homework. Address the pros and cons of each change and determine how each change will help generate more traffic and more revenue. Survey customers on how your store can be improved. Talk to your support staff on the type of Web-related support calls they receive. Examine your competitors' websites and see what they are doing. Put together a focus group and get feedback on design, experience, and ease of use.

When to Customize Your Store

So when is it a good time to start customizing your store? This mostly depends on how complex the customization is and how much time it will take. If you are planning to add a few advanced features, it shouldn't take long and you can do it anytime. If you are planning a major overhaul, adequate planning and implementation will be needed before you launch the new features or site.

Even if you hire a professional Yahoo! store design company to design or add the advanced features, it will still require some time and effort on your part.

Six main stages are involved when customizing your store:

1. **Analysis stage**—Define needs and goals. Develop documentation of requirements.
2. **Design stage**—Develop components and features according to design requirements and specifications.
3. **Evaluation stage**—Test and debug new features and components. Release beta version, if necessary.
4. **Launch stage**—Launch approved components and features. Can be phased into multiple launch dates.
5. **Feedback stage**—Request feedback from customers. Make additional changes and adjustments, if necessary.
6. **Redesign stage**—An ongoing stage based on continuous feedback.

Be sure to ask yourself a few things when planning to customize your store:

- How long will the development take?
- Will it take away resources from other essential duties?
- Can it be completed during non-peak times?
- Will I have enough time to work out the bugs?
- How experienced is the person or company in developing Yahoo! stores?
- Can the changes be launched in stages?

> **warning**
>
> **Making Changes in the Staging Area**
>
> Only one staging area is available for redeveloping or adding features to your site before it is published live. If you are hiring a development company, you will not be able to make other template changes while it is working on the changes to your site. You also cannot publish individual changes. When you publish the site, you upload all current changes in the staging area. If you are planning to release changes in stages, you can make changes to the template only in the current stage.

Different Options for Customizing Your Store

You have three main options when customizing your store:

- Use the current template, adjust variables, and insert custom HTML headers and footers.
- Do not use Store Editor; use Web hosting with store tags.
- Develop custom templates using RTML.

If you are a current Yahoo! store owner and have outgrown the standard template and functionality, you might want to consider either adjusting the variables and inserting custom HTML headers and footers, or continue building on the Yahoo! template using RTML. This is one of the biggest decisions you will make when taking your site to the next level. All three directions will take you down a different path, and switching back to a different method can be difficult, time-consuming, and costly. Talk to current Yahoo! store owners or Yahoo! store development companies, such as Solid Cactus (www.solidcactus.com), before you start your customization.

tip You can join Y Store Forums, provided by www.ystoretools.com, and post questions about the Yahoo! Merchant Solutions. This is also a great forum for other Yahoo! store owners and developers to review your store.

Let's take a closer look at all three methods and the pros and cons for each.

Web Resource

Yahoo! Store Designer Directory

Have an advanced feature that you want installed or need custom RTML programming help? Yahoo! provides a list of store developers and designers at http://smallbusiness.yahoo.com/merchant/designdir.php.

Yahoo! Talk

RTML

RTML is a proprietary real programming language used by Yahoo! store to describe websites. Yahoo! store templates are written using RTML.

Adjusting Variables and Inserting Custom HTML Headers and Footers

Instead of going through a major redesign and creating a new template, you can simply add custom HTML in the header and footer to give your site a new look. Also, adjusting variables such as font, color, background, button style, and type can give the standard Yahoo! template a custom feel. In addition, you can upload custom image buttons without any programming. Table 5.1 compares the pros and cons of using variables and inserting custom HTML headers and footers.

TABLE 5.1   Pros and Cons of Using Variables and Inserting Custom HTML Headers and Footers

Pros	Cons
This is an inexpensive way to customize your site design.	This applies only to the design "look and feel;" it does not add advanced functionality.
Changing variables does not require technical capabilities.	Some technical capabilities are needed to add HTML headers and footers.
Most Web designers and developers can add custom HTML headers and footers.	This might not give you the exact page layout you require.

Inserting Custom HTML Headers and Footers

To insert custom HTML headers and footers, just follow these steps:

1. In Store Manager, click the Store Editor link.
2. Click the red triangle to display the advance button set.
3. Click the Variables button.
4. Scroll down until you see the Page Properties section. Here, you can paste your custom HTML header in the Head Tags input box and your custom HTML footer in the Final Text input box (see Figure 5.3). If you are using images, you can upload your images to the hosting account and reference the images from the hosting account.

You can also use a style sheet by adding it in the Head Tags input box and then uploading the `.css` file to the hosting account.

FIGURE 5.3

A custom HTML header and footer can be added in the Head Tags and Final Text input box under the advanced variables settings in Store Editor.

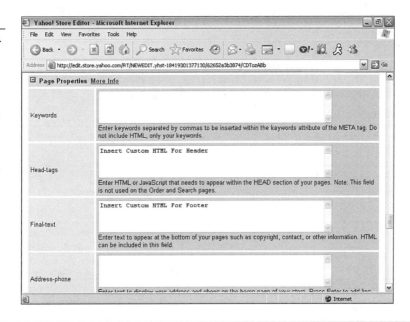

> **Yahoo! Talk**
>
> **Store Editor**
> The Store Editor is used to manage both storefront inventory and design.

Using Web Hosting to Customize Your Store

Web hosting lets you design your site using HTML building tools such as Yahoo! SiteBuilder and Macromedia Dreamweaver. When you're ready to upload your Web pages, you need to use an FTP client to upload your files. To add product data to your pages, you need to add special bits of custom code called Store Tags in the HTML of the page. The product data for the Web pages comes directly from Catalog Manager, where you add the product info.

Before you can even add the Store Tags to your page, you must create the product(s) in Catalog Manager. If you are using SiteBuilder or Macromedia Dreamweaver, you can use Merchant Solutions Extension tools to more easily import product data and create the necessary Store Tags automatically. Table 5.2 compares the pros and cons of using Web hosting to customize your store.

TABLE 5.2 Pros and Cons of Using Web Hosting

Pros	Cons
You're comfortable using WYSIWYG HTML software-building tools such as SiteBuilder or Dreamweaver.	You cannot dynamically generate product pages.
You want to build the website yourself and do not want to learn RTML.	Product pages must be created one by one.
You do not have a lot of products, and you do not need a robust database upload to add and edit your products.	You need to learn an HTML software tool to develop the pages.
	You might not be able to use future features developed by Yahoo!, which was built around RTML.
	You cannot use prebuilt advanced features built by other RTML Yahoo! store developers.

Using RTML to Customize Your Store

RTML is Yahoo!'s proprietary language for building the store templates. Any changes to the template, such as design or functionality, must be programmed in RTML. With RTML, you reap all the benefits of a dynamically generated site and a static HTML site. Dynamically generated sites tend to be easier to manage, usually with an administrative interface, but they do not fare well with search engines because their content does not reside on the page. The product pages are usually generated by some sort of database. Static HTML pages, on the other hand, are more optimized for search engines but require an HTML authoring tool to create and edit each page one by one. Creating product pages one at a time, as you would do if using the Web hosting side, can be quite time-consuming.

RTML enables you to continue managing your store and products using Store Editor and Catalog Manager, as you would do with a dynamically generated site. This will save you time, and you won't need technical knowledge of website programming. Although the product pages are generated dynamically when you perform a database upload of your products, RTML writes static HTML pages, which will help with search engine placement.

If the RTML templates are developed correctly, you will never have to look at the code again. You should have complete control over any product or data.

You should also be able to quickly add products, update products, and add sections. Table 5.3 compares the pros and cons of using RTML.

TABLE 5.3 Pros and Cons of Using RTML

Pros	Cons
You've already been working in Catalog Manager and Store Editor, and you don't want your efforts to go to waste.	If you do not know RTML, you will need to hire a company or programmer.
You want to continue to use the database upload feature to dynamically create your products and pages.	There are fewer RTML programmers and companies than there are HTML programmers and companies.
You want to use the RTML advanced features.	Not a lot of documentation on RTML exists.
You do not want to create product pages one by one, as in using Web hosting.	
You want to implement features, such as breadcrumbs, that can be generated on the fly.	

So which method is better? It is recommended that you either stick with adjusting variables and adding custom HTML for the headers and footers, or use RTML to customize your store. If you are going to start by just making changes to the variables, you will be able to upgrade and use custom RTML in the future. Avoid Web hosting, if possible. Yahoo! also recommends using RTML to customize your store for better performance and functionality. If Yahoo! is recommending it, you can bet it plans to build more features and functionality around the RTML concept.

The rest of this book focuses on RTML advantages and features, but does not go into detail on how to program using RTML. If you would like to learn more about RTML, go to Y-Times Publication, (www.ytimes.com) (see Figure 5.4). Y-Times Publication offers books, e-books, and newsletters on how to program using RTML.

FIGURE 5.4

Y-Times offers RTML books and e-books. If you're serious about learning RTML, take a look at its RTML Mega Pack; it comes bundled with a printed book and four e-books.

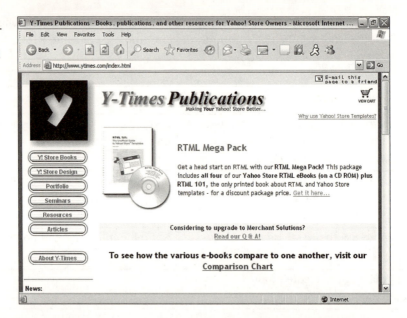

Customize: Design It Yourself or Hire an Expert

The decision of whether to customize the store in-house or hire a company to do so depends on a few things. Before you make a decision, ask yourself these questions:

- Does my staff or I have the time to do it in house?
- How much experience do I have in customizing the store, including knowledge of RTML?
- What is my budget for hiring an outside company?
- When do I need the new site or advanced features to be up and running?
- Would I rather spend my valuable time marketing my site to generate more revenue or trying to customize the site?

The old saying goes, "Time is money." If this is your full-time business and your time is better spent marketing the site or running the day-to-day operations, spend the extra dollars and hire a professional. Hiring a professional company will ensure that you get it done right the first time, and the company also will most likely know how to convert more visitors into customers with some of the advanced tools and features it can implement.

Companies such as Solid Cactus (www.solidcactus.com) (see Figure 5.4), have developed hundreds of successful Yahoo! stores in almost every industry. Using companies such as Solid Cactus ensures that the job is done right the first time. Solid Cactus can also help you market your site online with advanced marketing tactics.

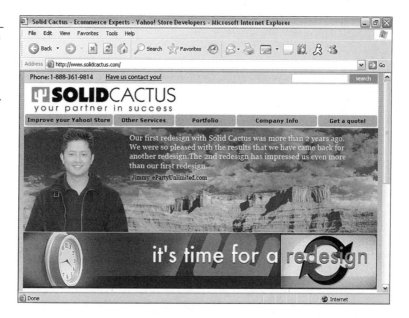

FIGURE 5.5
Solid Cactus has developed hundreds of Yahoo! Stores and is Yahoo!'s premier store developer and trusted partner.

For a list of other Yahoo! store development companies, visit www.myecommercesuccess.com.

Customizing your store and taking the site to the next level can be exciting and challenging at the same time. After all, you are probably moving from a part-time hobby into a full-time business. In the next chapter, we look at specific advanced layout, navigation, marketing, and search-engine optimization features.

> **warning**
>
> **Research-Development Company**
>
> Make sure the company you hire has experience developing Yahoo! stores. Ask to interview some of its clients, and review its portfolio of other Yahoo! stores. Hiring a company without the proper experience can cause more work and money down the road.

CHAPTER 6

Yahoo! Store Features and Advanced Techniques

In This Chapter

- What store features are available and why you should add them to your store

- How to create all your product pages by using the Database Upload feature

- How to upload multiple images simultaneously and have them automatically inserted on the appropriate page

With the basics of store layout under your belt, it's time to move on to more advanced Yahoo! store features and techniques. Changing how a product is presented and enhancing your store by adding marketing tools can increase your bottom line. Creating a description that sells and having a great product is only part of the formula. You want to enhance your store not only to close a sale, but also to upsell the total order. In addition, you want to make the buying process more user-friendly, avoid confusion, and give the customer the necessary information to buy from you, not your competitors.

This chapter covers features that you might want to consider adding to your store. Although these features are not part of the standard Yahoo! store and will cost additional money in programming, they will help convert more visitors into buyers. These features require RTML programming and will need to be implemented by a third-party development company or programmer. Most of the Yahoo! store development companies, such as Solid Cactus (www.solidcactus.com), have developed most of these features for quick and easy implementation. This helps reduce cost and does not require programming from scratch.

Advanced Store-Layout Options and Ideas

Store-layout features help present your product information in a clear and concise format. These give customers all the necessary information to make a buying decision. You do not want the customer to have to wait for additional research or need to contact you to clarify something before making a purchase:

- **Custom Add to Cart button**—Add a custom Add to Cart button (see Figure 6.1) to match your look and feel or to make the button stand out. The default gray order button does not bring attention to the customer and is somewhat camouflaged on the page.

- **Custom quantity pricing layout**—Customers enter the number of products they would like to purchase before going through the checkout process. This is a great way to get customers to purchase more, especially if you offer volume discounts (see Figure 6.2).

- **Click to Enlarge Image**—The default product image does not inform the visitor they can view an enlarged version of the image. The Click to Enlarge Image feature gives your customers a larger picture of your product and informs them that they can click the image to enlarge it. This is useful especially if the customer needs to see details of your product (see Figure 6.3).

CHAPTER 6 Yahoo! Store Features and Advanced Techniques

- **Product info table**—A professional, easy-to-read table format (see Figure 6.4) of product information such as pricing, discounts, shipping costs, and options can help accelerate the purchasing decision. Customers do not have to look all over your product page for vital information.

- **Multiple-product Add to Cart**—Customers can add multiple items with just one click of the button (see Figure 6.5). Multiple products, along with quantity ordered boxes, can be displayed on the same page. This is very convenient if your products are sold in sets.

- **Shipping policy pop-up chart**—Customers want to know how much shipping will cost and when will they receive their products before adding them to the shopping cart (see Figure 6.6). One of the main reasons customers abandon a transaction during the checkout process is that they do not like the shipping cost or timeframe.

- **Custom option display**—A simple-to-read and well-positioned custom option display makes it easier for customers to add options or customize their order (see Figure 6.7). This is a must if you have customizable products, such as engraving.

- **Custom contact form**—Allow your customers to quickly and easily contact you with a custom contact form (see Figure 6.8). You can control the questions by adding your own specific custom fields. An online contact form enables your customers to contact you without needing an email client.

FIGURE 6.1
A custom Add to Cart button stands out and draws attention. This makes it easier for customers to add the product to the shopping cart.

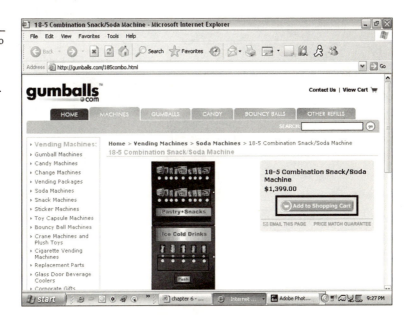

FIGURE 6.2

The custom quantity pricing layout shows customers volume discount pricing right on the page. This entices customers to purchase more items for greater savings.

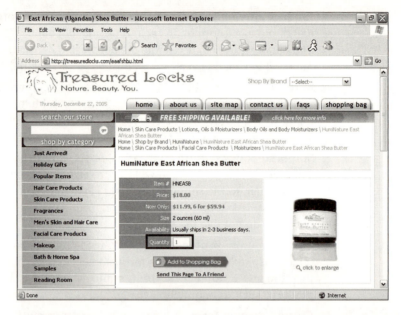

FIGURE 6.3

The Click to Enlarge Image feature enables customers to click on the product thumbnail to view a larger version of the image.

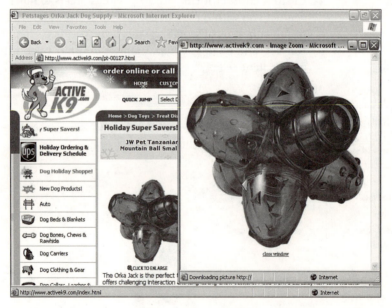

CHAPTER 6   Yahoo! Store Features and Advanced Techniques   **75**

FIGURE 6.4
A custom product info table can present your product information in an easy-to-read format. Most customers just skim your product information and do not like to read a long paragraph description.

FIGURE 6.5
The multiple-product Add to Cart feature enables customers to purchase multiple products with just a click of the button.

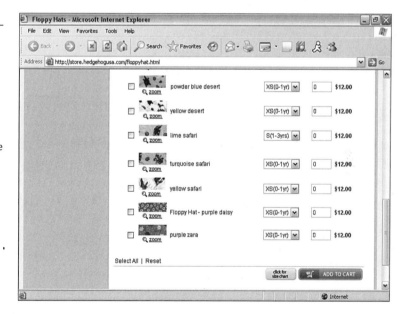

FIGURE 6.6

A shipping policy pop-up chart gives customers shipping options and rates without making them leave the product page or go through the checkout process.

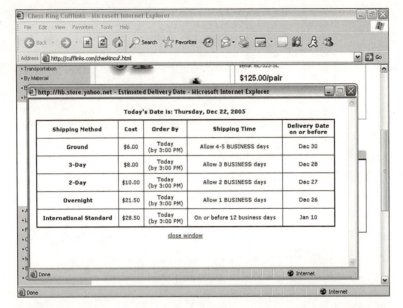

FIGURE 6.7

A custom option display shows your product option in a more user-friendly and easy-to-read format.

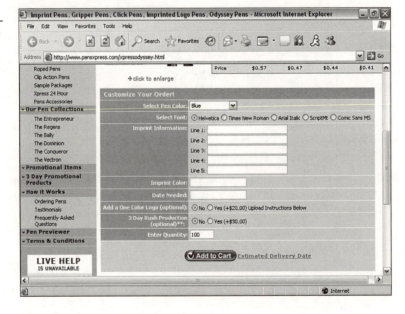

FIGURE 6.8

A custom contact form enables your customer to contact you or give you feedback without having to use an email client.

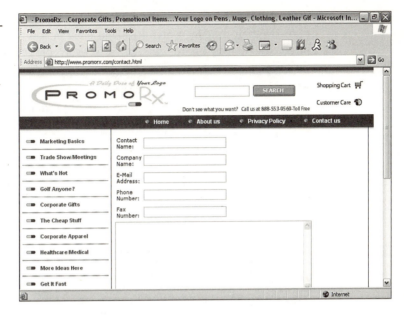

Advanced Store-Navigation Options and Ideas

Store-navigation features are designed to help your customers navigate your site quickly and efficiently. They help customers find the exact product they are looking for and create a user-friendly buying experience:

- **Breadcrumbs**—Breadcrumbs are a great way let your customers know where they are in your site (see Figure 6.9). They provide an easy way to backtrack to parent sections when viewing products. Breadcrumbs also help them remember which section they found that particular product in.

- **Multiple breadcrumbs**—Multiple breadcrumbs show multiple product paths (see Figure 6.10). These are useful especially if your product belongs in multiple categories.

- **Dynamic pagination**—For faster loading time and to eliminate constant scrolling, you can dynamically break up the number of products displayed into multiple pages (see Figure 6.11). Customers can skip between pages or have an option to view all products in one page.

- **Dynamic cascading menu**—A dynamic sliding submenu appears if the customer hovers over the main navigation link or button (see Figure 6.12). Customers do not have to click on the parent category to go to a subcategory.

- **Advanced search**—An advanced search can help customers search for or narrow their product search (see Figure 6.13). You can allow customers to search by brand, date, price, or even color.
- **Related items**—Displaying related items helps customers consider other similar products they might be interested in (see Figure 6.14). It's a great way to get customers to purchase other products.

FIGURE 6.9
Breadcrumbs let customers know where they are in your store.

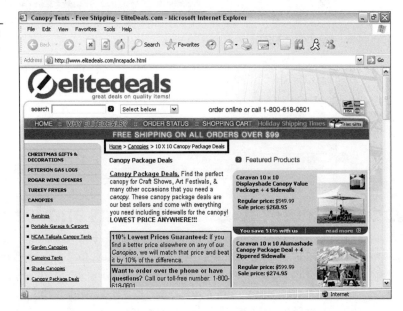

CHAPTER 6   Yahoo! Store Features and Advanced Techniques   79

FIGURE 6.10
Multiple breadcrumbs let customers know if products are located in other sections.

FIGURE 6.11
Dynamic pagination separates products into multiple pages to speed page-load time and reduce constant scrolling.

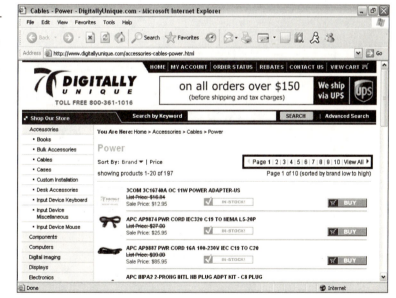

FIGURE 6.12

A dynamic cascading menu enables customers to drill down to subcategories without having to click on the parent category.

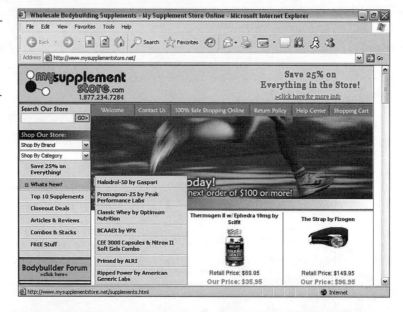

FIGURE 6.13

An advanced search helps narrow results.

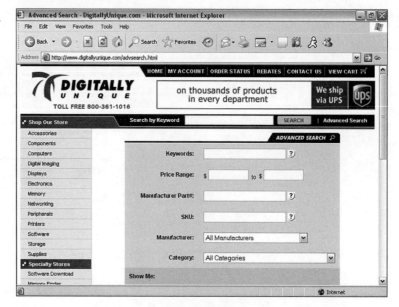

FIGURE 6.14
Related items show other products similar or complimentary to a product customers are interested in.

Advanced Promotional Options and Ideas

Marketing features help you increase your bottom line by selling more products. A site that is professional and well laid out helps customers make important buying decisions:

- **Send This Page to a Friend**—This enables a customer to tell friends about your site or product by completing an online form (see Figure 6.15). An email is sent to the individual with a link to the page and a message from the sender.
- **Multiple product image views**—Let your customers view multiple images of your product (see Figure 6.16). The default setting allows up to two product images. This is a great feature for products that come in multiple colors and for electronics; many buyers want to see the back of the product for input/output configurations.
- **You Save display**—Show a message and percentage of how much the customer is saving (see Figure 6.17).
- **Cross-selling**—Similar to the Related Items feature, cross-selling enables you to display other products the customer might be interested in (see Figure 6.18).
- **Random best-selling item display**—Randomly display best-selling or featured items. A different set of products appears every time someone comes to the site or refreshes the page (see Figure 6.19).

- **Recently Viewed Items section**—Customers can easily get back to items they were interested in or previously viewed. A list of recently viewed items is displayed at the bottom of the page (see Figure 6.20).

- **Secure Shopping graphic**—Let your customers know that your site and their credit card transactions are safe and secure. A Secure Shopping graphic enforces that message (see Figure 6.21).

- **Shopping cart cookie tester**—Test to see if customers have cookies turned off. If so, a message appears notifying them how to turn the cookies back on, or they will not be able to order from your store. This feature is standard with version 3 of Checkout Manager; no programming is required.

- **Randomly displayed testimonial**—Randomly display testimonials from your customers. A different testimonial appears every time the page is loaded. Customers feel secure when they hear that other customers were happy with you, your products, and your services.

- **Email newsletter subscription**—Customers can join your email newsletter by filling out an online form. Monthly email newsletters help you stay in front of your customer and new product releases and specials.

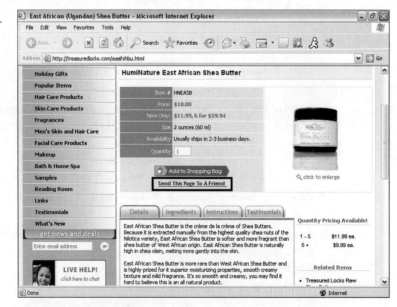

FIGURE 6.15
Send This Page to a Friend provides a convenient way to let customers tell their friends and family about your site.

CHAPTER 6   Yahoo! Store Features and Advanced Techniques   83

FIGURE 6.16
Multiple product image views enable you to upload multiple images of your product. It's perfect for products with multiple colors or if you need to show different angle views.

FIGURE 6.17
The You Save display shows the amount saved in either percentage or a dollar amount. This lets customers know exactly how much they are saving.

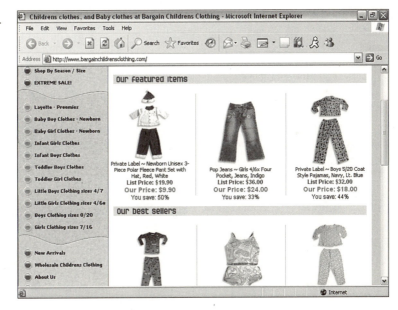

FIGURE 6.18
Cross-selling enables you to display other products to up-sell the total order package.

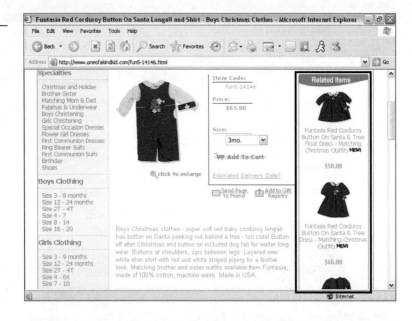

FIGURE 6.19
A random best-selling item display shows a list of the most popular items sold at your store. This gives customers ideas of which items are hot.

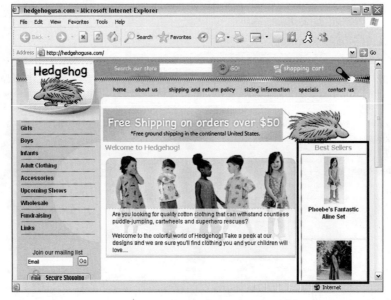

FIGURE 6.20
A recently viewed items section shows a list of products the customer previously viewed. This enables the customer to easily navigate back to previously viewed products.

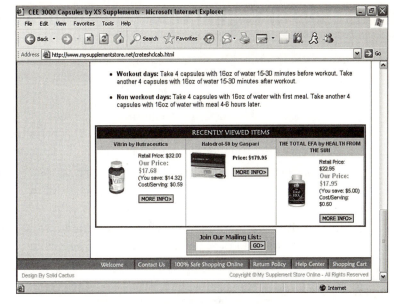

FIGURE 6.21
A Secure Shopping graphic lets customers know that your site and their credit card transactions are secure and safe.

Advanced Search Engine Options and Ideas

Search engine features help search engine spiders find your product pages easily and help you increase search engine ranking. Search engine traffic, besides pay-per-click, is free, and these are qualified leads that are looking for your particular product or information:

- **Related Items section**—Similar to the cross-selling function, other related items appear next to the product. This helps create internal keyword-rich content for search engines.

- **Breadcrumbs**—Breadcrumbs not only help customers navigate through your site, but they also contain keyword-rich content and keyword-rich internal links (refer to Figure 6.9).

- **Multiple breadcrumbs**—Multiple breadcrumbs shows multiple product paths (refer to Figure 6.10) and add keyword-rich internal links.

- **Text-based menus**—Instead of image menu buttons, text-based menus help with search engine ranking, especially if you have keyword-rich text in your menu. Search engines cannot read images. Switching to a text-based menu also helps create your menus dynamically.

- **Change page name to text**—By default, Yahoo! creates an image for the page name. Although it looks like text, it's actually an image. Changing the page name to text helps with search engine ranking. The page name usually contains keyword-rich text describing your product.

- **Image alt tags**—Some of your images do not have alt tags to describe your product. Adding a text description of your images helps with search engine ranking. Adding keywords in your alt tags helps with keyword density.

- **Dynamically generated metatags**—This feature scans your page to pull unique keywords and places them in your meta page description and keywords. This is a great solution if you don't have the time yourself to customize your meta descriptions and keyword phrases.

- **Custom 404 "Page Not Found"**—A custom "Page Not Found" message helps customers get to your site even if they clicked on a link that no longer exists on your site. Instead getting a blank "Page Not Found" message, they arrive at your custom page. This allows them to still navigate through your site.

- **Categorized site map**—A site map has categorized links to all your products. Search engine spiders can get to your pages from a link off

CHAPTER 6   Yahoo! Store Features and Advanced Techniques   87

your home page. This increases your chances of getting more pages indexed by search engines (see Figure 6.22).

FIGURE 6.22
A categorized site map not only helps customers find your products, but it also helps search engine spiders scan all your pages and hopefully index more product pages.

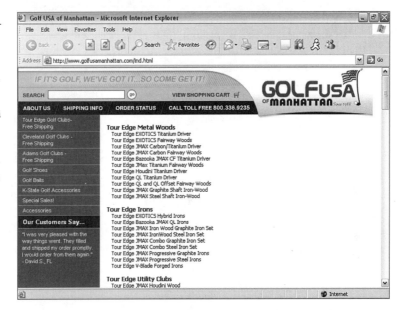

Creating Product Pages Using Database Upload

You can edit and add products in volume by using a spreadsheet program such as Microsoft Excel and uploading your product file into Catalog Manager. The Database Upload feature enables you to automatically create all your product pages and sections by simply uploading a `.csv` file. Using this feature saves you a tremendous amount of time and repetitive work. Although you can use a text editor such as Notepad to add and edit your products, it is recommended that you use Microsoft Excel so that you can more easily visually add, organize, and edit your product data (see Figure 6.23). Using a text editor can cause confusion when adding or editing products because there are no visually formatted columns. Database Upload is available for Store Editor—in fact, if you are building in Store Editor, you should use this feature because it enables merchants to include a path to create the hierarchy of a site, to avoid orphan product pages.

FIGURE 6.23

Microsoft Excel makes it easier for you to add and edit products because of the visual column and row structure.

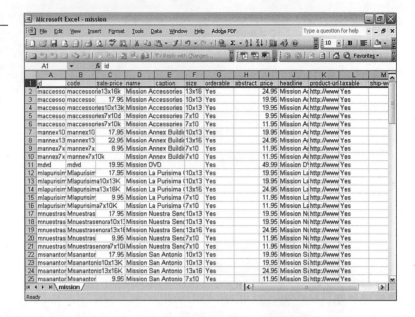

Take a look at this sample data file using a text editor:

```
code,price,path,name
S123,59.95,Shoes:Sneakers,Nike Air Jordans
F345,39.95,Shoes:Boots,Marc Nason
```

Database Upload also works with advanced features such as breadcrumbs, a site map, cascading menus, and more, if programmed properly. These features automatically are updated with your new product data file. You will want to speak to your programmer or development company about synchronizing those features with your database upload.

If you are using the Database Upload feature for the first time, it is recommended that you download the spreadsheet file and use it as your starting point.

To download the .csv file, follow these steps:

1. In Store Manger, click the Catalog Manager link under the Edit column.
2. Click the Upload Items link.
3. Click the Download button on the far right of the page.
4. Click the Download button with the default table selected.
5. Select the location where you want to save your file.

These required and optional fields are available in the file:

- **Name**—The name of your product. The name also is used as the `Title` tag for the product Web page.
- **Code**—A unique code. You can use a product SKU (Stock Keeping Unit), if available.
- **ID**—Another unique code that can contain only letters and numbers, no spacing. The ID is important because it must exactly match the image filename when using the multiple-image upload feature.
- **Price**—The amount you want to sell the item for.
- **Sale-price**—The discounted price.
- **Ship-weight**—The weight of the product only if you are using weight to calculate shipping price.
- **Options**—Product options, such as size and color.
- **Headline**—Any text in the Headline field replaces the page name. A more descriptive name can be added here for display.
- **Caption**—The text for the description of the product. The text is displayed underneath the Headline.
- **Abstract**—Used when text is needed for a description on another page.
- **Product-URL**—The exact Web page location of the product page. Because you are using the Database Upload feature, the URL is generated for you. The product ID is used as your page filename (www.yourdomain.com/id.html).
- **Path**—The section or category the product will be located in. By entering a name, the section button also automatically is created for you. You can create subsections by entering a colon—for example, Shoes: Sneakers.

When you have all the product information in your data file, you need to upload the file.

> **tip** You can also separate your products by creating more than one table or data file. Using multiple tables can help you manage your products better. This is also a great idea especially if you have products that are seasonal.

> **warning** Using the Database Upload feature can overwrite your entire site. When uploading a data file, you have the choice to add or rebuild the database. If you choose the rebuild option, all current products are deleted and only products in your new data file are available.

To upload the `.csv` file, follow these steps:

1. In Store Manger, click the Catalog Manager link under the Edit column.
2. Click the Upload Items link.
3. Click the Upload button on the far left.
4. Here, you are given two options (see Figure 6.24). The first option asks which table you would like to upload the file. If you plan to create multiple tables, you must create them before you upload the file. The second option asks if you would like to rebuild or add to the table. *Note:* The rebuild option completely erases all your products in the current table and replaces them with your new product in your data file. When you have selected the two options, you need to click the Browse button to locate your new data file.
5. When you locate your file, click the Upload button. This takes you to a

> **tip** **Reverting back to a previous `.csv` file**
>
> You can roll back to the last version of your data file if you made a mistake with the new data file. Simply click the Revert button on the upload page. Any new products in the new data file are erased because the previous data file did not include the new products.

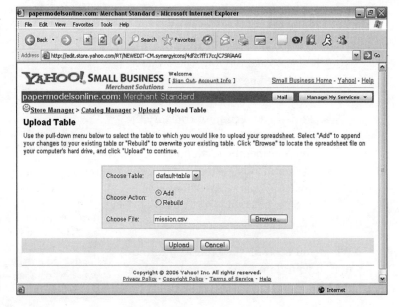

FIGURE 6.24
When uploading a `.csv` data file, you have an option to either rebuild or add to the database.

page to report any errors. If there are errors, correct the errors in the `.csv` file and upload the file again.

6. If there are no errors, click the Commit button. This takes you to a screen to confirm that you want to rebuild the product table. Click the Rebuild button. *Note:* If you are adding to the product table, an Add button appears instead of a Rebuild button.

Uploading Multiple Images at Once

If you have a lot of products, using the option to upload multiple images will help you save time. How does the system know where to put the images? The name of file must exactly match the ID of the product page.

The Yahoo! store supports both `.jpg` and `.gif` image formats.

For example, if your product ID is `zd100`, your image filename must be `zd100.jpg`. If it's a `.gif`, the image filename will be `zd100.gif`.

All images must be in a Zip file to be uploaded. This helps reduce the file size and speeds up the upload time. You can upload as many Zip files as you want, but only one Zip file can be uploaded at a time. If you don't have a Zip program, you can download WinZip (winzip.com) StuffIt (stuffit.com), or another Zip utility program:

1. When you have added all the image files into the Zip file, click the Store Editor link in the Store Manager control panel.
2. When the Store Editor home page appears, click the red triangle on the toolbar to display the advanced settings.
3. In the advanced settings, click the Controls button.
4. Scroll down until you see the Multiple Image Upload link, and click the link.
5. After you click the link, a dialog box appears where you can browse and upload your Zip file.

The next chapter looks at tips and tricks to customize your store and add advanced features.

CHAPTER 7

Yahoo! Store Tips and Tricks

In This Chapter

- How to enable the built-in breadcrumbs for the new store Editor
- How to add Cascading Style Sheets
- How to add related product items
- How to add a quantity box

In this chapter, we show you step by step how to implement the advanced features mentioned in the previous chapter. These features improve your store's navigation, marketing capability, and customer user experience.

Istvan Siposs and Michael Whitaker of Y-Times Publications (www.ytimes.com) have generously allowed us to share some of their step-by-step tips and tricks from their book *Yahoo! Store Tips and Tricks* (Y-Times Publications, 2005), which includes more than 100 useful tricks. Siposs and Whitaker are recognized Yahoo! store experts who have helped hundreds of merchants improve their Yahoo! stores through books, seminars, and consulting.

Enabling the Built-In Breadcrumbs

Breadcrumbs are a set of links to parent sections. This is a great way to let customers know where they are in your site and provide an easy way to backtrack to parent sections. The new Yahoo! Store Editor has the breadcrumbs feature built into it. This might come as a surprise, and, no wonder: No switch or variable in the editor lets you enable breadcrumbs. This is part of the body-switch template, as shown here:

```
Body-switch. (wid)
MULTI
   IF test @show-path.
      then MULTI
            TEXT "[ "
            WITH-LINK TO :index
               TEXT "Home"
            TEXT " &gt; "
            CALL :walk-up.
            TEXT @name
            TEXT " ]"
            LINEBREAK number 2
      else nil
   IF test EQUALS value1 @type
                  value2 :search.
      then CALL :search-body.
            wid
      else CALL :page-body.
            wid
```

In this template, if the variable `show-path.` is `true`, breadcrumbs will show up at the top of the page. The problem is, there is no variable or property called `show-path`. Let's create a custom variable by that name. However, notice that the variable in this template has a period at the end of its name. Because periods are not allowed in custom variables, you cannot add `show-path`. You can, however, modify the copy of this template. To turn on the built-in breadcrumbs, all you have to do is modify your copy of the `body-switch` template and change `@show-path.` to `up`. The template should then look like this:

```
MULTI
  IF test up
    then MULTI
           TEXT "[ "
           WITH-LINK TO :index
             TEXT "Home"
           TEXT " &gt; "
           CALL :yourstoreid-walk-up.
           TEXT @name
           TEXT " ]"
           LINEBREAK number 2
    else nil
  IF test EQUALS value1 @type
                value2 :search.
    then CALL :yourstoreid-search-body.
         wid
    else CALL :yourstoreid-page-body.
         wid
```

This makes sense because you want to show breadcrumbs only for pages that have parents (where `up` has a value). With this template modification, you get breadcrumbs that look something like those in Figure 7.1.

FIGURE 7.1

Breadcrumbs.

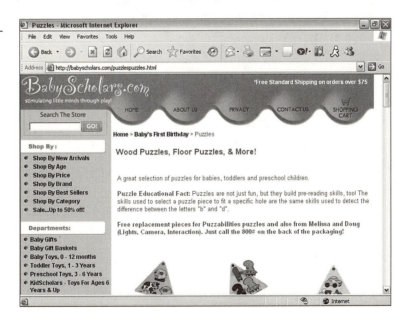

A couple of problems crop up with this: First, the font is the default browser font (Times New Roman, in this case). Second, the font is too big; breadcrumbs are usually smaller than the regular text font. To rectify this, first replace the second MULTI expression with a FONT, and paste that MULTI expression within the FONT operator:

```
MULTI
  IF test up
    then FONT size 1
              face @text-font
           MULTI
             TEXT "[ "
             WITH-LINK TO :index
                TEXT "Home"
             TEXT " &gt; "
             CALL :yourstoreid-walk-up
             TEXT @name
             TEXT " ]"
             LINEBREAK number 2
    else nil
  IF test EQUALS value1 @type
             value2 :search.
    then CALL :yourstoreid-search-body
             wid
    else CALL :yourstoreid-page-body
             wid
```

This is better, but the links between the home page and the current page are still too large. To fix that, edit your copy of the walk-up template. Originally, it looks like this:

```
yourstoreid-walk-up ()
FOR-EACH-OBJECT GET-PATH-TO dst id
                              src :index
                              nodst :t
                              nosrc :t
  WITH-LINK TO id
    FONT size @text-size
         face @text-font
      TEXT @name
  FONT size @text-size
       face @text-font
    TEXT " &gt; "
```

As you can see, FONT is set again in this template, so you have two choices:

1. Edit each FONT operator in this template and change size to 1.
2. Better yet, remove the FONT operators altogether.

This is what the finished template should look like:

```
Yourstoreid-walk-up ()
FOR-EACH-OBJECT GET-PATH-TO dst id
                                src :index
                                nodst :t
                                nosrc :t
    WITH-LINK TO id
      TEXT @name
    TEXT " &gt; "
```

Click to Enlarge

When an image is larger than the size specified by the `item-height` and `item-width` variables, the visitor can click on the image to view it full size. The problem is that unless the customer moves the mouse over the image, the customer will not know that the image can be clicked. Wouldn't it be more obvious if you could add the text "Click to Enlarge" right below the product image (see Figure 7.2)? To do this, you need to modify the `imexpand` template. The original, untouched template looks like this:

FIGURE 7.2

Click to Enlarge.

```
Yourstoreid-iImexpand (im orig hlimit wlimit align)
WITH= variable exp
      value CALL  :yourstoreid-imexpands
            RENDER image orig
                   hlimit
                   wlimit
  IF test NOT EQUALS value1 exp
                    value2 :no
        then WITH-LINK IMAGE-REF orig
              IMAGE source im
                    align align
                    alt WHEN EQUALS value1 exp
                                    value2 :yes
                        "Click to enlarge"
        else IMAGE source im
              align align
```

The bold line puts the image on the page using the `IMAGE` operator. That's the line you need to modify so that instead of simply displaying the image, you display the image *and* a text line that says, "Click to Enlarge." This can be achieved by replacing the `source` argument of the `IMAGE` operator with the image FUSE, together with the text line. The modified template looks like this:

```
Yourstoreid-imexpand   (im orig hlimit wlimit align)
WITH= variable exp
      value CALL  :yourstoreid-imexpands
            RENDER image orig
                   hlimit
                   wlimit
  IF test NOT EQUALS value1 exp
                    value2 :no
        then WITH-LINK IMAGE-REF orig
              IMAGE source FUSE axis :vertical
                                 im
                           RENDER text "Click to Enlarge"
                    align align
                    alt WHEN EQUALS value1 exp
                                    value2 :yes
                        "Click to enlarge"
        else IMAGE source im
              align align
```

To format the "Click to Enlarge" line to suit your needs, edit the RENDER operator and modify the `text-color`, `text-font`, `font-size`, and `text-align` arguments.

Cascading Style Sheets

CSS was introduced to define how to display HTML tags. Without CSS, the browser basically decides how to display common tags such as `<P>`, `<H1>`, and `<A>`, giving the designer little control over the appearance. CSS gives you more control and options over the appearance of your Yahoo! store. CSS is particularly useful for creating rollover effects for text-navigation links. Just as with HTML, you can create CSS by hand in a text editor, but it's easier to use editors such as Dreamweaver for that task. You can use CSS in a Yahoo! store in two ways:

- **Internal style sheet**—Paste the style sheet information directly into the `HEAD-TAGS` variable:

    ```
    <style type="text/css">
    a:link {color: #FF0000}
    a:visited {color: #00FF00}
    a:hover {color: #FF00FF}
    a:active {color: #0000FF}
    </style>
    ```

    This changes the appearance of every hyperlink in your Yahoo! store that uses the simple `<A>` tag. Remember to provide a proper opening (`<style....>`) and closing (`</style>`) tag.

- **External style sheet**—Upload your CSS file to your Yahoo! Web Hosting account and link to it as in the previous example:

    ```
    <link rel="stylesheet" type="text/css" href="http://site.your-domain.com/style.css" />
    ```

The preferred approach to using CSS is to use an external style sheet. After the external style sheet file is loaded into the browser, it is cached for subsequent pages and, hence, reduces page-load times. Also, from an SEO standpoint, the fewer nonvisible page elements there are in the HTML source code, the better. (For this reason, you should also put any JavaScript in an external file.)

Here is a practical example you can use right away: removing the default padding and margin from your page layout (see Figure 7.3).

FIGURE 7.3

Using CSS to remove padding and margin.

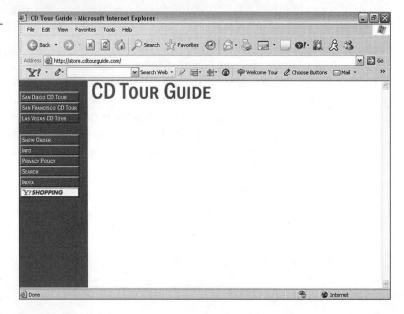

Without having to modify any templates, you can simply add the following instruction to your style sheet:

```
body {margin:0; padding:0;}
```

Naturally, you can also use this to add increase margin and padding.

It is beyond the scope of this book to cover CSS in any great detail. If you are not familiar with style sheets, you should consult the excellent tutorial at www.w3schools.com/css/css_intro.asp, or purchase *Sams Teach Yourself CSS in 24 Hours* (Pearson Education, 2002).

Bestsellers

The Bestseller feature is usually similar to the Specials feature (see Figure 7.4). Whereas specials are items you want to promote (typically because of reduced prices or other promotions), bestsellers are products that you sell a lot of—and that's exactly the reason you want to call your customers' attention to them. Bestsellers are usually not as important as specials; therefore, their placement is normally not as prominent. Bestsellers can appear in various locations on the home page depending on the design of the store. For most stores, a narrow column along the right side of the home page works well for this purpose. To see an example, go to www.notetools.com.

FIGURE 7.4
Bestsellers advanced feature.

Setting up the bestsellers is a task with two main parts: identifying and listing the bestsellers, and showing them on the home page. Identifying the bestsellers is very similar to identifying specials. You need a field like the `Specials` property of the home page. Because the bestsellers will most likely be displayed on the home page only, you can add a new property called `bestseller` of type `references` to the home page. To mark an item as a bestseller, simply enter its ID into this new Bestseller box while editing the home page. As in the case of the specials, you can enter the IDs of multiple bestsellers into the Bestsellers box. Multiple IDs must be separated by spaces.

To show the bestsellers, you need a template that will create the thumbnails and links for the bestsellers, and then you need to place this template on the home page. The template that creates the bestseller thumbnails, `show-bestsellers`, is listed next. For each bestseller, it shows the thumbnail of the bestseller, the name (or label) of the bestseller, and its price. It also hyperlinks both the thumbnail and the name to the bestseller's page:

```
Show-bestsellers ()

TABLE border 0
       cellspacing 0
       cellpadding 0
       width "100%"
  TABLE-ROW valign :top
    TABLE-CELL align :center
```

```
TEXT-STYLE :bold
  TEXT "BESTSELLERS"
LINEBREAK number 2
FOR-EACH-OBJECT @bestsellers
  FONT size 2
       face @text-font
    WITH-LINK TO WHEN @template
                  id
      WHEN IF test @icon
            then @icon
            else @image
      IMAGE source RENDER image IF test @icon
                                     then @icon
                                     else @image
                    max-height WITH-OBJECT :index
                                   @thumb-height
                    max-width WITH-OBJECT :index
                                   @thumb-width
            hspace 3
            alt @name
      LINEBREAK
      FOR-EACH-BUT variable line
                sequence LINES IF test NONEMPTY @label
                                 then @label
                                 else @name
                    last LINEBREAK
        TEXT line
    WITH= variable price
         value OR
                @sale-price
                @price
    WHEN price
      LINEBREAK
      FONT size 2
           color @emphasis-color
           face @text-font
        TEXT PRICE number ELEMENT position 0
                                    sequence price
                     currency @currency
  LINEBREAK number 2
```

A number of small details require further explanation:

- Notice how the thumbnail is created. First, if the item has an icon, it is used as the thumbnail; otherwise, it is the image. The maximum size of the thumbnails is determined by the thumb-width and thumb-height variables *as defined on the home page.* That's what the WITH-OBJECT :index business is about. There, you take the value of the thumb-width and thumb-height variables from the home page. Without that (if you simply used thumb-width or thumb-height), your bestseller list could end up with various thumbnail sizes if either of these variables was overridden for any of the bestsellers.

- The way the hyperlink is created (the `WITH-LINK TO...` part) might seem a bit strange, but here is what's going on: You want to hyperlink to the bestseller only if the bestseller has a page to hyperlink to. Every item in a Yahoo! store that has a page also has a template. Conversely, if an item has no template (if its template is `nil`), the item has no page generated for it.

- I use either the `label` property (if provided) or the `name` property to show the title of the bestseller. That's what the `IF test NONEMPTY @label` expression does. This way, you can have different text appear for the bestseller on the home page than on the bestseller's own page. This can come handy if the name of the item is too long.

- Finally, you can simplify the way prices are displayed. Show the base of either the sale price or the regular price. Don't worry about quantity pricing here, although you can change this if you need to show quantity discounts.

Now that you have a way to display the bestseller block, you need to add it to the home page. You can do this by modifying the copy of the `home.` template. Where you modify the template depends on the style of your home page: whether it uses top buttons or side buttons. The side button arrangement is easier. In this arrangement, you can simply add a new table cell before the part dealing with `RIGHT-MODULES` (this section is at the end of the `page-body` template in the old Yahoo! Store Editor, but it is missing from the new editor) and then call your `show-bestsellers` template. The entire cell is within a `WHEN @bestsellers` block so that you show the bestseller block if there are bestsellers to be shown. The relevant part of the template is listed here:

```
:side-buttons
TABLE border 0
      cellspacing 0
      cellpadding 0
   TABLE-ROW valign :top
      CALL :yourstoreid-side-nav
         vnav
      TABLE-CELL
         FONT size @text-size
              face @text-font
           WITH= variable wid
                value (@page-width - 26) - vnav-wid
              CALL :yourstoreid-home-body
                 nil
```

```
                    nil
                    wid
          WHEN @bestsellers
            TABLE-CELL
              CALL :show-bestsellers
          WHEN @right-modules
            TABLE-CELL width 10
              SHIM height 1
                   width 10
            TABLE-CELL valign :top
                       width 150
              CALL :yourstoreid-right-modules
                @right-modules
```

If the store has a top navigation bar, adding the bestseller box is a little trickier. In this case, you want to put the entire page inside the left cell of a table, and put the call to `show-bestsellers` in the right cell of the same table.

Quantity Box

You might have seen online stores that let the customer type a quantity right on the item's page before clicking the Order button. Although this feature is not readily available in the Yahoo! Store Editor, it is easy to add in RTML (see Figure 7.5).

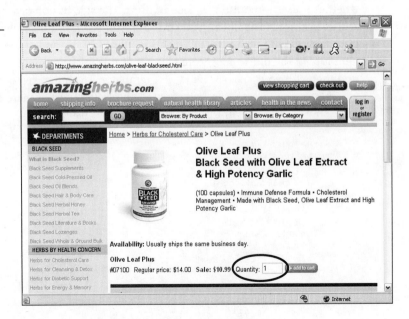

FIGURE 7.5
Quantity input box.

The quantity box is a simple text box. Its name makes it work as a quantity box. If you name a text box vwquantity and submit it to the shopping cart page, the Yahoo! store system takes the value in this box as the order quantity.

The key to add this feature to your store is the template called order. To add the quantity box, you must modify your copy of this template. Toward the bottom of the order. template, locate the part that reads as follows:

```
INPUT type :submit
      value @order-text
```

This RTML expression generates the Order button. You have to add the quantity box before this expression. To begin, click the New button, select INPUT from the operator list, and click Create. Next, click the INPUT expression just above the one that creates the Order button. The one to click reads as follows:

```
INPUT name :vwcatalog
      type :hidden
      value account
```

After you have selected this INPUT expression, click the Paste After button. This inserts the blank INPUT operator you created earlier right above the Order button. Now click Edit and fill in the parameters as follows:

- For name, enter :vwquantity.
- For type, enter :text.
- For value, enter 1.
- For maxlength and size, enter 3.

Note that the entries for name and type have no quotes around them and both begin with a colon. In addition, the number 1 you entered for value is the default quantity that will appear in the quantity box on your item pages. You might need to change this if another number makes more sense for your store. When you have entered these values, click the Update button. The finished INPUT expression should look like this:

```
INPUT name :vwquantity
      type :text
      value 1
      maxlength 3
      size 3
```

Now you have a functioning quantity box next to the Order button. You might want to add a TEXT Quantity expression just before the box or tweak the appearance a little to suit your particular needs.

Radio Button Options

You can also change the default drop-down option boxes to radio buttons (see Figure 7.5). The radio button input element does the same thing as the drop-down list: It enables the user to select one of a number of choices. To do this, again modify the `Order.` template. Locate the following block in the `Order.` template:

```
else MULTI
      TEXT ELEMENT position 0
                  sequence set
      TEXT ": "
      SELECT name ELEMENT position 0
                       sequence set
            options ELEMENTS sequence set
                             first 1
```

Replace the entire block starting with MULTI with the following:

```
CALL :radio-options
   set
```

Because you do not have the `radio-options` template, you will need to create it as follows:

```
Radio-options (set)
WITH= variable name
      value ELEMENT position 0
                   sequence set
  TEXT name
  TEXT ":"
  LINEBREAK
  FOR-EACH variable option
         sequence ELEMENTS sequence set
                             first 1
    INPUT name name
          type :radio
          value option
    TEXT option
    LINEBREAK
```

These modifications to the `Order.` template change all the drop-down options to radio buttons. If you want the option to selectively change the options to radio buttons, you can modify the `Order.` template, based on how we did it for the check boxes, to indicate whether you want radio buttons or standard drop-downs. (We leave the details of this change to you as an exercise.)

One additional note: For this to work, you might have to go to Order Form in the Store Manager, scroll down to the bottom, and change the Item Option Validation setting to allow items with unrecognized options. But try it first: If your radio buttons work without that setting, you won't need to change it.

FIGURE 7.6
Radio button options.

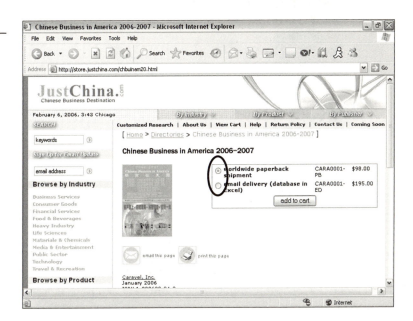

Free Forms (Email Form)

The Catalog Request feature provided to every Yahoo! store is a great way to collect information about visitors who haven't made up their minds to actually make a purchase in your store. Those who fill out an online information request form are usually very "hot" leads because they are close to clicking that Order button. The Catalog Request form is not just to request a catalog; you can call it anything that makes sense in your store: More Information, Online Newsletter Signup, and so on. On the Variables page, you can change the Request-text variable to reflect whatever you use that feature for. Under Order Form in the Store Manager, you can change the title of the Catalog Request form and add your own message. The problem is, there is only one such form and you cannot tell what fields you want to collect. What if you would like a separate sign-up form for a newsletter or another form for those interested in your affiliate program (see Figure 7.7)? The answer is an undocumented CGI script available to all store owners. This script can process any

FIGURE 7.7
Free forms (email forms).

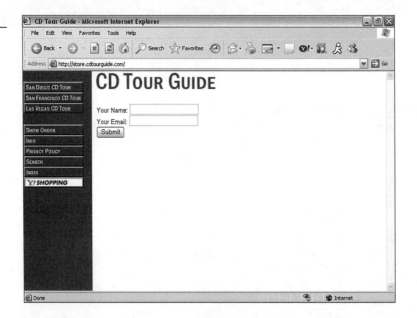

form and email the form's fields (as filled out by a visitor) to the email address you specify. Here is how you can use it.

Copy the following in the `Caption` property of a page where you want the form to appear:

```
<form method="POST" action="http://store.yahoo.com/cgi-bin/pro-forma">
Your Name: <input type="text" name="Name"><br>
Your Email: <input type="text" name="Email"><br>
<input type="submit" value="Submit">
<input type="hidden" name="owner" value="type your email here">
<input type="hidden" name="newnames-to" value="type your store's Yahoo! ID here">
<input type="hidden" name="continue-url" value="target page">
</form>
```

For `target page`, enter the URL of a page you want to send your visitors after they have filled out the form. If you leave out that entire hidden variable, visitors will be sent to the home page of your store. You can add other fields the same way as `Name` and `Email`. You can also include drop-down boxes, check boxes, radio buttons, and anything that can be part of a standard HTML form.

List of On-Sale Items

Using RTML, you can create a page that automatically lists all the items in your store that are on sale. With this trick, you can add an On Sale Now page to your store without having to manually copy all the sale items into this page.

First, create a new section for the sale items. You can call this section On Sale Now or Sale Items or Clearance Items, or whatever else you think sounds good. After you have created this section, make a note of its ID.

Next, create a custom template called `sale-items`, as shown here:

```
Sale-items ()

YANK element nil
     sequence FOR-EACH variable item
                   sequence WHOLE-CONTENTS
             WITH-OBJECT item
                WHEN @sale-price
                   id
```

After this template has been set up, edit your copy of the `page-body`. template. Toward the bottom, you'll find the following block:

```
WHEN @contents
   WHEN OR
         side-im
         NONEMPTY @caption
      LINEBREAK
   CALL :contents.
      @contents
      wid
   LINEBREAK
```

Paste the following after that block, replacing `:saleitems` with the ID of your Sale Items section:

```
WHEN EQUALS value1 id
          value2 :saleitems
   CALL :contents.
      CALL :sale-items
      wid
   LINEBREAK
```

> **warning**
>
> This template makes use of the WHOLE-CONTENTS operator. Besides being slow for stores with a large number of pages, WHOLE-CONTENTS has a minor issue: Pages that use WHOLE-CONTENTS aren't flagged automatically for regeneration. This means that if you change prices, for example, even though the on-sale page you set up using the previous example looks right in the editor, after publishing, the on-sale page won't be updated on the published site. You can fix this in two ways. Before publishing, either edit the on-sale page and, without changing anything, click the Update button, or click Variables and then click Update without changing any variables.

Now you have a section that automatically lists all items in your store that are on sale. There is no need to manually add or remove items from this page.

Related Items

Related items and cross-sells are a way of suggesting related items (see Figure 7.8). Until recently, the Yahoo! store cross-sell feature was rather limited. You could create some families by entering their names in the `Families` variable and assign items to these preset families. Then, when a customer placed one of these items in a shopping cart, the related items were listed as hyperlinks at the bottom of the shopping cart page. This was quite limited and uninteresting.

The current cross-sell functionality is a lot more complex and is now located in the Store Manager, in the Promote section. Here, you can set up complex cross-sell rules to offer discounts, for example. When such an item is placed in the shopping cart, the item's thumbnail is shown in addition to the hyperlink. Additionally, if a discount is offered, it is mentioned on that page, making the cross-sell feature more useful to the merchant and more interesting to the customer.

One feature still missing from this, however, is the capability to show related items on the item pages themselves. Luckily, this limitation—like many others—can be solved using RTML.

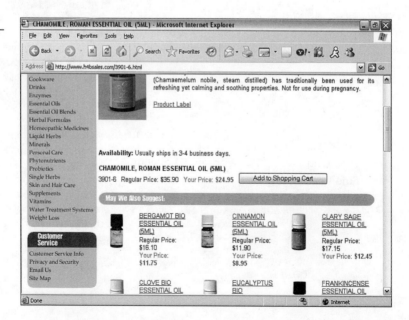

FIGURE 7.8
Related Items feature.

Like the bestsellers, the cross-sell has two main parts: identifying the related items and showing them on the page.

```
Find-family ()

YANK element id
     sequence YANK element nil
                   sequence WITH= variable family
                                  value @family
                          WHEN AND
                                family
                                NOT EQUALS value1 family
                                           value2 :none
                          FOR-EACH-OBJECT WHOLE-CONTENTS
                             WHEN EQUALS value1 @family
                                         value2 family
                                  id
```

The first template, `Find-family`, returns a list of all the items that are assigned to the same family as the current item. Because you don't need the current item (it is definitely part of its own family), you use the YANK operator to pull its ID of the list of the family members.

The following YANK expression removes all `nil`s from the list of family members. You need that because the FOR-EACH-OBJECT block at the end of the template produces a list that has as many elements as there are objects in the store. For each object that is in the same family as the current page, this list has the ID of the object. For all other objects, the list contains `nil`.

To display the elements of the family, you could use the same approach as with the bestsellers. In fact, you could use the exact same template, Show-bestsellers, with the only change being replacing the variable `@bestsellers` with CALL `:find-family` (and perhaps changing the title of Bestsellers to `@cross-sell-text`). However, I would like to show a slightly different method.

In this method, you use a built-in template called Contents that is used to show the contents of a section or an item. This template comes in handy because you want your cross-sells to show thumbnails and links just like the regular content. Contents takes two parameters: a list of IDs and a width. For your cross-sells, the list of IDs consists of the IDs of the family members.

The most convenient place to call this template is in `page-body`. At the very end of that template, it already makes a call to `yourstoreid-contents` (where `yourstoreid` is the Yahoo! ID of your store) to handle the regular contents of the page. To show your cross-sells right after that, paste the following after the WHEN `@contents` expression:

```
WHEN @contents
  WHEN OR
        side-im
        NONEMPTY @caption
    LINEBREAK
  CALL :yourstoreid-contents
    @contents
    wid
  LINEBREAK
WITH= variable family
      Value CALL :find-family
  WHEN family
    LINEBREAK
    TEXT-STYLE :bold
      TEXT @cross-sell-text
    LINEBREAK
    CALL :yourstoreid-contents
      family
      wid
```

In this example, the variable `cross-sell-text` serves as a heading for the cross-sell section, but you could get creative and format it more nicely, perhaps using a nice banner or graphical letters. The great thing about this small feature is that it is completely automatic. From now on, all you have to do is define your families (using the `Families` variable); as soon as you have at least two items in a family, they will be shown at the bottom of the item page, formatted the same way as your regular contents. (To add an item to a family, edit the item and select the appropriate family in the Family drop-down list.)

One final note about the previous example: If you want to show the cross-sells in multiple columns as shown in **"Error! Reference source not found."** using the `contents` template, you also need to click Config and change the `Leaf-columns` variable from 1 to the number of columns you need.

Using WHOLE-CONTENTS is quite slow, especially in stores with a large number of pages. An alternate solution is not to use the Family feature at all, but rather add a custom property called `related-items` to your items. This new property should be set up as type `references`. Then, for any item, you can enter the IDs of the related products into the `related-items` property. To make this work, simply change the `find-family` template to this:

```
Find-family ()
OR
  @related-items
  YANK element id
      sequence YANK element nil
              sequence WITH= variable family
                      value @family
```

```
              WHEN AND
                    family
                 NOT EQUALS value1 family
                            value2 :none
          FOR-EACH-OBJECT WHOLE-CONTENTS
              WHEN EQUALS value1 @family
                          value2 family
                   id
```

Text Page Titles

As we discussed earlier, a Yahoo! store always creates an image for the name of the item or section. Although a Yahoo! store also generates an "alt text" for these images, pictures are no match for text when it comes to search engine optimization (SEO). Although the Yahoo! Store Editor does not provide you with any way to show item and section names as text (instead of automatically generated images), it is quite easy to tweak a template to give yourself this feature.

The key is the template called `head` (or your copy of it, that is.) This template is used to create the heading for any item or section page (it's also used by the info and privacy policy pages). Before modifying this template, create a new template called `show-title`. We use this template to display the name of the page in text. `show-title` is listed here:

```
Show-title (title)

FONT size 3
     color @display-text-color
     face @text-font
   TEXT-STYLE :bold
     FOR-EACH variable line
             sequence LINES title
       TEXT line
       LINEBREAK
LINEBREAK
```

Feel free to modify this template to suit your needs. The example uses text size 3 for the heading here; the same color is set for the display title (the graphic titles are replaced here). When you have this template, bring up your copy of the template called `head`. In this template, locate the following expression (you will find it in three places):

```
IMAGE source textim
      alt text
```

When you have located these expressions, replace them with the following:

```
CALL :show-title
  text
```

This does the trick. The template `show-title` preserves line breaks you might have in the `headline` field just like the generated graphical headings would. However, whereas the generated graphic headings don't let you use any HTML tags in the name or headline parameters, `show-title` has no such problems because it deals with text. When you have these modifications in place, for example, you can include a trademark sign next to a trademark by entering this into the `headline` field:

```
My Trademarked Item<sup><small>TM</small></sup>
```

If you tried doing the same without these template changes, you would end up with something like this on your page:

```
My Trademarked ItemTM
```

You can do other things, including changing the color of certain words in the page heading by simply including the `<font color=...>...</font>` tags in the `headlines` field (you should never include HTML tags in the `name` field. `name` is used as the title tag of the page and is also used by Yahoo! shopping's search engine.)

Being able to format those headlines any way you want is certainly a plus, but the most you can gain from not having graphical headlines is better search engine placement. Remember, search engines can't see images, but they can read text. In fact, that's all they do.

Shipment Status Form

Keeping the customer up-to-date on the status of an order is an integral part of good customer service. Yahoo! store makes it easy to keep your customers informed about order status. Simply log into the Store Manager and click Shipment Status in the Order Settings column to enable and configure the store's shipment status-reporting function. Of course, this feature by itself doesn't do any good; you need to update the status of your orders either manually (by opening the order in the Store Manager and changing the shipping status) or automatically (see http://store.yahoo.com/vw/uptracstatau.html).

When shipment tracking is enabled, each time you update the status of an order (say, the order was shipped or will ship in one day or two days), Yahoo! automatically sends a status update email to the customer (the email is somewhat configurable in the Store Manager under Shipment Status). However, customers sometimes miss these emails; the messages can be ignored or these days even caught by some spam filters. When a customer wants to find out about the status of an order, chances are, the customer goes to your store and then goes to the Info page to look up your customer service email or phone number. Why not make it easy for customers and provide an order-tracking form that will save time and customer support calls or emails (see Figure 7.9). Setting this up is rather simple, and you can do this with no RTML or even HTML knowledge.

FIGURE 7.9
Shipment status form.

First, decide where you want the order-tracking form to reside. As mentioned earlier, an obvious place for it is on the Info page, but you might want to put it on a separate page and perhaps add an Order Status link to the navigation bar. In this example, we show you how to add the order-tracking form to the Info page.

Edit the info page, and wherever you want the order-tracking box to appear (in the `Greeting` or `Info` fields), enter the following HTML (but replace `your-storeid` with the Yahoo! ID of your own store):

```
<form name="vw-form" method="post"
action="https://order.store.yahoo.com/cgi-bin/wg-order-status">
  Enter Your Order ID<br>
  <input name="oid" type="text" size="20" value="yourstoreid-">
  <input type="submit" value="Show">
</form>
```

The HTML will produce a form on your Info page. When a customer enters the order number in this form and clicks the Show button, he or she is sent to Yahoo!'s built-in order tracking screen. If the customer is logged in with a Yahoo! ID, the order status is displayed immediately. If the customer has no Yahoo! ID, unfortunately, the only message that customer gets is that the order has been placed. In this case, you will get that customer service call or email after all. For an example of what such an order-tracking form looks like, go to www.efunctional.com.

If these tips and tricks were useful and you would like to learn and implement additional features, consider purchasing the book *Yahoo! Store Tips and Tricks* (Y-Times Publications, 2005), available at www.ytimes.com. The book contains more than 100 tips and tricks. If you need assistance or would rather outsource the implementation of these advanced features, contact Monitus (www.monitus.com).

Now that you've learn how to implement a handful of advanced features yourself, in the next chapter, you'll learn how to design your customized Yahoo! store to sell.

CHAPTER 8

Designing Your Customized Yahoo! Store to Sell

In This Chapter

- Eighteen tips every Yahoo! store owner needs to know
- Fifty-one words that will help you sell
- Eight design pitfalls you need to avoid

We've covered quite a bit of information so far that will help your customized Yahoo! store sell. In this chapter, we sum up some tips and some important words that will help "sell" your Yahoo! store. In addition, we show you how to steer clear of design pitfalls.

Eighteen Tips Every Yahoo! Store Owner Needs to Know

Have you ever received a suggestion or tip from someone that changed your life? Well, these 18 tips will change your store. Keep these tips in mind when designing your site: They will help turn visitors into buyers and increase your average sales amount. You can also find additional and new tips at www.myecommercesuccess.com.

Cross-Selling

Recommend other similar or related products on your product pages, so visitors can more easily compare products and navigate to other products. This way, they do not have to either click the Back button or find the link to take them back to the product list page. For example, you can offer accessories, add-ons, upgrades, replacement parts, and even warranties. Cross-selling is also a great way to increase your total average order.

Upselling: Offering Packaged Deals

Grocery stores and retailers do it all the time: "Buy one and get the second for half off." "10 for $10." Why do they do this? It's because they want you to purchase more than one product. You always end up with more than you need because it was a "good deal." You can do the same with your online store. Package related items together and offer a substantial discount. Make it easier for the customer to purchase multiple items by allowing them to click one Buy Now button. It's easier than having them click one button that takes them to the shopping cart and then making them click the Continue Shopping button to add more products.

Using Colors to Make Your Important Information Stand Out

Looking at a bunch of text on a white background is confusing and overwhelming. After all, visitors are scanning your site. If they want more detail, they will happily read the long description of your product. Create little tables with color backgrounds and text to make your site stand out. Don't add all your copy: You need just a few important pieces of product information or benefit phrases. Put this next to your product image, along with the Buy Now button. You can leave the long product description underneath.

Getting Visitors to Click the Buy Button

Customize your Buy Now button; don't use the built-in one. You want your custom Buy button to stand out, so you can draw in customers. Make visitors feel like if they click on it, they can get the product immediately. They shouldn't have to guess how to purchase your product. Also, be sure that you move the Buy button to the top, next to your product image and above the screen fold. If you have a long product description that requires a visitor to scroll, make sure you add a second button at the bottom of the page.

Note: Customizing the Buy button requires RTML programming.

Considering What Visitors See and Don't See

Website designers usually forget that people scan sites instead of reading them. It's just like billboards: You're driving 80 miles per hour down the highway, and all you have time to do is read large headlines. It's the same concept while surfing the Web. Instead of driving down the highway, you're driving down the information highway at a greater speed. Websites are like billboards, not brochures. Graphics, images, colors, bold text, headlines, and color text catch a visitor's eye at first. Everything else is a blur. Use that to your advantage. Make your "what's in it for me?" copy standout. Find that perfect image to convey your message. Remember the old saying, "A picture is worth a thousand words." Add graphic text to your image, if you have to.

Implementing Tell a Friend

Free advertising! What better way to advertise than to have your visitors spread the news about your store and how much they like your product or service? Word-of-mouth is the holy grail of marketing. Make it easier for your visitors by adding a Tell a Friend link on your website, so they can simply click a link and fill out a form instead of having to pick up the phone to call someone or leave your site and open their email program. Your visitors can tell their family and friends about your site without having to *leave* your site.

Not only should you add a Tell a Friend link on your homepage, but you should add it to every product page. This way, your visitors can refer individual products. You can also see what customers are telling their friends about your company and product by requesting for a copy of each email sent.

Adding Special Offers

Everyone loves to get a discount. Add special offers on your home page, and rotate them frequently. You might also want to let your visitors know how often you change your special offers. Instead of using the headline "Special Offers," use "Weekly Special Offers." This tells visitors to come back every week for other offers. You can also add a sense of urgency by applying an expiration date to the special offer.

Designing Above the Fold

Make sure your unique selling position, logo, and main navigation are above the fold line—that is, what visitors see when they visit your site without scrolling. Depending on the computer monitor resolution, this varies for each user. Test your site using the minimum 800 × 600 resolution to see what your site will look like. Rearrange your layout if you have to; a lot of computer users still use the 800 × 600 resolution.

Customizing the Shopping Cart Page

Yahoo! Store Checkout Manager enables you to customize the checkout page by adding HTML for the top navigation, side navigation, and footer. You can incorporate your unique look and feel to the checkout page to carry your branding throughout the process and help your customers navigate back to your site to continue shopping.

To customize your checkout pages using Checkout Manger, follow these steps:

1. From Store Manger, click Checkout Manger under the Orders column.
2. Click the Global Settings link.
3. Click the Checkout Wrapper tab.
4. Scroll down until you see the Checkout Regions. Here, you can paste in HTML (see Figure 8.1).

FIGURE 8.1
You can customize the checkout page in Checkout Manager by adding custom HTML for the header, side, and footer.

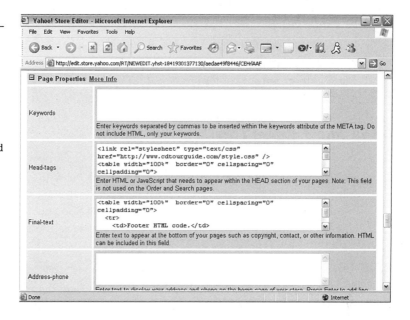

> **Yahoo! Talk** Checkout Manger enables you to customize the pages, sections, and fields displayed to buyers during checkout.

Considering Product Positioning

Positioning your products in certain locations can affect what people buy and don't buy. Why do you think grocery stores put the milk in the back of the store? They want you to walk down the aisle and pick up other products. They also move featured or nonselling items to the front of the store for additional exposure. In an online store, the same concept applies. Product placement can take the form of special offers on the home page, cross-selling items, related items, and packaged deals.

Getting Them to Return

Why should your customers become repeat customers? Is it for weekly specials, new products, or great customer service? Not only should you provide a great buying experience and a superior product, but you also need to let your customers know. It doesn't hurt to tell them why they should come back. Remember, it cost less to keep a customer than to find a new one.

Creating the Page So It's Printable

People like to print product pages so they can show others the product, study it, read up on it later, or give the page to someone for approval. You don't want your important content to be cut off if it's printed. If it is, have an optional print version.

Formatting Your Content Copy

Do you know why news sites limit the number of words per line? Because it's easier to read. Don't stretch your Web copy across the entire screen; that makes it harder to read and scan. You can use columns, but make sure your content continues to flow down. It's not a book or brochure, so you don't want to continue your copy on the next column, where visitors have to scroll back up.

Managing Content Flow

Visitors shouldn't have to guess what to do next. Lead them to where you want them to go or what you want them to do. Consider this a call to action. Do you want them to click a link for more information, or do you want them to click the Buy button? Don't be afraid to make it obvious. It's not a hard sell—they'll appreciate it. To help you plan your website content flow, draw a flowchart with all pages leading to the shopping cart. After all, you're here to make money.

Creating a Professional-Looking Website

If you don't know how to design websites, hire a Yahoo! store designer or development company. You don't want your website to appear amateurish or look like it was done by someone who is learning website design. You want your visitors to think that you're a real business, not a fly-by-night company. A professional website design makes you look like one of the big boys and positions you to compete on their level. With a professional website design, visitors will not be able to distinguish whether you are a one-man operation or a 500-person corporation. A good design also will increase sales.

For a list of Yahoo! store–development companies, go to http://developernetwork.store.yahoo.com.

Performing Usability Testing

It's important to find out how others are using and navigating your site. Are they confused? Are they having difficulty finding a product? Is your site user friendly? Do you need to improve something? It doesn't take a computer lab or a ton of cash to administer a usability test. All you need are some warm bodies and a video camera. You can even stand behind the person, if you don't have a video camera. You simply want to find out where the bottlenecks are.

Adding Product Guarantees

What's your customer satisfaction return policy? Do your products come with store or manufacturer warrantees? If so, make them known. People feel more comfortable purchasing products that come with guarantees and warrantees. One of the biggest fears about purchasing online is the ease and cost of returning items. With retail stores, you can just go to the store and return the item. With online stores, you have to package and ship back the product. And because most of these stores are privately owned or small, they usually do not have a great return policy; customers are usually stuck with the cost of shipping and maybe a restocking fee.

Adding Credibility

Trust. You're asking your customers to take out their wallet, give you their credit card information, and then hope that they will receive your product. They are also hoping not to have their personal and credit card information misused. That's a lot to ask for. Make your customers feel comfortable doing business with you.

You can do a few things to add credibility to your store (see Figure 8.2):

- Add testimonials.
- Put your contact information, especially phone numbers (toll and toll-free), on every page.
- Add a 128-bit encryption button. You can download an official e-commerce by Yahoo! button at http://help.yahoo.com/help/us/store/aboutms/aboutms-29.html.
- Offer options—both phone numbers and email address—for customers to contact you if they have questions or issues with your product.
- Add a Yahoo! hosting button for credibility. Nobody will know that you are using Yahoo! as your hosting and shopping cart unless you tell them.

FIGURE 8.2
To add credibility, PalzzoPaintings.com displays a customer testimonial, a "30 day money-back guarantee" seal, a e-commerce by Yahoo! 128-bit encryption badge, and a "Hosted by a Yahoo!" graphic.

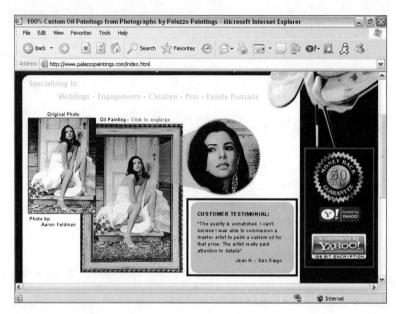

You're Not Done Designing Yet

If you think you're done working on your site when it's launched, think again. Technology is always changing, the psychology of buying is always changing, and your customer interest is always changing. A simple copy change or product placement can mean the world. Using current buzzwords or images can increase sales. Your competitors are also looking to outdo you, so you need to be on top of your game. Don't be afraid to test different layouts, sales copy, and color schemes. Making little improvements can mean huge returns.

Eight Design Pitfalls You Need to Avoid

Mistakes can be costly. You've spent a lot of money, effort, and time to get visitors to your site. The last thing you want is to have them leave because of design flaws that you could have avoided. You must avoid these eight design pitfalls.

Don't Make Your Visitors Think

Your site should be clear and to the point; visitors shouldn't have to figure out what you are selling or how to get additional information (see Chapter 12, "The Power of PARM: Positioning Your Business"). But design also enters the picture here. It's too easy for someone to say, "It's too confusing" and then click the Back button or close your page. Make sure your unique selling position (USP) is available, and have product images on your home page. Visually, customers need to see what you're selling and read how your site will benefit them.

Don't Make Them Guess Where They're Going

Don't make your visitors guess where they need to click to get to certain sections or products. It's okay to be descriptive, and it's okay to add more product category links. You can also cross-link by putting products in multiple categories, if it applies. The worst thing you can do is make visitors click a couple layers deep only to find out that the product or information they are looking for is not there.

Avoid Shopping Cart Abandonment

In shopping cart abandonment, a shopper adds products to the shopping cart and initiates the checkout process, but then leaves the site before completing the purchase. It's equivalent to shoppers in grocery stores adding a bunch of products in the shopping cart and then just leaving the store. So how can you reduce shopping cart abandonment?

Shopping cart abandonment happens for these reasons:

- Shipping prices are too high.
- Delivery time is too long.
- The total cost of items is too high.
- Shipping is not included.
- They don't want to pay tax.
- The checkout process is too confusing.

Knowing why shoppers abandon their cart will help you plan and design your store accordingly.

Avoid Content Overload

Not enough content can hurt, and too much content can overwhelm visitors. Don't make your pages look like a big blob of text or a never-ending site map; keep it simple and clean. Break up the content into multiple pages or organize the content by sections. You don't want your visitors saying, "What do I do next?" or "What should I focus on?" or "Where am I?"

Avoid Sending Your Visitors to Your Competitors

Try to avoid placing banner ads and other affiliate-related ads all over your website. You spent all that time, energy, and money getting people to visit your site, and now you want them to leave your site so you can make a few cents on banner advertisements? Some of these automated advertisement programs even put competitors' advertisements on your site (their keywords match yours). If you have to advertise others, remember to send the link onto a new window. This way, your website will still be available if the visitor exits the other window. Reciprocal links are okay because there is a mutual benefit and usually the two sites do not compete.

Avoid Changing the Location of Your Main Navigation

Make sure your main navigation menu and overall layout are at the same location on every single page. This creates consistency and makes it easier for visitors to navigate your site. Also, make your navigation menu visible and obvious. Don't use small text for your main navigation links. Incorporate tabs, graphics, or colors into your menu.

The FerretStore.com (see Figure 8.3) has a great main navigation. It's consistent on every page, color makes it stand out, and the image tells you what it's all about without making you read the menu title.

FIGURE 8.3
FerretStore.com's main navigation is consistent on every page, uses color to make it stand out, and uses images to tell you what it's all about, without making you read the menu title.

Avoid Graphic Overload

You might have a high-speed Internet connection and be able to blaze through Web pages at the speed of light, but not every visitor has a connection like yours. Don't go crazy with too many and too-large images. This can bring your pages to a screeching halt because they will be too slow to load. Create thumbnails of your products, and offer larger versions of the image that open in a new window. This way, the image can load while the visitor can still navigate your site.

Avoid Using Technology That Users Need Plug-Ins For

Incorporating cutting-edge technology can be cool, but it usually requires visitors to download a plug-in. Unless visitors can automatically install the plug-in quickly, they most likely will decline the plug-in download. Then, instead of seeing the cool effect, they will see a big red "X" where the technology is supposed to be displayed. Give visitors options and let them know that a particular plug-in is required. Then, offer a link to the plug-in on your site.

Fifty-One Words That Sell

Can your copy sell the product on its own? Grab a pen and write down as many sentences or phrases as you can to sell your products. Ask others to help you refine them. Test them on your site and see which one produces more sales. Also look at other sites to sell how they crafted their sales copy.

Here's a list of words that will help you sell:

- Gain
- Health
- Value
- Happy
- Healthy
- Advice
- Trustworthy
- Safety
- Announcing
- Comfortable
- Right
- Your
- Proud
- Security
- People
- Amazing
- Winnings
- Why
- Sensational
- Fun
- Fast
- Remarkable

- Discover
- Win
- Revolutionary
- Bargain cash
- Startling
- Hurry
- Results
- Miracle
- Free
- Easy
- Magic
- New
- Proven
- Offer
- You
- Guaranteed
- Quick
- Sale
- Love
- Challenge
- Introducing
- Benefit
- Compare
- Save
- Alternative
- Improvement
- Money
- Now
- Suddenly

Use these words in your copy, and surely you will see your closing ratio increase.

Now that you've learned tips and tricks on how to design your website to sell, let's deconstruct a few websites to find out what makes them tick and why they are so successful.

Part III

Deconstructing a Yahoo! Store

9 Digital Product Store

10 Manufactured Product Store

11 High-Volume Product Store

CHAPTER

9

Digital Product Store

In This Chapter

- How selling digital products works
- Pros and cons of selling digital products
- How to sell both PC and Mac file format products

The best way to learn about running an online store is from others who have online businesses. Learning tips, tricks, and even mistakes from experienced owners not only saves you time and money, but it also guarantees you business success. You need to learn real-world experience in today's market.

How do you build a store? Why did you use this product compared to other products? What advanced features did you use, and did they help with conversions? How do you set up your inventory? Which development company did you use, and were you satisfied with them? How do you import order information into your accounting system? How did you design your warehouse and packaging process? What shipping provider(s) are you using and why? What marketing tactics have you tried, and did they work?

Unless you work for an online business or have a good friend in the business, you won't likely get answers to these questions. So, you're left making the same mistakes, throwing money away on unsuccessful marketing campaigns, and spending too much time tweaking your store and not working on obtaining more customers. You can try to consult with a development company, but unless the company has its own successful online store or has built and marketed an online store in your industry, you might not get that real-world experience advice you're looking for.

In this chapter and the next two chapters, we deconstruct three separate Yahoo! stores: a digital product store, a manufacturer product store, and a high-volume product store. All three of these online stores have generously agreed to give you the inside secrets and tactics they have been successfully using for years. You will learn advanced tactics in today's market, where you will be competing with hundreds, if not thousands, of other websites. You will also learn mistakes they have made so you can avoid the same pitfalls.

We look at everything from the user interface to marketing strategies. After all, the best way to learn is to learn from others with experience. Surfing the Internet and just looking at competitors' websites will not give you the behind-the-scenes strategy that you will need to successfully run your online business.

In this chapter, we deconstruct a digital product store by WriteExpress (www.writeexpress.com). Yahoo! Merchant Solutions enables you to sell digital or downloadable products. You can sell software, e-books, articles, PDFs, how-to information, photos, music, and more. Anything of value that can be digitized can be sold online. The great thing about selling digital products is that you don't have inventory and don't need to ship the product. When you create the digital product, you can sell it over and over again—they're virtual products with real profits! The process is all automated. After you upload your digital product, customers can purchase and receive the product immediately.

The Yahoo! store has made it easy for anyone to sell digital products. With the Internet and the fast-paced environment we live it, consumers want their products *now*. For example, the online music industry has seen an explosion of downloadable music. Consumers want it immediately: They don't want to have to go to the music store or wait for a CD in the mail; they want to be able to listen to it immediately on their iPods or other MP3 portable music player, in their cars, and even on their cell phones.

General Company Information

Company name: WriteExpress

Year business started: 1994

Year Yahoo! store started: 2002

Company main URL: www.writeexpress.com

Number of unique visitors: More than 900,000 per month

Number of products: More than 100

Product Information

WriteExpress offers letters and templates for using Microsoft Office, writing novels, drafting wills and legal documents, using grammar software, and using a variety of related writing software and e-books. The company creates all its products in-house. CD versions of the products are also available for those who want the product shipped. The CD version is slightly more expensive because of the cost of the CD and handling and shipping.

How Do Digital Products Work?

Before we get started deconstructing WriteExpress.com, let's look at how selling digital products works. Setting up your website to sell digital products is just like setting up your site for manufactured products. The only extra step is to upload your digital product file. After you do that, the Yahoo! store automatically knows it's a

> **warning**
>
> Because digital products are fulfilled immediately, before the order can be personally reviewed and processed, these types of products experience a higher-than-normal fraud rate. The customer will receive the product even if the credit card is later found to be invalid.

digital product. When a customer purchases a digital product, a Download button appears next to the product information on the confirmation page during the checkout process (see Figure 9.1). The complete process is automated. The only thing left for you to do is process the order. Think about it—no fulfillment. You might need to deal with support emails or calls, but you can be anywhere in the world and still operate your store.

How to Upload a Digital Product

You cannot use Database Upload to upload digital products; you must do this individually. A digital product upload feature is provided at the Edit Item page:

1. After you create your product(s) either by uploading your product data file or creating the product in Store Editor, go back and edit the product. Scroll down until you see the Download section, and click the Upload button. You can also do this while you're creating a new product in Store Editor.
2. Locate your digital product by clicking the Browse button.
3. Enter a name for the file (see Figure 9.2). Make sure you also add the file extension, such as .pdf for Adobe PDF files.
4. Click the Send button. This sends the file to the server and then returns you to the Edit Item page.
5. In the Edit Item page, click the Save button.

> **warning**
>
> Each digital product has a file size limit of 16MB. So, if you have digital products that are larger in size, this might not be the solution for you. You might want to try to compress the file to reduce the file size by using software such as WinZip. Also, keep in mind that consumers with slow Internet connection speeds will not be able to download your file if it's too large. Let the consumer know how big the file size is, and maybe offer alternatives, such as CDs. WriteExpress uses another shopping cart for products of a larger file size. It's not the best solution, but it's a temporary fix until the Yahoo! store can increase the file size limit.

CHAPTER 9 Digital Product Store 135

FIGURE 9.1
A red Download button appears next to the product data on the confirmation page during the checkout process.

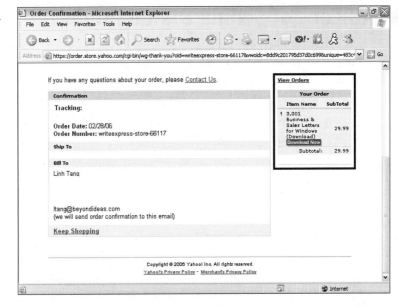

FIGURE 9.2
When assigning a filename to the digital product, make sure you add the correct file extension, such as `yourfile.pdf` for Adobe PDF files.

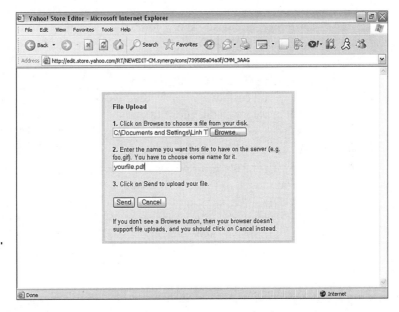

Pros and Cons of Selling Digital Products

Before diving into selling digital products, you want to be aware of some of the pros and cons of selling digital products.

Pros:

- No physical fulfillment is involved.
- No inventory must be maintained.
- You can repeatedly sell the same product.
- Customers enjoy immediate fulfillment.
- Customers can redownload the product if they cannot find the file or lose the file.
- You can operate your store anywhere in the world.

Cons:

- Customers can easily share your product with others.
- The possibility of fraud increases. Because the order is fulfilled immediately, the customer receives the product before credit information is verified.
- You might need to create multiple forms if your file is for a specific operating system (Mac or PC). Note that PDFs, JPGs, GIFs, and Word, Excel, PowerPoint, and other common files are completely cross-platform-compatible.

> **tip** **Using PDF Files**
>
> If you are selling PDF files, you might want to give your customers instructions on how to download and save the file on to their computer. You can add the instructions on the confirmation page and in your FAQs. When a customer clicks the Download button, the PDF file will open in the same window. It will not prompt the customer to save the file. If you have a large PDF file and your customer has a slow Internet connection, the screen appears blank until the file is completely downloaded. The customer will think the file doesn't work. This might help reduce technical support calls and emails. Also, if the customer purchased multiple PDF files, this ensures that the download confirmation page won't be lost because the PDF files open in the same window. Putting PDF files into a ZIP file can be a workaround for this issue. This also has the benefit of a smaller file size if the buyer is not on a broadband connection.

Selling Both Mac and PC Platform File Formats

If you are selling software or have files that are specific to the operating system (OS), you need options for your customers. If your product caters to only one particular OS, make sure the customer is aware of this. Include text to inform your customers that your product works for only a certain OS. This might help you avoid returns, chargebacks, support emails and calls, and bad reviews. In Figure 9.3, you can see that customers can choose a PC or Mac file format for the Easy Letters downloadable product.

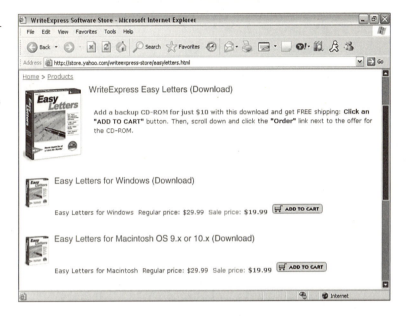

FIGURE 9.3
WriteExpress.com offers digital products in both PC and Mac file formats.

The Evolution of WriteExpress's Website Design

You should constantly change or improve your website design, layout, and structure. What seems to be effective today might not be as effective tomorrow. Continuously evaluate your site to see if you can make any improvements to increase your ROI or close more sales. Some say that you have a 45% chance of turning a visitor into a customer in a retail store and only 2% in an online store. It's too easy for a consumer online to visit your competitor with just a click of a button. You want to do everything you can to immediately grab customers' attention and make them want to further investigate your site.

WriteExpress.com has gone through many variations of its website "look and feel" and layout. Let's take a look at three designs, including the current one.

One of the earlier versions (see Figure 9.4) did not offer a professional look. Your visitors need to be convinced that you are a legitimate corporate business. A professional look and feel can offer the impression that you can compete with the big boys and that you mean business. This Web design also lacked a logo, easy-to-read sales copy, a sense of product identity, a unique selling position (USP), and creditability. You don't want to leave your customers asking, "What's in it for me?" or "Why should I purchase from you?"

FIGURE 9.4
WriteExpress.com's first design concept.

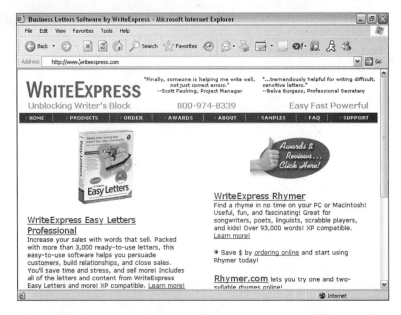

The second major redesign (see Figure 9.5) had a more professional look. Other changes included a custom logo, a product search capability, an easy-to-read product format with bullet points for scanning, a striking image, and a USP. Although this particular design change was leaps and bounds from the previous one, it did not convert as well as expected.

FIGURE 9.5
The second iteration of the site has a more professional look and feel, but it still wasn't as effective as the one you see today.

The third major redesign, which is in use today (see Figure 9.6), includes a change not only in "look and feel," but also in color. In the second design, the main colors of the site were gray, red, and black. After reviews and research, WriteExpress found that red was a negative color. Although it stood out, it didn't give consumers a sense of confidence or a feel-good experience. So, they decided to go with the safe blue tones. Immediately after launching the new site, they saw a major increase in sales. This is probably why most websites use blue tones in the site color schemes.

FIGURE 9.6
After many iterations of site design, this current design has proven to be the most effective.

For WriteExpress, advanced features were not as important as site layout. WriteExpress treats the site as a billboard, not as a brochure. The purpose of a billboard is to get the customers' attention, inform them of a product or service, and to get them interested enough to seek more information. You don't have time to sit in your car and spend even 10 seconds reading, especially if you are going 80 miles per hour. It's the same concept with websites. Visitors are scanning your site. They're looking for benefits copy and attention grabbers (WII-FM). They want to make sure they are at the right site and that they can benefit from your website. They don't want to be sold—they want to be informed.

The products are also laid out in a column format (see Figure 9.7) with a short description and product image—no more than six words per line. This makes reading and scanning easier. Unless space is an issue and the consumer is requesting detailed information, never have text span the entire website: It makes the text too overwhelming to read.

FIGURE 9.7
WriteExpress laid out products into columns with short descriptions. Limiting six words per line also helps reading and scanning of information.

> **Web Resource**
>
> **Color Combos**
>
> Color Combos (www.colorcombos.com) offers a Combo Tester that allows Web developers to see how different color combinations work together. The site also offers a color combo library with preset color combinations.

Testing Your Site Design Effectiveness

So how did WriteExpress.com know how and when it needed a site design change? Here are a few tips that helped them decide:

- **Focus groups**—Find people to evaluate your site. Watch them surf your site and listen to them talk about the site out loud.
- **Customer feedback**—Don't ignore your customer feedback, especially if it's negative. Learn from your customers. Ask why did they not like your product or site.
- **Look at your competition**—Analyze your competitors' websites. See what they are doing and why. Try to find out what's working and not working for them.

■ **Talk to your worst enemy**—Take your harshest critics to lunch. Pick their brains. Ask them why they did or didn't like your website. Your worse critics can become your best friends. If they have issues with your site, others might have the same problem.

Marketing

Besides placing products in retail locations, such as Fry's Electronics and Office Depot, most marketing is done online with pay-per-click (PPC) advertising. WriteExpress uses hundreds of keywords as part of its PPC campaign with Google Adwords and Yahoo! Search Marketing (formerly Overture). The company also uses the tracking functionality to see the conversion rate for each keyword campaign. When you sign up with Google Adwords or Yahoo! Search Marketing, you get a special HTML code to place on your Yahoo! confirmation page. This allows the PPC system to track which keyword(s) generated a sale.

WriteExpress also has an affiliate program that other website owners can join to earn a commission. Website owners can place a banner or text link on their site with special code to enable visitors to jump from their sites to WriteExpress.com. The website owner shares a percentage of all sales that are generated from that link or banner. The revenues from the WriteExpress affiliate program have accounted for less than 4% of total revenue.

Additional Tips from WriteExpress

Website owners and developers sometimes take too much pride in their website layout and design. Remember that you are designing not for yourself, but for your targeted market. Just because you like the design and have poured a lot of sweat into it doesn't mean it will work for your potential customers. Test different layouts—change fonts, sales copy, USPs, and photos.

Indeed, the right photo can make or break a sale. In its second design (see Figure 9.5), WriteExpress used a photo of a woman with a laptop that looks like she's having too much fun. The image didn't quite portray the message of a writer with writer's block. In the latest design, the woman looks frustrated (see Figure 9.6). Customers seem to relate more to this particular image. With the latest design, WriteExpress has seen a better conversion rate.

A lot of websites miss the concept of content flow. What do you want your visitors to do? Help lead your customers to what they should do next. Do you want them to click to another page? Do you want them to click the Purchase button? Do you want them to contact you? Use focus groups and watch how they navigate through your site. It might be clear to you, but not as clear to visitors. A focus group can be just a bunch of friends and family; it does not have to be formal, expensive, or even a group.

Now that we've deconstructed a digital product store and you've learned how downloadable products work, let's deconstruct a manufactured product store.

CHAPTER

10

Manufactured Product Store

In This Chapter

- What marketing techniques worked for Pacific Pillows and why
- How adding simple features can increase sales
- How outsourcing your task can save you money
- How to use eBay in conjunction with the Yahoo! store to increase orders

In the previous chapter, we deconstructed a digital product store. But the majority of online stores sell manufactured goods—physical products produced by either another company or you that must be shipped or picked up by customers.

In this chapter, we deconstruct Pacific Pillows (www.pacificpillows.com), a manufactured product store. Before starting Pacific Pillows (see Figure 10.1), owners Craig and Abby Clark owned DealCat.com, selling electronic goods such as digital cameras and computers. While selling electronics, Dealcat.com decided to stock a few hotel pillows. Sales of the pillows started to increase: Pacific Pillows was born and proved to be a much more successful business. Owners Craig and Abbey later shut down the online electronics store and focused on their new niche selling pillows and bedding that luxury hotels use.

One of the great benefits about selling online is that you can inexpensively test whether there is a market for your product. By using such methods as pay-per-click advertising, you can get immediate exposure of your product and online store. Like Pacific Pillows, a lot of companies have also changed their product line. What they thought was the hottest thing on the market did not perform as expected; the product that was added as a filler unexpectedly made the most amount of money for the store. Because most of your store infrastructure is already in place, changing products is as easy as adding new products.

FIGURE 10.1
Pacific Pillows sells pillows and beddings used by luxury hotels.

General Company Information

Company name: Pacific Pillows

Year business started: 1999

Year Yahoo! store started: 2004

Number of employees: 5

Company main URL: www.pacificpillows.com

Number of websites: 1

Number of unique visitors: More than 25,000 per month

Number of products: More than 45

Number of orders per day: 22

Product Information

Pacific Pillows carries luxurious pillows, down comforters, and bedding that you find at luxury hotels such as the Ritz-Carlton, Marriott, Hilton, DoubleTree, or Hyatt Hotel. Now, guests of these hotels can own the exact same down pillow or bedding they enjoyed during their stay. Pacific Pillows has more than 45 products to choose from. Customers can easily search for pillows or bedding by hotel name.

Website Layout and Advanced Features

PacificPillows.com started out with the basic easy Yahoo! point-and-click default template, with minor customization done in-house. When business proved itself as profitable, they reinvested profits into creating a more professional look. The investment was made four months after opening the online store.

Besides unique website design, some advanced features and layout modifications were implemented on the site:

- **Breadcrumbs**—Using breadcrumbs is a great way to let your customers know where they are in your site (see Figure 10.2). Not only does it provide an easy way to backtrack to parent sections when viewing products, but it also helps with search engine ranking.
- **Relocation of the Add to Cart button**—Instead of defaulting the Add to Cart button to the bottom of the text, Pacific Pillows repositioned the button at the top and created a copy at the bottom of the page (see Figure 10.3). Positioning the button in both locations made it easier for customers to see and click to purchase.

- **Color background of product thumbnail**—Pacific Pillows added a light blue background to the product selection to make it stand out a bit more (see Figure 10.4).
- **Newsletter signup button**—Visitors can click on the newsletter signup button on the home page (see Figure 10.5).

FIGURE 10.2
Not only do breadcrumbs help visitors know where they are in your site and help them navigate to parent sections, but they also help with search engine optimization.

FIGURE 10.3
Relocating the Add to Cart button helped increase sales.

FIGURE 10.4
A light blue background color was added to the product thumbnail and link to make it more visible.

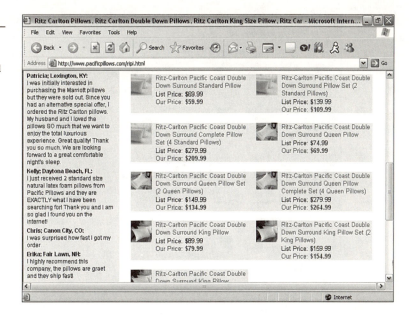

The overall layout and features are simple and effective. The goal is to make it easy for customers to get your vital information and make the buying process effortless. Some websites overdo their sites with too many advanced features that make it too complicated for customers.

Product Package Deals

Pacific Pillows saw an increase in sales when the company started selling its pillows in packages (see Figure 10.5). Customers were able to purchase an individual pillow, a package of two pillows, or a package of four pillows. Creating the packages and offering an extra discount incentive resulted in an increase in the total sales order. The packages made it easier for customers to make a single-purchase transaction of multiple products.

FIGURE 10.5

Pacific Pillows was able to increase the average sale amount by offering pillows in sets at a discount.

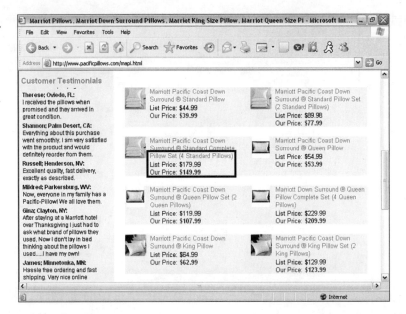

Before implementing the choices of the packages, customers ordered one pillow 58% of the time. After the packages were implemented, a set of four pillows was ordered 43% of the time, a package of two was ordered 39% of the time, and individual pillows were ordered only 18% of the time.

> **tip** Another alternative to offering packages is to offer multiple quantity discounts. The discount must be easily readable for customers to know that there is an incentive to ordering more of the product. Consider putting your quantity discount in a color-coded table format.

Adding Credibility Banners

Customer service constantly received emails and phone calls asking if the website was secure to process credit cards. Instead of just adding a FAQ (frequently asked questions) page and telling customers that the site is secure, Pacific Pillows added a "Tested for Safety" banner on the home page (see Figure 10.6). The site security is tested by a third-party company, Safe Shopping Network (www.safeshoppingnetwork.com), which provides a directory of security-tested websites. Such banners add consumer confidence, resulting in sales. Since the banner has been online, customer service has not received an inquiry regarding site security. Although it is not part of the standard Yahoo! store feature, the seal is included with the purchase of a paid yearly listing.

Pacific Pillows also added banners for the Better Business Bureau Reliability Program and Yahoo! Shopping Rating. Similar to the Tested for Safety banner, both add credibility to a site.

FIGURE 10.6
Adding banners such as Tested for Safety, BBB Reliability Program, and Yahoo! Shopping Rating brings credibility to your store.

Testimonials

Including testimonials is a way to show potential customers how much other customers have enjoyed your products (see Figure 10.7). The scrolling text on the Pacific Pillows home page not only draws attention, but it also helps save space to include additional testimonials. Pacific Pillows receives at least one email per week from a customer who made a purchase because of the testimonials. So they work! Testimonials are a great way to get customers to make a purchase, especially if they are on the fence about purchasing. Some customers even ask to have their testimonial included on the website—maybe it's their five minutes of fame, similar to having your name mentioned in a newspaper.

tip Don't be afraid to solicit testimonials from customers. Try to approach the customers whom you know had a great experience with your website and enjoy the products.

FIGURE 10.7
Pacific Pillows added testimonials to the home page.

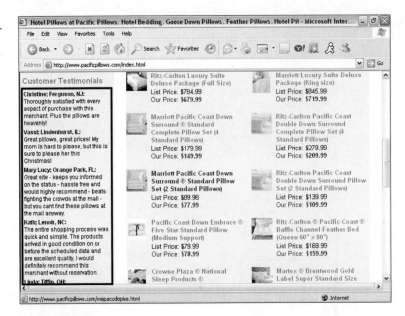

Website Development

Instead of hiring a Yahoo! store development firm, Pacific Pillows decided to hire individual programmers. Hiring programmers for specific tasks has proved to be a cost savings for the company. Pacific Pillows turns to Elance (www.elance.com) for developers. Elance (which is part of eBay) lets you post your available projects online. After you describe your needs and requirements, you receive proposals from professionals with bid on your project. You review all the bids and select the person who best fits your requirements and budget. Elance also offers a way for you to pay the programmer through the Elance website.

Before using Elance, Pacific Pillows received a few bid proposals from other development firms, but the company found hiring individuals to be more cost-efficient.

> **warning**
>
> Hiring freelance programmers through websites such as Elance can be cost-effective, but those programmers might lack the required RTML experience. Developers in the developer directory (www.developernetwork.store.yahoo.com) have been screened for their knowledge and are more accountable because they want to remain listed. If you plan to use freelance programmers, check for references. Otherwise, merchants could end up paying once to do work initially and then paying again to fix work done by a developer with not enough experience.

Outsourcing

Pacific Pillows tries to outsource as much of the tasks and projects as possible, to keep overhead low. Unlike hiring full-time employees, subcontracting and outsourcing do not require paid employee benefits, such as health care. Outsourcing also enables you to pay on a commission or project base.

Some outsourcing of services includes website design and development, newsletter creation, affiliate program management, graphics design, 25% of the shipping and warehousing, email campaign management, and toll-free customer service.

Additionally, four employees do most work from their homes (two in San Diego, one in Los Angeles, and one in Buffalo, New York).

Outsourcing Your 1-800 Customer Service

If you support and respond to your own customer service phone calls but would like a backup plan, outsourcing your customer service as a backup could be the route for you. Pacific Pillows uses a 1-800 number that they can manipulate. During working hours, the phone first rings to a woman they hired through elance.com. If she is not available, it rings to another customer service person. If he is not available, it rings to the outsourced call center operated by Sunshine Communications (www.sunshine1.com). Call center packages start at $29.95, which includes 40 minutes and 75¢ for each additional minute. Other discounted packages are available for higher call volumes. During nonbusiness hours, calls just ring to the call center, which takes orders and handles minor customer service issues. For major issues, the call center takes a message and promises a call back by a certain time. Pacific Pillows maintains a log with tickets created so reps can call back all customers with any major issues.

Backend System

The built-in backend system the Yahoo! store provides has been sufficient for Pacific Pillows. Orders are retrieved and processed from within the system. For accounting purposes, orders are exported from the system and imported into QuickBooks Retail Edition.

Online and Offline Marketing Strategies

Pacific Pillows operates a $20,000 monthly advertising budget for both online and offline media advertising. The company continually tries different marketing techniques to test the return on investment (ROI) of each method. When the target ROI has been achieved, Pacific Pillows continues to increase the dollar amount for that particular marketing method.

Email Marketing—Newsletter

Not only do you have to generate new customers, but you need to create recurring customers. The monthly email newsletter (see Figure 10.8) has proven to be a great advertising avenue to develop customer retention and attract new customers. The customer email database is collected from only past customers. Pacific Pillows purchased emails list in the past, but this did not prove successful. Sending a coupon code with a significant discount in the monthly email newsletter has been a very effective way to get customers to continue to purchase products.

Pacific Pillows uses Campaigner by Got Marketing as its email newsletter–management program. Campaigner enables you to seamlessly create, track, and manage your email newsletter with the Yahoo! store. Customer email accounts are easily and automatically imported into the email newsletter program.

FIGURE 10.8
An email newsletter that includes coupons and special offerings is sent to customers monthly.

Using eBay

Pacific Pillows also offers 70% of its products on eBay (www.ebay.com), as shown in Figure 10.9. eBay has accounted for approximately an additional 20% in sales. Pacific Pillows outsources the management and listing of the products on eBay to an individual. Revenues from eBay not only pay for the salary of that person, but they account for a good portion of total company sales.

> **tip** You can find individuals who are willing to post and manage your eBay product listings on a commission basis. You can post a request on sites such as Craigslist (www.craigslist.com) or find one of those local drop-off centers that will post your listings for you.

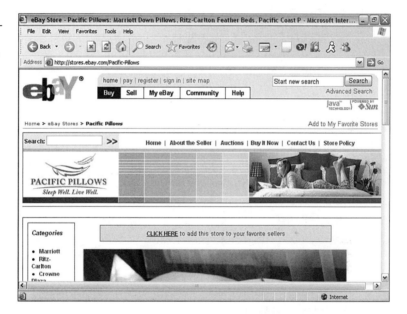

FIGURE 10.9
In addition to the Yahoo! store, Pacific Pillows opened an eBay store to increase exposure.

Pay-Per-Click Marketing

Pay-per-click marketing has been by far the most successful form of advertising. Pacific Pillows manages more than 1,000 targeted keywords across the GoogleAd and Overture (now Yahoo! Search Marketing) network.

> **tip** When signing up with price-comparison sites such as PriceGrabber.com, ask them to waive the setup fee. Most sales reps have the capability of waiving certain fees as an incentive for you to use their service. It doesn't hurt to ask—the worst thing they can do is say no.

Marketing through price-comparison websites such as www.shopzilla.com, www.bizrate.com, www.shopping.com, www.pricegrabber.com, and www.nextag.com has also been successful.

Using pay-per-click advertising has allowed Pacific Pillows to directly reach targeted customers who are specifically searching for an exact product—and it's "pay on performance."

Print Marketing

Print advertising in magazines has been the least effective form of marketing. Pacific Pillows has currently ceased all print advertising campaigns.

Television Commercial Marketing

Television has also not been successful. Pacific Pillows spent more than $18,000 worth of television ads, but they resulted in only a few orders. Advertising media might not be fruitful. Hopefully, you do not have to shell out $18,000 to test it, but you never know until you try it.

Affiliate Marketing

Pacific Pillows uses Commission Junction (www.cj.com) as its affiliate software system. Yahoo! store has partnered with Commission Junction to allow Yahoo! store customers to seamlessly integrate the affiliate software. You can sign up with Commission Junction by simply going to the Affiliate Program link in Store Manager.

Seventeen percent of sales is generated by affiliates. Pacific Pillows has hired PepperJam Management (www.pepperjammanagement) not only to manage its affiliate campaign (pay affiliates, tech support, create banners and links, and so on), but also to recruit super affiliates. Super affiliates are those affiliate marketing gurus who usually make up the majority of your affiliate sales. These super affiliates are serious about helping you generate sales and also know how to send you traffic. The average affiliate simply puts an affiliate link on its site. Super affiliates create advanced online marketing strategies to increase your traffic. Initial Pacific Pillows budgeted a total of $8,000 for the service but now spends $5,000 per month because of the effectiveness of the campaign and PepperJam's capability to perform.

Tips and Recommendations from Owner Craig Abbey

First, e-commerce in general is not a scheme or the holy grail of capitalism. Running an e-commerce store takes a lot of hard work, experimentation, commitment, and desire. The key is to keep trying different business models and marketing techniques until you find a business model that works. Our first store, DealCat.com, was marginally profitable. We worked with this business for years, and it proved not to be worth our time. However, Pacific Pillows grew from this experience and has proven to be a phenomenal success.

I also would like to note that the key to marketing is to invest a little in the different advertising opportunities you find. Be conservative. When a marketing method proves itself as a rain maker, throw your money at that method. We once spent $3,000 for email marketing, and it was a total flop. But I don't worry about this type of loss. You have to try the different methods with an amount of money you can afford to lose. Only by trying different types of marketing will you find marketing methods that work. And when you do find such methods, increased profits will flow. We are always on the lookout for new marketing opportunities and are willing to take a risk in the hopes that any given marketing opportunity will prove to be sustainable over the long term.

Now that you've learned how a midsize-volume manufactured website is constructed and marketed, you'll deconstruct a high-volume website in the next chapter.

CHAPTER 11

High-Volume Product Store

In This Chapter

- Benefits of using an advanced backend order-management system

- How to create multiple niche websites without adding products

- How to set up your warehouse and bin location system

- What marketing tactics are working and not working for Neeps

The third online store we deconstruct is Neeps, a pioneer in the e-commerce field. Neeps launched its first online store back in 1994, even before there was a Yahoo! store service. It couldn't even purchase a domain name at that time because domain names were so expensive. Instead, Neeps had to use a folder within its Internet service provider's domain (www.epix.net/~neeps).

General Company Information

Company name: Neeps, Inc.

Year business started: 1994

Year Yahoo! store started: 1999

Number of employees: 24

Company main URL: www.ferretstore.com

Number of websites: 12

Number of unique visitors: 450,000 per year

Number of products: 5,400

Number of orders per day: 400

Product Information

Neeps currently carries more than 5,400 pet-related products. It sells everything from dog products to exotic pet products for animals such as ferrets. Neeps carries more than 93% of its products in its warehouse, and the manufacturers drop-ship the other 7% (that is, the manufacturer or a third-party distributor ships the product directly to the customers). The benefit of drop-shipping is that the company does not have to carry or purchase inventory in advance. When an order is placed, the drop-shipping company is notified and ships the order on your behalf.

Website Layout and Advanced Features

Getting visitors to your site is only half the battle. You need to be able to turn visitors into customers. Not only do you need a site that's easy to navigate, but you also want to add advanced features to improve your customer acquisition ratio. Let's take a look at TheFerretStore.com navigation layout and some of the features implemented to help increase the number of customers and improve the total order revenue:

- **Easy navigation menu**—The top navigation menu enables users to get to other pet type products; the left menu displays the entire ferret product categories (see Figure 11.1). The top menu animal illustrations and color separation easily identify the buttons and make them buttons stand out.
- **Specials with percentage saved**—Percent Saved lets customers know exactly how much they are saving from the retail price (see Figure 11.2). This enables customers to see the retail price, the sale price, and the percent saved all at once.
- **Easy-to-read product table**—Placing product information in a color-filled table has helped TheFerretStore.com customers easily read product details (see Figure 11.3). The product tables make your vital information stand out.
- **Free Shipping icon**—A Free Shipping icon (see Figure 11.4) visually lets customers know that the product includes free shipping. The icon makes it easy for customers to see, compared to plain text that says "Free shipping." Orders of more than $35 also include free shipping. A display above the products in the shopping cart page lets customers know how much more they will need to spend to receive the free shipping (see Figure 11.5).
- **Quantity savings and input box**—The quantity savings input box lets customers easily purchase multiple quantity of a product for additional discounts (see Figure 11.6). Customers can type in how many items they would like to purchase even before the checkout page.
- **Advanced product search**—The advanced search also has a price filter (see Figure 11.7). Customers can view products within a certain price range. This is extremely helpful for customers who are looking for a gift in a certain price range or if the search results displays too many listings.
- **Real-time order tracking**—Real-time tracking lets TheFerretStore.com customers track their own packages (see Figure 11.8). This reduces lots of emails and phones calls asking when customers will receive their order. The current status is instantly pulled from the UPS real-time tracking database.
- **Live support**—The live chat support has been very well received. A customer can chat instantaneously with a customer representative about anything from product information to assistance with ordering online. Having a live support not only gives customers better customer service, but it has saved the company money on incoming 1-800 calls. Customers can also chat and receive advice live with a ferret owner expert.

Solid Cactus (www.solidcactus.com) developed these features; they are not part of the standard Yahoo! store.

FIGURE 11.1
A navigation menu with recognizable illustrations and different-color buttons makes it easier for users to identify their options.

FIGURE 11.2
Percent Saved text lets customers know exactly how much they are saving.

CHAPTER 11 High-Volume Product Store 161

FIGURE 11.3
An easy-to-read table with color backgrounds helps displays vital product information.

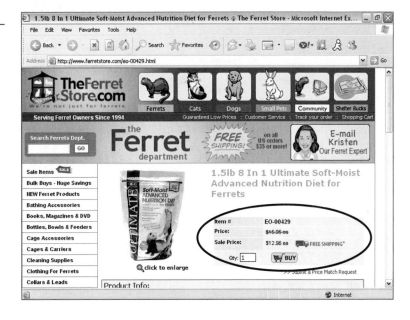

FIGURE 11.4
A Free Shipping icon visually lets customers know that their order will be shipped for free. An icon is more noticeable than plain text.

FIGURE 11.5
If you set a minimum order amount for free shipping, let customers know how much more they will need to spend to receive the free shipping.

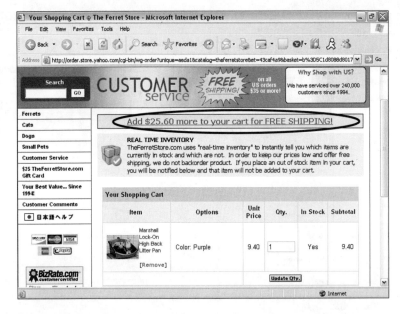

FIGURE 11.6
Encourage bulk orders by letting customers input how many items they would like to purchase and show quantity discount pricing.

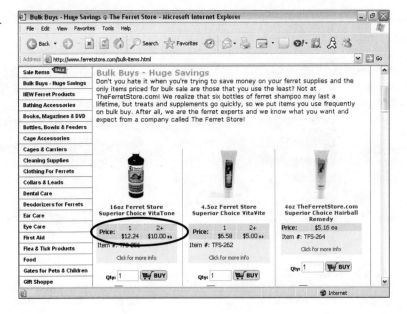

CHAPTER 11   High-Volume Product Store   **163**

FIGURE 11.7
An advanced search capability helps customers narrow their search results.

FIGURE 11.8
Real-time order tracking puts the package status inquiry in the hands of the customer.

Creating Multiple Website Niches with the Same Product Line

Creating multiple sites is like having your own chain of stores. The more chains you have, the more money you will make. Opening a second or even a third store can give you more exposure, and you also can try different marketing tactics with minimal expense. For Neeps, the main website is www.theferretstore.com (see Figure 11.9). The website URL targets only a niche market of ferret owners, but the company also sells products for dogs, cats, rabbits, and other critters. Neeps wanted to target other pet owners who would otherwise avoid the site because the website domain name is too specific. So, it started www.petcarecentral.com (see Figure 11.10) to target the general pet owner market.

But what about the pet owners who would rather buy from websites that cater to their type of pet? Some customers would rather purchase products from websites that they think are the industry experts on their type of pet. Specific product-related websites can also make it easier for the customers to find products that relate only to them. Neeps added 11 more websites, including www.rabbitcentral.com (see Figure 11.11), www.activek9.com, www.thecritterstore.com, and others to do just that. If you go to ActiveK9.com, for example, the home page shows only dog-related products. Although you can purchase other types of pet products, the focus is on dog products. Creating additional sites that segment your product line creates a niche within your general product website. This is an advantage especially if you have a large product line with lots of product categories. Creating a niche website gives your customers the perception that you are an expert in that industry.

Another reason you should create additional stores is to experiment with marketing techniques. For example, one store will have products that are cheaper but will have a shipping fee. The other store will have products that are a little more expensive but will include shipping. You can also tinker with your layout, look and feel, and marketing pitch.

Yes, you are competing against yourself, but who best to compete with? You win either way.

CHAPTER 11 High-Volume Product Store **165**

FIGURE 11.9
TheFerretStore.com specializes in ferret products. You can purchase other types of pet products by clicking the buttons on the top navigation bar.

FIGURE 11.10
PetCareCentral.com focuses on the general pet product market. The website caters to all types of pets.

FIGURE 11.11
RabbitCentral.com focuses on only rabbit products. The products are pulled from the same product data file as the other websites owned by Neeps.

Managing Multiple Websites

Managing multiple websites sounds like a lot of work, right? Not really, if properly designed. The 12 sites that Neeps owns all pull from the same product data file. Yes, folks, *one* product data file. The data file contains all 5,400 products. Each site is programmed to pull certain product categories and display them accordingly. For example, ActiveK9.com places only dog products on its home page, and RabbitCentral.com places only rabbit products on its home page.

Although you will need to upload the product data file to each Yahoo! Store Editor, it will be the same file.

> **tip** If you plan to use the multiple-niche website strategy, make sure your Yahoo! store–development company or programmer is aware of this. The programmer will need to add special identifiers so the website will know which products to display.

Neeps Backend System

When you start receiving more than 30 orders a day and start hiring helpers, you will find that the built-in Yahoo! management system might not adequately suit your needs. Having a fulfillment-management system that can handle large numbers of orders and help streamline your order and shipping process can either make or break your company. Getting lots of orders is great, but not being able to handle them is not—and could cause more unnecessary work. A good backend system not only streamlines your process but also reduces personnel cost. Neeps chose OrderMotion (www.ordermotion.com) to handle its backend processing. OrderMotion integrates seamlessly and in real time with the Yahoo! store.

About OrderMotion

Like the Yahoo! store, OrderMotion is a Web-based system. Let's take a look at some of the benefits of using OrderMotion:

- **Real-time inventory checking**—Your Yahoo! store retrieves the current inventory level in real time and lets your customers know whether the product is in stock.

- **Multiple websites**—You can have multiple websites accessing the same product data file and inventory level. All orders are stored in one account.

- **Customized packaging documents**—If you plan to have multiple websites, the system will know which site the order came from and print the appropriate shipping document with the correct company information and logo. The system can also send shipping confirmation emails with tracking numbers.

- **Fully automated payment processing**—Orders can be authorized in real time, and credit card payment can be processed and settled from within the system.

- **Repeat customer notification**—OrderMotion can flag orders based on first-time or returning customers. Neeps uses this feature to include a product catalog for first-time customers.

- **Targeted mailings**—The system allows Neeps to send catalogs to customers who bought certain products. This allows Neeps to customize and send to targeted customers.

For additional information about OrderMotion or to see an online demo, go to www.ordermotion.com.

Automated Drop-Shop Notification

More than 7% of Neeps inventory is drop-shipped to the customer. If an order is placed that includes a drop-shipped product, the backend system, OrderMotion, notifies the supplier via email. When the supplier fulfills the order, the order status is updated in the OrderMotion system.

Accounting

Neeps uses the Peachtree software to track revenues and expenses. Neeps's accountant recommended this as an easy-to-use and robust accounting system. Daily inventory, sales, and refund totals are recorded into the system daily. Sales data is exported from the OrderMotion back-end system and then imported into Peachtree. Peachtree is not directly tied into the OrderMotion system.

Setting Up Your Warehouse and Bin Location System

Having an easy-to-navigate system for your warehouse is crucial to your fulfillment process. Not only will it give you more control over your inventory, but it will also help you save time. A well-planned warehouse and system also helps with new hires and seasoned employees.

Neeps has developed a system and warehouse layout that has streamlined its fulfillment process. Here's an article from the SolidCactus September 2005 newsletter written by Scott Sanfilippo, co-founder and chief operating officer, on how to set up your warehouse:

> If you're selling products and stocking them in your warehouse, you probably have some type of location system in place to make picking easy for your employees. You don't? Well, then, read on!
>
> If you're just starting out and have a few employees who know where products are located by memory, it may seem like a good system to have. Don't be fooled. For instance, what happens when those employees take jobs elsewhere or you need to quickly hire new people to take care of the influx of holiday orders that suddenly crept up on you? Chances, are you'll be wasting a lot of valuable pick/pack time having those employees walk around aimlessly searching for products. The solution to your warehousing evolution is bin locations.
>
> Bin locations are simply the places where products are housed in your warehouse. This is a crucial system for every e-business to develop, and you should organize your warehouse right down to the exact location on every single shelf. Taking the time to set up bin locations now, before the holidays, will save you time and money, improve your order turn-around time, and eventually lead to greater customer satisfaction down the road. Here's how you start.
>
> For the purposes of these examples, I will assume that your warehouse is set up with racks making up aisles, which we call pick lanes. The

first thing you need to do is find a starting point for your pick route. A good origination point is the spot where you keep your pick tickets and baskets or carts for picking products. The second step is to label your pick lanes. Pick lanes should be labeled alphabetically. The aisle closest to the start of the pick route can be labeled A, the second-closest can be labeled B, and so forth.

When you have a map of your pick lanes, it's time to label the racks that are located in each of those aisles. To maintain a flow, racks are labeled in such a way that your picker will start at the beginning of the pick route, walk up the first aisles, down the second, up the third, and so on, eventually ending up back at the start of the route, ready to pick another order. For obvious reasons, we call this a serpentine layout.

Labeling your racks along the pick aisle is simple. Let's assume there are three racks in each aisle. Starting at the beginning, assign the first rack on the right the number 01 (put a zero in front of single-digit numbers to maintain consistency and allow for future growth), the second 03, and the third 05. On the left side of the aisle, assign the first rack 02, the second 04, and the third 06 (see Figure 11.12). When your racks are labeled, it's time to drill down to the details of each rack.

FIGURE 11.12
Example warehouse floor plan.

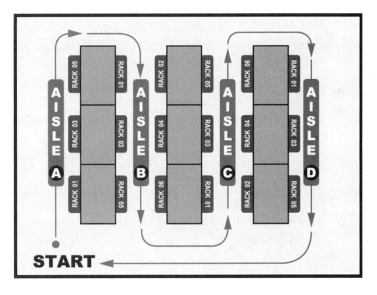

The first rack in aisle A is called A01 (aisle A, rack 01). Let's assume that rack 01 has three shelves. Starting at the floor, label the bottom shelf as A, the middle shelf as B, and the top shelf as C. On those shelves, your product is contained in boxes or "bins." Starting left to right, each bin can be labeled 01, 02, 03, 03, and so on. You do this for each shelf, so, in this example, products in the fourth bin on shelf B of rack 02 in aisle A would have a bin location of A02B04 (see Figure 11.13). The key thing to remember is that the bin location is not tied to an item—it's tied to the rack.

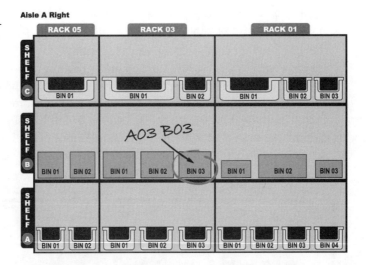

FIGURE 11.13
Example of rack setup.

At first, organizing your warehouse may sound confusing and look like a lot of work, but, believe me, it will pay big dividends over time! As TheFerretStore.com quickly grew from Joe and me picking out orders by memory to hiring our first employee and ultimately dozens more, it became necessary for us to have a system in place to make picking easy, while at the same time making it easy to teach others in a short time. Today the time spent training new employees on how to pick product takes no more than 5 or 10 minutes because the system is easy to learn. With a system in place like this, when you need to bring in temporary help to pick and pack during the holidays, your training is minimal.

When your bin location system is up and running, you can tweak it even more to improve warehouse efficiency. For example, you may want to put your most-picked products right at the beginning of your pick route so your pickers don't have to go three aisles back to get the most popular items they pick on a constant basis. Or if you have items that sell only in the winter, move them to the end of the pick route and put your summer merchandise at the beginning during the spring and summer months.

Establishing a bin location system is essential as your business grows.

Shipping and Packaging

Neeps uses United Parcel Service (UPS) to ship all orders. With an average of 400 packages per day, UPS makes two trips daily to the warehouse for pickup.

All packages for the first pickup are placed on a crate and wrapped. UPS loads the entire crate onto the truck.

Negotiating Shipping Cost

Anything you can do to cut cost without cutting quality is more money in your pocket. If you are shipping enough packages per day, the shipping company will do whatever it can to keep you as a customer, including giving you a steep discount rate or giving you computers, software, and even bar code–scanning equipment. UPS, FedEx, and DHL are all competing for your business. Get rates from all three, and use that as your negotiating power. Neeps was able to get a discounted shipping rate, computer equipment, and software for free.

> **tip** You can request refunds or discounts for late packages. You can simply do it yourself by calling the shipping company or use a third-party company such as www.refundpackage.com or www.shippingrefunds.com to do it for you. There is no up-front cost, and you pay only 50% of whatever they recover.
>
> If you are shipping hundreds of orders per day, that can mean thousands of saved dollars per month.

Online and Offline Marketing Strategies

Neeps uses a combination of online and offline marketing to drive traffic to a site. Even if your business is completely online, it's still a good strategy to use traditional marketing, such as print advertisement.

Print Advertising

Print advertising is also an effective marketing strategy of Neeps. TheFerretStore.com, ActiveK9.com, and RabbitCentral.com all run quarterly printed catalogs.

Pay-Per-Click Advertising

Neeps uses and manages more than 11,000 keywords/keyword phrases as part of its pay-per-click advertisement campaign for all its websites. It primarily uses Overture (www.overture.com) and Google Ad Words (Google.com) to manage its pay-per-click advertising. Neeps also uses www.bizrate.com and www.shopping.com for additional product exposure.

Affiliate Marketing

Neeps has more than 3,000 affiliates throughout its group of websites. As we mentioned earlier, affiliates are website owners who agree to place a link or advertisement banner on their websites, in hopes of driving sales to your website in exchange for a set percentage or sales amount. Of the total number of affiliates, about 10% are currently active, meaning that 10 out of 100 affiliates usually produce constant sales. Affiliate marketing accounts for approximately 25% of the total number of orders.

PepperJamManagement.com manages all its affiliates, from acquiring new super affiliates to handling payment for affiliates. This is a great service for anyone who has a large number of affiliates or would like to start a successful affiliate program.

> **tip** Product reviews help customers make purchasing decisions especially if they are on the fence about a particular product. Positive reviews can help push customers into making the purchase.

Email Marketing

For Neeps, email marketing has not been effective as in previous years. Even with an opt-in email list, email marketing has not resulted in many sales. With the amount of spam and better spam filters, people don't pay as much attention to email advertisements anymore. Of all the online advertising strategies, email marketing has been the least effective.

Creating Repeat Customers

Having a niche market, such as ferret products, means that the customer base is very limited: There are only so many ferret owners. It's important that Neeps keep its customers happy and that they continue to purchase from the store. To encourage repeat business, Neeps not only wanted to be number one in customer service, but it knew the importance of staying in front of customers.

To keep customers thinking about the company, Neeps incorporated a few marketing tactics:

- **Product catalog**—Every first-time customer gets a product catalog along with an order. This is easily done with OrderMotion, which tags the shipping slip for new customers.
- **Product samples**—Repeat customers get a product sample—anything from food samples to pet toy products—included with the package. This lets customers try different products.
- **Monthly newsletter**—This newsletter includes reviews and announcements about new products. It also includes tips on pet care.
- **Discounts**—These are discount codes to encourage repeat business. Everybody loves a sale.
- **Community message board**—This interactive online message board helps ferret pet owners communicate with each other. You can read articles, get tips, send e-cards, view a photo gallery of other owners and their ferrets, and more (see www.ferretstoreinteractive.com).

Now that we have deconstructed three individual websites and looked at how they have successfully positioned themselves, let's look at how you can successfully position your own store.

Part IV

Growing Your Online Business

12 The Power of PARM: Positioning Your Business

13 Acquiring Customers (Part 1)

14 Acquiring Customers (Part 2)

15 Retaining Customers

16 Monetizing

17 Monitoring Site Sales and Performance

18 Public Relations

CHAPTER 12

The Power of PARM: Positioning Your Business

In This Chapter

- The power of PARM
- How to position your business in the digital marketplace
- How to create a brand
- The Big 5 of branding

William James, the famous nineteenth-century philosopher, once compared the universe to a "blooming, buzzing mass of confusion." Internet marketing can also resemble a mass of confusion to those trying to understand and use an almost infinite variety of marketing tools and tactics. Search engine submittals, placement and optimization, keyword purchases, promotional emails, text, HTML and rich media newsletters, opt-in list building, database email marketing, affiliate marketing, strategic partnerships, link exchanges, banner exchanges, newsgroup and forum postings, community building, and websites, newsletter, and electronic magazine advertising are just some of the many marketing tools available to you to market and promote your Yahoo! store.

These are only the ones we use today. With the advent of the "always on," always connected Internet to every digital device, we're sure to see marketing strategies and tactics that we haven't even thought of yet. What we need is an "organizing concept" that can make sense of this blooming, buzzing confusion and make this vast variety of e-marketing tools work in concert to achieve your company's e-commerce goals and objectives.

In this chapter and the three that follow, we discuss the power of PARM (positioning, acquiring, retaining, and monetizing) as an organizing concept for your Yahoo! store marketing strategy.

The Power of PARM

The many marketing tools and tactics available might seem confusing at first, but if you stack each of them up under the elements of PARM, you can create a well-planned and effective marketing plan for your Yahoo! store.

PARM is a marketing strategy: positioning, acquiring, retaining, and monetizing. Positioning sits atop acquiring, which rests upon retaining; all three sit atop monetizing.

By *positioning*, we mean how your Yahoo! store positions itself in the digital marketplace. After you've positioned your business and when you know who your target audience is, it's time to *acquire* customers. You then need to *retain* those customers. It's well known that it costs 10 times more to acquire a new customer than to retain the ones you have, so retention becomes an important objective of your marketing program. Finally, all this positioning, acquiring, and retaining is for naught if you can't make a buck from customers. So, *monetizing* all this traffic to your digital presence is obviously your ultimate goal.

Any one of the marketing tools in itself will not make your company's Internet marketing plan a success. The slow and steady, consistent combination of them all wins the e-commerce race. Keep in mind that the tools we offer in this chapter and the ones that follow are only a start. By thinking long and hard about your digital business strategy, you can come up with even more marketing tools and tactics to apply to your particular Yahoo! store.

We take a closer look at each one and see which marketing tools and tactics you can use when creating a marketing strategy for your business. The details of each marketing tool are covered later in this chapter and in the ones that follow.

Positioning Your Business

Positioning your business is the first step when creating your marketing plan for your Yahoo! store. This includes reviewing how your communications and collateral material—such as your letterhead, business cards, brochures, and advertising copy (print, radio, TV)—are integrated into your digital strategy solution. For example, all your offline collateral materials and activities should include at least an email addresses and a reference to the URL of your website. You might even consider offering readers, viewers, and listeners the ability to sign up for your informative newsletter or for further information on your company. If you have a printed catalog, advertise and promote it on your website.

> **Web Resource**
>
> **Do-It-Yourself Logos**
>
> InstaLogo (www.instalogo.com) can help create your business logo for as little as $89. You can choose from a variety of images from an extensive catalog, use the company's online logo-creation tool, and get your logo on the same day you create it.

Positioning also includes reviewing your website's search engine placement and ranking in the search results, and analyzing site traffic logs, your business positioning, and your communication process with site visitors.

That last piece is important: How do you communicate with your site visitors? In fact, how do you communicate with any visitor who communicates with you through your digital presence? The phrase *digital presence* reflects the many more ways a business today can communicate its presence than just in a website.

> **Web Resource**
>
> **Find Out How Your Site Ranks**
>
> It's a good idea to check periodically to see where your Yahoo! store ranks in the top search engines. At Mike's Marketing Tools (www.mikes-marketing-tools.com/ranking-reports), you can see where your site ranks with the six top search engines—Google, Yahoo! Search, MSN, AOL, AltaVista, and AllTheWeb—and the top three Web directories—Yahoo! Directory, Open Directory (Dmoz), and LookSmart. And it's *free*!

Finally, there's the importance of branding. . ..

The Alphabet of Branding: USP, ESP, OSP, and BSD

How you position your product or service in the digital marketplace is your brand. Now, branding has many definitions. The best we've found is from the free Wikipedia (www.wikipedia.org):

> A brand is the symbolic embodiment of all the information connected with a product or service. A brand typically includes a name, logo, and other visual elements such as images or symbols. It also encompasses the set of expectations associated with a product or service which typically arise in the minds of people. Such people include employees of the brand owner; people involved with distribution, sale, or supply of the product or service; and ultimate consumers.

Examples of great brands are Nike, Coca-Cola, Pepsi, IBM, Amazon, Ben & Jerry's, Starbucks, and Priceline.

> **Web Resource**
>
> **Who's Talking About Your Brand?**
>
> Find out the buzz on your brand by going to Cymfony (www.cymfony.com). This site tracks what's being said about any brand in discussion boards and chat rooms, in media mentions, and even in blogs. It can tell you what consumers are saying about your brand and how often they're talking about it.

As you can see, a company's brand is not just its name, its logo, or its packaging. It's also a set of shopper expectations and the service you supply your customers. Let's take a closer look of what makes up a company's brand.

First, the positioning and branding of your Yahoo! store should reflect your company's unique selling position (USP). Your USP tells a potential customer the uniqueness of your product or service, how your business differs from your competition, and, above all, what's in it for them. In other words, you need to answer that burning question of every shopper: "What's in it for me?" (WIIFM)

CHAPTER 12 The Power of PARM: Positioning Your Business

Several studies have shown that when a customer looks at your ad or website, you have 1.54 seconds to convince them of the WIIFM before they close your window. Then if you do, you have less than 5 seconds to keep them there.

So, what makes the business unique in the market and in the eyes of a potential customer? To do that, you need to ask yourself the following questions:

- What gives your company a unique *advantage* over your competition?
- What is the distinct *reason* for consumers to buy from you?
- Can you portray in the consumer's mind a compelling *image* of what your business will do for them that others can't?

For example, maybe it's your no-questions return policy, like Nordstrom's. Or maybe your delivery policy matches that of Dominoes: You get it within 20 minutes, or it's free. Or you might offer service that matches the latest Best Buy guarantee: Place your order online and pick it up at the nearest Best Buy store in 23 minutes, or you get $23.

Too many companies believe that it's about them. It's not. It's about the customers. Remember this cardinal rule: *Consumers could care less about you. They want to know what you can do for them.* Then they will hand over their hard-earned cash.

Vincent Flanders, who runs *Web Pages That Suck*, advises e-commerce sites to write the following two sentences and post them near their computer so they can see them every day:

1. "The only reason my website exists is to solve my customers' problems."
2. "What problems does the page I'm looking at solve?"

Consumers care only about getting their problems solved. They're looking for information. They're looking to make a purchase. They're looking for entertainment. Fill those needs, and you will have a successful Yahoo! store.

> **tip** Include Keywords in Your Tagline
>
> You should be able to reduce your USP into keywords that you can later to optimize your Web pages for search engines and in your search engine marketing campaigns. A good tagline that appears on your home page should contain these keywords. If your keywords do not describe your USP—your value proposition to the shopper—then rethink your keywords.
>
> A good tagline should include the keywords you're targeting on your home page. If you find that you can't use your targeted keywords to describe your value proposition, you might be using the wrong keywords. A good example is "Ray's Rare Books: More Signed First Editions Than Any Other Online Bookstore."

Martin Lindstrom, a recognized branding guru by the Chartered Institute of Marketing, adds some other elements that you should consider when branding your Yahoo! business. Besides your USP, you should consider an ESP, an emotional selling proposition. He cites Coke and Pepsi as good examples of ESP. They differentiate themselves from each other not on rationale logic and product attributes (after all, a soft drink is a soft drink, no matter what the "taste challenge tests" say) but by calling on the feelings, identity, and values they promote in the consumer's mind. Kevin Roberts, Worldwide CEO of Saatchi & Saatchi, has stated that "the brands with legs are those that create an emotional connection with customers."

Another of Lindstrom's branding elements is your organizational selling proposition, or OSP. This type of branding is reflected in the organizational structure of the business itself. Lindstrom cites Nike as an example of OSP. Nike promotes a sports culture among it employees, and encourages them to use Nike's products and make sports a big part of their lives, both at work and away. The offices of Nike are more than just a workplace; they're a sports lifestyle for its staff.

> **Web Resource**
>
> **Building Your Brand**
>
> Building Brands (www.buildingbrands.com) can give you real feedback and direction when building your brand, for a small fee.

Lindstrom's final element of branding is the brand selling proposition, or BSP. With BSP, the product or service itself is irrelevant. He cites the Harry Potter brand as an example. Although only the books have been sold, thousands of related products (toys, clothing, lunch boxes, and more) sell only because of the brand name "Harry Potter" on them. George Lucas created this type of branding, now called merchandising, with *Star Wars*.

So, when you're creating your company brand, keep this alphabet soup in mind and apply the different elements of branding, where appropriate, to your positioning strategy.

Underpromise and Overdeliver

A big part of branding—and, thus, the positioning of your Yahoo! store in the digital marketplace—involves consumer perception. That is, it involves the set of expectations that arise in the consumer's mind about your product or service. One of the best ways to do this is to underpromise and overdeliver.

One way is to respond to customer inquiries faster than you promise. For example, you might claim on your customer service and frequently asked questions (FAQ) pages (you do have a separate FAQ page that answers many of a potential customer's questions about your product or service and company policies, right?) that you answer all email inquiries within 48 to 72 hours. But let's say you actually answer your inquiries in 24 hours. The consumer now expects that if he or she buys from you, you will go the extra mile for that customer if a problem develops. Or perhaps you add a small present of nominal cost in each order that the customer was not expecting. Remember, it's not the cost, but the thought that counts.

If you deliver a quality product with better service than the customer expects, you will win the most important promotional tools that a business can have: positive word-of-mouth that builds a valuable brand in the minds of consumers.

Martin Lindstrom offers a good example of this.

A man purchased a barbeque grill as a gift for a friend. After spending the time to assemble the grill, the man's friend said that he could not accept the present. So the man returned the grill to the store for a refund. The merchant gladly accepted the grill, and the man was refunded the full amount—plus $30. The man asked what the $30 was for, and the merchant replied that because he had taken the time to assemble the grill, he should be compensated for it. The salesperson replied, "You've used most of the day collecting and assembling this grill, so you've made life easier for its next owner. You should be rewarded for this."

You can bet that the next time someone asks the man for a recommendation on where to buy a barbeque grill, that store will be his first suggestion. Surprise your customers by underpromising and overdelivering, and your brand will reap the benefits.

Tips for Online Branding

Larry Chase Web Digest for Marketers (www.wdfm.com) is an excellent resource for marketers. Chase's weekly newsletter is always packed with marketing tips and resources that you can use to promote your Yahoo! store. Chase has compiled a list of branding tips that you should review when creating your brand, to make your positioning message stand out among your competition.

First, look at your tagline—those few words or one phrase that quickly tells a visitor to your Yahoo! store about your USP. Does it really differentiate your business from the competition? Remember, you don't have very many seconds

(1.54) to grab a visitor's attention, so your tagline must be short and effective. "Our prices can't be beat" and "We are the lowest price" don't sell the shopper. Customers need to know *why* you are the lowest and *why* it's important to them.

Michelin's tagline is an example of one that focuses on the customer's need: "Because so much is riding on *your* tires." This tagline personalizes the USP and answers the question in the consumer's mind, "Why should I care? What's in it for me?"

Your objective is to create a solid, exact, and usable USP that both positions you in the marketplace and convinces a consumer to buy from you.

> **Web Resource**
>
> **Create Your Own Tagline**
>
> AdSlogans.com (www.adlogans.com) is a tagline database service that can help you create an effective tagline that will not compete with your competitors'. The company's services include BizCheck, to help you research all the taglines in your brand category; Mission Statements, which provides all the mission statements and strategic intent of key players in your category; PosCheck (short for PositionCheck), which compares and contrasts the brand positioning of your competitors to spot weaknesses and overlap; TermCheck, which checks the use of specific terms, concepts, or ideas; LineCheck, which checks prior or current use of a proposed new tagline; and Sloganalysis, which assesses the content of your slogan against a series of branding benchmarks. Some of the tools, such as Sloganalysis, are free to use. Others, such as LineCheck, are available for a fee (this one runs $500 and promises 24-hour turnaround).

Second, don't be perceived as a "me, too." Marvin Honig, well-known creative director who was responsible for the classic ads for Volkswagen, warns against losing your business in the Sea of Sameness. As an example, he once took the soundtrack from one noted soft drink ad and placed it over the visuals of a second noted soft drink ad. They synched up perfectly! His focus groups proved that people could not tell the difference between one soft drink ad of that time and another.

Third, show customers—don't tell them. Talk is cheap, so *show* your shoppers how you will anticipate their needs and meet their expectations. Again, this is the idea of underpromising and overdelivering.

Fourth, find a personality for your site, otherwise known as your voice. Don't make your product or service (even your company polices) sound like boring spec sheet. Talk to your shoppers. Get in their shoes. If you can do that, you go long way toward answering their question of WIIFM: "What's in it for me?"

Fifth, ask for criticism. Show your worse critic your Yahoo! store. In fact, show it to as many critics as you can. Tell them to be fair but brutal. Take their criticism to heart, and make the appropriate changes.

Finally, you can't please everybody. That's why you have chosen a target audience. Market to those consumers, position your business, and build a brand for those you want to sell to.

Branding with the Big 5

In our previous book, *Launching Your Yahoo! Business* (Que, 2006), we spoke about the Big 5 of e-commerce: price, selection, convenience, service, and security. These five elements can help you define your brand and separate it from your competition.

Briefly, you can brand on price, selection, or experience (convenience, service, and security).

Price is no longer king on the Internet. Yes, it's important, but with a consumer's ability to shop for the best price using search engines, comparison-shopping sites, and auctions, it has become very difficult to compete on price alone. So how do you avoid the lowest-price trap? By adding the other four of the Big 5 to your branding mix.

Free Info Download the free informative article titled "Flexible Pricing: A Concept Whose Time Has Come at www.myecommercesuccess.com.

First, start with your target audience and focus on selection. You can't be all things to all people, so sharpen the focus of your product or service selection. More sales to more people outside your target market will not necessarily bring you profitable customers. Choose your selection and then add value to it. Are you selling a price-sensitive commodity such as books, CDs, or videos? Don't try to be the lowest. Find ways to add value to the product, such as free shipping or packaged deals or knowledgeable recommendations—anything that you can use to raise your price a bit and still make a good margin.

Value is in the eyes of the consumers. If they feel that they are getting a good deal because you went the extra mile for them or made their purchase more convenient, they will pay more. Amazon is a good example. Why not pay a little more than their competitors if you know you can purchase your product quickly and easily with a "one click" purchase?

Construct a brand that incorporates your version of the Big 5, and you will create a USP for your Yahoo! store.

In the next chapter, we cover some of the best marketing tools for acquiring visitors in your Yahoo! store.

CHAPTER 13

Acquiring Customers (Part 1)

In This Chapter

- Using watering-hole marketing to find customers
- Advertising your Yahoo! store on the Net
- Using email marketing to attract customers to your Yahoo! store
- Doing internal store marketing

The second word of the marketing concept of PARM is *acquisition*. You've positioned your business in the digital marketplace, you've created a unique brand, and you have a dynamite product or service offer. Now it's time to promote that offering to consumers and attract them to your online storefront.

Acquiring customers has to be the most important and the most challenging job of any e-commerce business. Not only must you determine which of the many available acquisition tools to use, but you also must use those tools properly. Here's a list of the most important tactics and tools for customer acquisition covered in this chapter:

- Watering-hole marketing
- Advertising
- Email marketing
- Internal marketing

But before we go into these in detail, we need to first discuss where to find the prospects of your target market.

> **Web Resource**
>
> **Are You Marketing Savvy?**
> Take the quick 10-question quiz on marketing at www.microsoft.com/smallbusiness/resources/marketing/customer_service_acquisition/quiz_are_you_marketing_savvy.mspx to see how you rate. Then, focus on the areas of marketing that you need to better understand.

Watering-Hole Marketing

We've learned that developing a unique selling position coupled with a target market is the most efficient way to market your online storefront. But what's the most cost-effective way? That's where the concept of watering-hole marketing comes into play. That's the person, place, or thing that already has attracted your potential customers' attention and credibility. If you find these sources, you find not only your potential customers, but also a strategic partner that could market your product for you—for free!

If you know where to find the watering holes of the target audience you want to reach, you are halfway toward your goal of acquiring customers who would respond to your product or service offering. If you find the correct watering hole, you will have the drinkers' attention.

Here's an example of watering-hole marketing. Suppose you run a company that sells telephone equipment to apartment complexes and small businesses. One way to find potential customers is to do cold calls and buy lists of companies that just received business licensees. But cold-calling can be very inefficient and costly—and by the time a company has its business license, in most cases, it has already purchased its phone system.

> **Free Info** Download the free informative article titled "Contests, Giveaways and Promotions" at www.myecommercesuccess.com.

A better way is to talk to title companies. Any commercial building or apartment complex that is being built needs to have a title search. Title companies guarantee that the title to the property being built on is free and clear of liens. Because this search must be done on any property before a bank will extend a construction loan, it makes the title company a watering hole for businesses that need a new phone system for the building or for future tenants.

Using a title company does one other thing for your business: It positions the title company as a credible source of information, one that has the attention of those at the watering hole. In this situation, you could approach a specific title company and offer an exclusive program to commercial property developers and businesses—perhaps a discount on a phone system or a free extended warrantee. The title insurance business is competitive, so title companies love these kinds of deals that differentiate them for the competition. And because the major title companies are nationwide companies, working with them to help find prospects would give the telephone business national coverage for their product.

Here's another example. Suppose you owned a pet clothing company. Where's the watering hole where pet owners congregate? Veterinarian offices, for one. You might put sample brochures in the waiting room with your company's logo, telephone number, and Web address.

What's Your Marketing Goal?

Before you rush out and begin spending money on marketing your Yahoo! store, make sure you know what you expect to accomplish with your marketing plan and which marketing tool will provide it. That is, decide what you expect for your return on investment (ROI) from your marketing endeavourers.

That ROI could mean more than just increased sales. You could also spend money on marketing to achieve the following:

- More inquiries
- Sales leads
- Repeat customers
- Attention from the media
- Registrations

You can use many of the marketing tools discussed here for a variety of results; your ROI might not necessarily be a sale right out of the chute.

Finally, whatever the goal of your ROI is, you mustn't forget the call to action (CTA). An actionable CTA asks the reader of your marketing piece to take an action there and now. For example, "learn now" is a much better call to action than "learn how." Use active voice when writing your CTA. Do customers know what is expected of them when they read your promotion? Is it to buy? Register for a contest? Download a file? Join a club? Subscribe to a newsletter? Ask for further information? Don't be vague about the action you require from your customers or prospects.

Advertising

The old adage goes, "Early to bed, early to rise, work like a dog, and advertise." But what advertising works best? John Wanamaker, manufacturer and dry goods pioneer once said, "I know half my advertising is wasted. I just don't know which half." The good news is that you can get immediate and real feedback on your marketing tactics when you're marketing online.

Let's first clear up some confusion over the differences between adverting and marketing. As you can see by the organization of this chapter, advertising is a subset of marketing—just another tool in the marketing toolbox. But unlike online print advertising that talks *at* the consumer, online advertising talks *to* the consumer and gives you the necessary feedback of whether you are meeting the ROI goals of your advertising.

You can use a number of advertising vehicles—some free and others that have a cost. These online advertising vehicles are available to you:

- Banner ads
- Contextual ads
- Electronic newsletter and e-zine ads

So, what will it cost? Most marketing experts agree that you should devote 3% to 8% of your annual sales to your total advertising and promotional budget. And that's not including any promotional start-up costs. Look at the amount of money that Travelocity, Orbitz, and Expedia spend just to build brand. This is why strategic partnering and media partnering are important. But before you pull out your wallet and get ready to spend ad dollars, you should know how to speak the lingo of Net advertising.

The Language of Net Advertising

Internet advertising has split, combined, and multiplied into a bewildering array of approaches to advertising on the Net. Abbreviations such as CPM, CPC, CPA, CPT, and CPS make the novice Net advertiser's eyes glaze over.

Let's go step by step through this seemingly incomprehensible zoo of letters. We first define them and then show how you can make the best use of your Internet advertising dollar. There's a new world out there for advertisers on the Net.

Today's Net delivers accountability it in spades—not just audience estimates, as in the real world. When you advertise on the Net, you know exactly how well your ad campaign is doing by the number of impressions, click-throughs, and responses that you get from your advertising efforts. You must measure to see these results.

Impressions are correlated with awareness or brand advertising. You count impressions by how many times your ad is presented to a viewer. If the intent of your advertising campaign is to raise awareness of your product, service, or brand, the number of impressions per dollar is of prime importance—that is, you want the most impressions you can get for the lowest ad dollar.

Click-through, in response to an ad by a consumer, simply indicates interest or intent. When a consumer clicks your ad or goes to a URL that you've advertised in an email message or newsletter, click-through provides you with an opportunity to offer something for sale or to even complete a sale. Other uses include filling out a survey or asking the viewer to take some other kind of action (conversion). You can equate this with a potential buyer opening a direct-mail envelope to read the offer inside. The better the ad, the more potential it has to be acted on. If your intention is to have the viewer click your ad or go to your site, the number of clicks (or visitors to your site) per ad dollar is of prime importance.

A *response* is indicated by either providing leads for future sales or completing sales themselves. A response also could include a software download. If your objective is to actually make a sale or have the viewer complete an action, the number of responses per ad dollar is of prime importance.

Now, let's see how impressions, click-throughs, and responses play out in the alphabet soup of Net advertising:

- CPM (cost per thousand impressions) is the number of times your ad is viewed. Another way to say it is the number of times the ad is displayed. When you buy based on CPM, you're paying each time a consumer views your ad. Click-throughs to your site and sales are not your prime objective here; brand or image awareness is.

- CPC (cost per click) is the number of times your ad is clicked or how many people actually go to the URL you are advertising. Your objective is to have them "open your direct mail envelope" and view your offer.

- The last group of abbreviations in this advertising alphabet soup is CPA, CPT, and CPS. All three of these fall, more or less, under the same umbrella. Using these schemes, you pay for only an actual response to an offer, not just a view or click-through. CPA (cost per action) is the number of times the desired action takes place on your site, such as a sale, a registration, or a download. CPT (cost per transaction) is the cost per lead. This type of banner ad is similar to CPA, but you pay only for people who click your banner ad and either fill out a registration form or are sent to a page on your site where they can view the full offer. CPS (cost per sale) is similar to CPA, but you pay for only leads that generate a sale.

Not every one of these approaches is perfect for everyone. Decide first what type of action you are willing to pay for and then negotiate your best deal.

Common Advertising Vehicles

Banner ads, sponsorships, contextual ads, and electronic newsletter and e-zine advertising are the basic advertising vehicles that you can use to promote your Yahoo! store.

A *banner ad* is like a small billboard that resides on a Web page. Buying banner ads from individual sites is one way to get your message out. Another is to buy ads on a banner network. But you can also run banner ads for free if you join a banner exchange network. Banner exchange networks trade banners ads on your website with banner ads from other websites on a rotating basis. A third-party banner ad server delivers and rotates your ad and others throughout the network. The only thing you have to do when joining one of these networks is add some code on your website to display other members' banner ads on your site.

Generic and industry-specific banner ad networks exist. For targeted traffic, it's best to join an industry-specific network. To find your industry-specific network, go to Yahoo.com and search for *"your industry banner exchange network."* You can also go to some industry-related websites to see if they have joined a banner exchange network and find out how you can also join. But heed this warning: Because you do not have control over what ads are displayed on your storefront, a competitor's ad (or other inappropriate ad) might appear on your site because your competitors are likely using the same keywords you are displaying on your site. A network might eliminate a lot of the work of negotiating deals for individual banner ads, but there is a risk that you will end up displaying ads for your (possibly bigger) competitors and driving visitors away from your site.

Contextual advertising is a way to place your promotional ad next to related content, such as a news article or a product review. Why are contextual ads a good advertising vehicle? Well, people use the Net for more than just searching for products to buy. In fact, the largest use of the Internet is to find information. If your banner ad or text ad shows up next to or within an informative piece that a consumer is reading, you might enter the consumer's mindset of a *targeted market*, which would get that person to visit your storefront. It also creates a perceived endorsement of your product or service.

Advertising in newsletters and e-zines can be a cost-effective way of reaching your targeted audience. The cyberworld has its equivalent of the printed media of the real world: email newsletters and e-zines (electronic magazines). You can advertise in any of thousands of newsletters and hundreds of e-zines, each focusing on a particular market niche. And don't forget the many forums, discussion boards, and blogs. Forums can be very specific, so they're great for going after niche markets. Blogs are newer but might be worth targeting, depending on the quality of the blog and the market you are targeting.

Is advertising effective? Should you consider using it as a promotional tool? One story tells of a businessman who did not believe in advertising. When his e-business did not fare well, guess what he did? He advertised it for sale.

Advertising is a necessary evil that, if used properly, can help you reach your company's marketing goals. It's all about the ROI.

Email Marketing

What could be better? A marketing piece that's easy to use, costs no money to produce, costs next to nothing to send, and reaches millions of prospects in a matter of minutes. That's email marketing, one the most cost-effective ways for an online business to market and get people to purchase goods and services. There simply isn't an easier, cheaper, more direct way to talk to someone online.

Though it sounds easy, email marketing takes a lot of work to do right. You start with a clean email list of people who have confirmed their willingness to receive your email offer (have opted in). Then, you target and personalize that offer for the best response. And that's the most important part of email marketing—sending only to those who have asked to receive your offers. With your Yahoo! store, you can sign up for Campaigner by GOT, an integrated Web-based email-marketing tool that enables you to collect opt-in emails during the checkout process. You can sign up for an account by clicking the Email Marketing link in the Store Manager's Promote column.

Spam is the opposite of responsible, or opt-in, email marketing. And spam is the bane of any good email-marketing program. Though sales might be made from spamming email addresses, your online business reputation can be harmed in the process. In addition, spamming violates the Yahoo! store Terms of Service. Spam can get your store closed. But you don't need to spam to mass-mail. If you follow the CAN-SPAM Privacy Act of January 1, 2004, you can still market through unsolicited mail. It's easy to abide by the law, and you might see a response rate of 15% to 25%.

So before you plan your grandiose email-marketing scheme, be aware that opt-in email marketing is really permission marketing. It's a good idea to find out how to get that permission and the ways to get the best results.

> **tip** **What's Opt-In Email?**
>
> Opt-in email is the direct opposite of spam (unsolicited emails). People who opt into an email list have said in advance that they are willing to receive unsolicited email from companies on the Net that meet the list criteria. For example, someone who wants to be kept informed of newly released software might opt into an email list that announces new software products. With Yahoo! store, you can also include and customize a Catalog Request form to collect opt-in emails. Visitors who click on the Request button are taken to a page where they can enter their name, email, address, and any comments to request a catalog or join your newsletter. Merchants can also customize the request form to collect other customer information or data for marketing purposes.

Best Practices of Permission Marketing

So just what is meant by permission marketing? Permission marketing means getting the consumer's permission to email an offer *before* it shows up in the email box.

Sound simple? But that's not all.

First of all, if at any time the consumer wants to opt out of your email-marketing pieces, he or she needs to be able to easily do so by visiting your website or clicking an automated link in the email. Either set up an automated system that removes an email address from your database when a recipient clicks on it, or create a separate opt-out URL on your site where recipients can go to remove their email address from your list. The law also says this must be processed within 10 days.

Second—and very important—these consumers gave *you* permission, not anyone else, permission to email them. Don't give or sell email addresses (that is, consumers' permission to be emailed) to any other company or person. If you do, you need to clearly state your intentions in your privacy policy.

With permission marketing, you get by giving. Although spammers are currently getting good response rates on their email spams, that's changing fast. Consumers are wising up and are demanding that the spammers be curbed. That's being done in two ways:

- The Realtime Blackhole List (RBL)
- The CAN-SPAM Privacy Act

If you're thinking about spamming, think about these first. Antispammers rarely complain just to their Internet service provider (ISP). They complain to your ISP, your ISP's backbone provider, and just about everyone else who is in between you and the electronic path to the recipient. These providers will often terminate your Net connection, if only to stop the complaints.

> **Web Resource**
>
> **ROI Calculators**
>
> You can use these free ROI calculators to track your advertising and promotion results. (You must have a Flash program on your computer to use them.)
>
> - Conversion rate calculator at www.bplans.com/common/calculators/conversionrate.cfm
> - Pay-per-click ROI calculator at www.bplans.com/common/calculators/ppcroi.cfm
> - Email ROI calculator at www.bplans.com/common/calculators/email_roi.cfm
> - Break-even calculator at www.bplans.com/common/calculators/breakeven.cfm

tip Email-Marketing Tips

- Make it personal: "Hello Bob. Here is the next...."
- Be sure it has specific value content for the specific demographic you are sending it to.
- Send with the appropriate frequency: too long, and it's not enough; too often, and it might be annoying.
- Put a price on the front. If you have two newsletters on your desk and you notice a $19.95 or $9.95 price in the corner on one, and nothing on the other, which has the higher perceived value?
- Keep it succinct. A really good one-page newsletter might be better received than a nine-page one.
- If it's an HTML email, add some graphics. A photo can quickly summarize the content, and an email with a photo has a 60% higher response rate than one without.
- Write "What's in it for me?" headlines, like this: "The Five Things YOU Need to Know About..." or "What You Don't Know Can Cost You."
- Use sans-serif fonts.
- Include all of your contact information throughout: your name, physical address, URL, 800 number, and so on.
- Include all of your branding: logo, colors, graphics, and so on.
- Include your "call to action" conversion message.
- Add hyperlinks to "More Information" and "Buy Now" or other conversion.
- Use hyperlinks to drive consumers to a particular Web page, the home page for branding, the catalog page for searching, or the product page for buying.
- Include your Opt Out radio button or link.
- Include your privacy policy or link.
- Make your subject truthful and compelling.
- Be sure that the "from" email address is legitimate and contains "What's in it for me?" keywords, such as "Success Department."
- Put your "What's in it for me?" message in the first five words so it shows in a preview pane.
- Keep phrases such as "Discount," "Save," and "Lowest Rates" out of your subject.
- Check your newsletter email with a free spam checker, such as the one at www.ezinecheck.com/check.html.
- Use columnar format or mimic the look and feel of an industry publication, such as the *Wall Street Journal*, the *New York Times*, or *Scientific American*.
- Offer links to supplies and other noncompeting companies you do business with in exchange for reciprocal links on Web pages to you.

If losing your Internet connection is not scary enough, then listen to this: The Mail Abuse Prevention System, at www.mail.abuse.org, runs the Realtime Blackhole List (RBL). They have compiled a list of IP addresses of known spammers and offer this list to their subscribers. Who are these subscribers? Email administrators. Using the RBL list, these administrators reject any email that originates from those IP addresses. That's right, any email—not just bulk email!

The CAN-SPAM Privacy Act went into effect on January 1, 2004, and comes with some stiff penalties; however, compliance is easy. Requirements include "The subject line must be truthful" and "the return email address must be real" and "There must be a conspicuous Opt-Out." At several websites, you can paste your emails to have them checked against all the SPAM Checker rules. The sites analyze your email and comment on how to correct them to be sure they go through.

Here are a few sites:

- www.enetplace.com/spam-checker.html
- www.lyris.com/resources/contentchecker
- http://spamcheck.sitesell.com

Getting permission is extremely important for your email-marketing strategy and the reputation of your e-business. Plan to do it right.

Choosing a Proper Opt-In Email List

When you have your email marketing campaign ready to go, you need a list of prospects to send it to. Keeping in mind the CAN-SPAM Act and the Realtime Blackhole List, you want to make sure that recipients on the email list you rent have given the list broker permission to email to them.

This called an opt-in email list. An opt-in email is the direct opposite of spam. People who opt into an email list have said in advance that they are willing to receive unsolicited email from companies on the Net that meet the list criteria. For example, someone who wants to be kept

> **tip** **Don't Precheck Permission**
>
> When collecting information from the consumer as a way to build your customer database, make sure you ask the consumers' permission to send them emails. Even if they have bought from you, answered a survey for a free gift, or given you information for whatever reason, you still should provide a check box on the form asking if they would like to receive further emails form you. Do not automatically precheck the box; have them check it manually.

informed of newly released software might opt into an email list that announces new software products.

If you want to email responsibly, use the services of the opt-in list companies on the Net to prospect for new customers. The first company to collect, categorize, and offer for sale nonspam opt-in email lists is Postmaster Direct, at www.postmasterdirect.com. The company offers for rent lists of 30 million consumers in more than 400 categories and demographic breakdowns.

So what is double opt-in? According to the New Zealand marketing Association, "Double opt-in is an email subscription practice that allows marketers to ask new email subscribers to confirm (via email) that they want to be added to an email distribution list for promotions, before the subscriber actually receives the information. The double confirmation is the best guarantee of user interest."

Here are some keys rules for doing email permission marketing:

- **Identify yourself**—Let your prospective customers know who you are right up front. If you've rented an opt-in list, remind consumers that they opted in. Include a sentence reminding them why they're receiving your email. Also, if you're mailing to another business, send your email from either a real person in your company or at least an alias with a title.

- **Always provide a "from" line**—Give recipients a valid address to which they can reply.

- **Keep the subject line short**—The subject line is the outer envelope of an email campaign. This is the vehicle that decides whether your message will be read. Your choice of words—and the length of the message—is critical. Keep the number of words in the subject line to no more than 35 characters.

- **Keep the message short**—Keep your message less than one page: Email is most effective when it's short and simple. After you introduce yourself, give a brief description of your offer. Capture consumers' attention the first two or three lines. Within the offer, give them a link to click or refer them to the URL of the buying page. Keep the message to 500 words.

- **Provide value for their time**—Make it a compelling or limited-time offer. Offer something that consumers couldn't already buy from your site: perhaps an exclusive offer made only through your email. Offer coupons or a free sample. According to Forrester Research, two-thirds of consumers like free samples, but only one-third of merchants offer them.

- **Be ready to apologize**—People's memory can be short, and they can forget that they opted into the list. Additionally, consumers' tastes or needs might have changed. If they complain or ask to be removed from your list, respond immediately and politely through an auto-responder. You have 10 days to remove a customer after such a request.
- **Make it easy to unsubscribe**—Place your unsubscribe instructions at both the beginning and the end of your email message. Don't make consumers call a phone number to unsubscribe. The law says you must provide a link to quickly and easily unsubscribe.

> **Web Resource**
>
> **Stay Up-to-Date**
> Check out the free weekly newsletters offered by DMnews to stay up-to-date on email issues affecting marketers today. The newsletters also cover case studies of successful email campaigns.

Email marketing for prospects and customers can be a valuable addition to the acquisition strategy of your marketing plan. Keep in mind the important points of what you've read here, to help build a successful email-marketing program.

Internal Marketing

E-commerce sites spend a lot of time and money attracting potential customers to their site. Yet, once there, they cease to market to them. That's where internal marketing tactics come into play. Here are some to consider:

- **First-time visitor page**—Create a page where you can direct first-time visitors from your home page (see Figures 13.1 and 13.2). This simple page can be a powerful marketing tool that gives you an opportunity to restate your unique selling position and tell why a visitor should by from you, offer a small set of frequently asked questions on why visitors should buy from you company, and then a special offer to first-time buyers, such as free shipping or a special discount.

FIGURE 13.1
CouponSurfer.com offers a link on its home page for first-time visitors.

FIGURE 13.2
A "first-time visitor" page gives instructions on how to use the website and coupons.

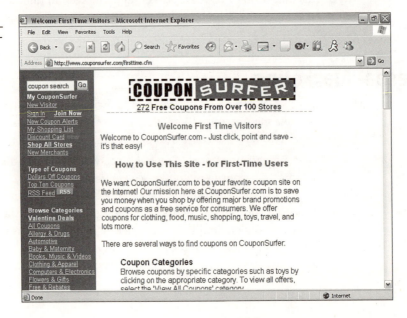

- **Online surveys and polls**—If done right, online surveys and polls can be useful tools for acquiring leads from visitors to your Yahoo! store to market to later. Create a poll with an intriguing question. Visitors might answer the question to see how their opinion compares with others. In the process, they can share some of their interests with you so you can further target potential customers. For example, if you sell fashion clothing, you might ask, "Who will *The Bachelor* eliminate this week from the show?," because you think that people interested in fashion might watch *The Bachelor* TV show. You then can connect the poll to a survey that asks what category of fashion clothing on your site they feel would make the female contestants more desirable to the bachelor. This would give you a window into their fashion preferences.

- **Referrals**—One of the best ways to acquire a visitor's attention and provide an objective third-party review of your business, product or service is the referral. Just doing a good job servicing a customer is not enough to generate a referral: You need to ask. The best time is just after the customer has received the ordered product or service. Don't wait a week or so to ask in a follow-up email how customers rate your company and if they would allow you to use them as a referral or a testimonial on your website. Do this immediately. And don't worry about rejection. If you ask every customer to respond to your email request, you will gather enough referrals and testimonials for your use. If necessary, even offer an incentive to reply to your email survey, such as free shipping on their next order, a discount coupon, or even a free sample.

- **Additional marketing materials**—Use the space in the product boxes to include materials such as a catalog or information on special offers.

Now that you've learned how to attract prospects and customers to your Yahoo! store using some of the basic marketing tools, it's time to learn how to use the most popular way to attract visitors to your Yahoo! store: Internet search engines and directories.

CHAPTER

14

Acquiring Customers (Part 2)

In This Chapter

- The importance of website submissions
- How to optimize your website for search engines
- How to use search engine marketing
- How to use microsites to market your Yahoo! store

When discussing the acquisition of prospects and customers, one phrase comes up constantly: *search engines*. Why? Because when shoppers are looking for products or services on the Net, the most common place they turn to are the Internet search engines.

When consumers turn to this popular shopping tool looking for places to shop, your online storefront must be there to grab their attention. This chapter shows you how to use the different types of search-engine strategies to bring your Yahoo! store front and center on the Net:

- Website submissions
- Search-engine optimization
- Search-engine marketing
- Microsites

Using Search Engines for Marketing

Marketing through search engines can be confusing because this can be done in so many different ways. Some ways are free; others can cost a substantial amount of money. But because search engines are the prime way that people look for products and services on the Internet, a good search marketing strategy is important to the promotion of your Yahoo! store.

Two basic approaches to search engine marketing exist. The first is search-engine submission and optimization; the second is search-engine marketing. *Search-engine submission* is just that: submitting your Yahoo! store to search engines and directories to get listed—that is, search-engine registration. *Search-engine optimization* involves optimizing your Web pages so they will rank high in the search results. *Search-engine marketing* is a marketing tool to guarantee placement high up on the search results or purchase pay-per-click ads. Figure 14.1 shows an example of both of these.

FIGURE 14.1
You can purchase ads on major search engines, such as Google. You can purchase either guaranteed-placement ads or pay-per-click ads.

Getting Listed at the Search Engines and Directories

So what are the differences between search engines and directories?

A *search engine* spiders, or crawls, your site; scans your content; and then indexes your web pages. This works with specialized software. List your storefront with the top five accounts for the majority of the search engine market:

- Google (www.google.com)
- Yahoo! (www.yahoo.com)
- MSN (www.msn.com)
- AOL (www.aol.com)
- Ask (www.ask.com)

A directory is like a search engine, but humans, not software, usually handle the indexing of sites. Directories are sometimes called organic search engines. The top two are Yahoo! and Open Directory (www.dmoz.com). When you are submitting to a directory, you must identify the appropriate category that your site should be listed under. Directories are kind of like Yellow Pages; everything is categorized by the type of business. Consumers who use directories like the fact that they can browse a list of websites in the same category.

In the not-so-distant past, getting registered with search engines and directories was free. Although it is still possible to do it for free (Google and Froogle are still free), if you want a guarantee that you'll be listed (especially in a reasonable amount of time), you have to open your pocketbook. Given this, you need to set up a budget for search-engine submittal.

> **Free Info** Download the free informative article titled "Peters, Limbaugh, Jones? Eat Your Heart Out: Using Media to Market Your Business," at www.myecommercesuccess.com.

So what will this cost you? Here is a minimum budget suggested by Search Engine Watch (www.searchenginewatch.com):

Yahoo Express: $300 for the year

Yahoo! Search Marketing (Formerly Overture): $50 per month

Google Adwords: $25 per month

Total = $375

Although this is a minimum suggested budget, your actual search engine marketing and pay-per-click (PPC) campaign budget depends on how many searches are performed using your particular keywords and the cost per click. Merchants need to be aware of their cost per acquisition (CPA) in terms of average order amount. In other words, if you spend $10 to acquire 10 shoppers and only 1 converts, your average order size had better be more than $10 net. If the average order size is small, merchants should be aware that they need to pay less to acquire leads. Some Yahoo! stores actually spend tens of thousands of dollars in PPC per month because their CPA is far less than their average net income order.

tip Search-Engine Submission Tips

Search Engine Watch (www.searchenginewatch.com/webmasters/) offers a marketers' guide on search-engine submission, placement, ways to optimize for search-engine crawlers, and other marketing ideas.

You can get listed for free—such as at Mozilla Open Directory (www.dmoz.org)—but if you want your online store to be listed quickly, you will need to pay the minimum amount.

Another method of getting listed with search engines is to let them find you. Sites with backlinks from other sites already indexed will be found and do not need to be submitted. You should be actively working to have your site found by crawlers by securing external links. Getting links is ultimately a long-term strategy, whereas submitting is a short-term tactic.

Remember, even when you do get listed, that doesn't mean you will rank high in the search results. For that, you need to optimize your website and pages.

Search-Engine Optimization

So, what main things does a search engine look for when ranking your site?

- **Keyword-rich content**—Include your keywords in your content. Your Web page copy should have between 200 and 350 words. When writing your Web copy, keep your targeted keyword list handy to make sure you include those keywords. Place your keywords in the first few lines; search engines give priority to keywords found near the top of the Web page. Also, use style tags, such as `<b>`, `<strong>`, `<i>`, `<em>`, and `<li>` on your keywords. Not only do search engines respond favorable to these style tags, but it makes the keywords more visible to the reader.

- **Header tags**—Create header tags for your inside-copy titles. Header tags are headlines for your Web page or paragraph. Headers are specified with the following HTML code: `<h1>`, `<h2>`, `<h3>`, `<h4>`, `<h5>`, and `<h6>`. The `<h1>` tag is more important than the `<h2>` tag, and so on. Create a keyword-rich title for your paragraphs.

- **Link popularity**—The popularity of your site is determined by the number of external links pointing to your site. The more links, the better. You should exchange links with sites within your industry theme.

- **Link anchor text**—Link anchor text is the visible text in your link. Search engines give keywords in the link text higher priority.

- **Page title**—Put your keyword phrases in your page title. Unless your company is well known (branded) and people are using your company name as the search phrase, don't just use your company name in the title. If you have to include it, put it at the end of the title. Choose a couple of keyword phrases to include in your title. Also, make sure the keywords you use are included in your content. If you have a bunch of targeted keyword phrases, group them and create unique page titles for each page. Keep your page titles to less than 80 characters, and remember that the first few words are extremely important to MSN and Google. Don't stuff your title with keywords after keywords; your title also needs to be enticing enough for someone to click on your link.

- **Metatags**—Many debates have arisen over whether search engines still consider metatags to be important. The answer is yes, especially the description tag. Some search engines use the description tag as the summary description of your page on their results page. You should create a unique meta description for each page. Approximately 200 to 250 characters can be indexed, but only a portion of the characters will actually be displayed on the search result page. Try to keep your keywords at the beginning of the description, in case your entire description is not displayed.

Take a look at this example of meta keywords and meta description:

```
<meta name="description" content="Your keyword rich description here">
<meta name="keywords" content="keyword 1, keyword 2, keyword phrase 1, keyword phrase 2, keyword phrase 3">
```

Make Your Site Spider-Friendly

So how does the search engine spider crawl through your site? What does it look for? What does it ignore? The spider first visits your Web page and reads it, and visits links to other pages within that site. The spider then reports everything it finds to the search engine and then indexes it. If your content changes, the spider reports the new changes when it revisits your pages.

So what do these spiders like and don't like?

- **Popularity**—Spiders like lots of other quality sites pointing to your site. It's easier for spiders to find your site, and you must be important for others to link to you.

- **Buried Web pages**—Spiders don't like to go three, four, and five levels deep. Spiders go through billions of pages daily and need to visit other sites. If you have pages that go too deep, create a site map to all your pages. With the Yahoo! store, this is usually not an issue because all the pages live at the same level, but it can be a concern if you are using the Web hosting side.

- **Load time**—With billions of pages to visit, spiders do not have time to wait for your site to load. Keep the graphics to a minimum. Make sure you optimize your images before you upload them. Uploading your 2MB images direct from your digital camera is a sure way to kill page-loading time.

- **Dynamic pages**—It's too hard for spiders to index database-driven pages. They prefer HTML pages with links and keywords that can be easily read. One of the advantages of having a Yahoo! store is that all pages, including product pages, are static HTML.

- **Scripts**—When possible, keep the Java scripts to a minimum or create an external Java script file (server side). Spiders don't like to sniff through all that code to get to your content.

Top 10 Tips to Increase Link Popularity

Although getting links to your site is technically not optimizing your Web page, it's an important element of getting your site ranked high. Getting links to your site is not automated: Real people make decisions to either add or not add your site. These are the top 10 tips on how to increase your chances of building referral links:

1. **Network with others**—When going to networking mixers or industry conferences, ask the people you meet to exchange links. You have a better chance of getting a link exchange when you ask someone in person as opposed to emailing.

2. **Submit to directories**—Submit your site to important directories, such as DMOZ, Yahoo!, and LookSmart. Also, don't forget industry-specific directories.

3. **Identify your target market**—Search engines rank you higher when your sites come from industry-related websites.

4. **Write news releases**—Not only can you put your news release on your website, but you can also submit it to news sites such as PRWeb.com. You never know which sites will pick up your news release and add it to their site.

5. **Write articles**—Ask other industry-related websites if you can contribute an article to their sites. Not only will you give value to their websites, but you also will create creditability for yourself, and you will be able to add your website URL as part of your signature.

6. **Create value**—What's in it for me? Let the people you are requesting a link exchange with know what's in it for them in your email. If your website offers great resources, let them know. How will their visitors benefit from going to your site as a resource? This will make your recipients more inclined to review your website for a possible link exchange.

7. **Monitor your referrer stats**—Other sites might be sending you traffic: Review your log files and find out why. Maybe you can use the reasoning to approach other sites. As a courtesy, you can also offer a link back to them or even ask for better placement.

8. **Create a link page**—Make it easy for others to link to your site. Create copy that you would like link partners to use. This way, all they have to do is copy and paste. Let others know that you do want link partners. Some might think that you are unapproachable, and some might not even think about trading links with you until seeing your link page.

9. **Use keywords in your linking text**—Lots of sites make the mistake of using their company name or "Click here for more info" as their link. Using keyword phrases in your link gives you a boost with that particular keyword phrase in search engines

10. **Add partners' links first**—Sites will be more eager to add your link if you already place their link on your site. Don't forget to mention this, and have a link where they can find their link in your email.

> **warning**
> Don't add your site on link farms. Link farms are websites that accept any link and duplicate links on a bunch of other link farm sites. This is a sure way to get search engines to ban your site.

Search-Engine Marketing

At first glance, search-engine optimization (SEO) and search-engine marketing (SEM) seem to be the same thing. This stems from the marketing mindset that anything that has to do with search engines must be a programming function. It's not.

The two activities are very different: SEO is a programming function, whereas SEM is purely a marketing function. Briefly, search-engine marketing consists of two types:

- **Paid inclusion**—For an example of paid inclusion, look at a page of Yahoo! search results. At the very top of the list, above all other search results, you probably see one, two, or three listings with a tinted background (see Figure 14.2). These organizations have paid to be listed in the top of the search results when a particular search term is used.

FIGURE 14.2

You can pay to have your advertisement listed on top before the search results on Yahoo.com.

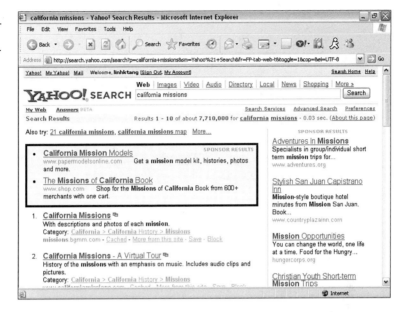

- **Paid placement or pay-per-click**—For an example of paid placement, look at just about any search results page from major search engines such as Yahoo! (see Figure 14.3). The paid placements appear in the right column of the page. But unlike paid inclusion systems, advertisers don't pay for these link listings to appear; they pay only when the listing is clicked. This is called *pay-per-click* (PPC) or *pay-for-performance* marketing. With PPC marketing, you choose a search term and bid on the term—that is, how much you're willing to pay if someone clicks your listing. The higher your bid, the higher your listing appears in the search results of search engines that use PPC search engine services, such as Yahoo! Search Marketing or Google's AdWords.

The action today in search-engine marketing is in the pay-per-click arena. But before you can create your SEM campaign, you need to provide the following:

- Thirty to 60 keywords and keyword phrases
- A listing title of the required length
- A listing description of the required length
- A designated Web page on your site to point to from the listing
- How the Web page will be relevant to the keywords, title, and description in the listing

Let's examine these one at a time.

FIGURE 14.3
Pay-per-click advertisements are displayed on the right column on Yahoo.com.

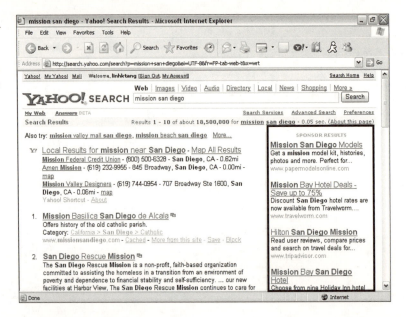

Choosing Appropriate Search Terms

By now, you should have some experience choosing targeted keywords and phrases for your Web pages. But a half-dozen keywords that target your organization's message are not enough for a strong SEM campaign. Choosing your keywords—or, in the language of SEM, your *search terms*—is the first and most important step in establishing a PPC marketing campaign. For your SEM campaign, consider three key issues related to the search terms:

- Number of searches for the term
- Relevancy of that term in relation to your product or services
- Cost (the bid amount you're required to spend for that term)

> **Web Resource**
>
> **Get the Lowdown on PPC Search Engines**
>
> PayPerClickGuru (www.payperclickguru.com) offers a guide to the main PPC search engines and a description of their programs. Check out its Pay Per Click Search Engine Comparison Chart, which details the top PPC engines and explains their minimum bid, initial deposit, and statistics.

How can you find help in choosing good search terms—and how many should you choose?

The best strategy is to find the search terms that Web surfers already use. Your IT staff should keep two free keyword tools in its bag of tricks to help your marketing staff:

- **Yahoo! Search Marketing Search Term Suggestion Tool** (www.inventory.overture.com/d/searchinventory/suggestion/)—Enter a search term related to your site; the results show both related searches that include your term and how many times that term was searched for in the previous month. This tool is quick and easy to use, and doesn't require any download or installation.
- **Good Keywords** (www.goodkeywords.com/)—This free Windows program (which you must download and install) helps you find the perfect set of keywords for your Web pages. Good Keywords is more than just a search-term suggestion tool, and it goes far beyond what the YSM tool provides. Good Keywords helps you think like a customer, analyze the competition, and monitor the progress of your SEM campaign.
- **WordTracker** (www.wordtracker.com)—Although WordTracker is not free to use, it's worth the money. WordTracker not only helps you find related keywords, but it also tells you exactly how many Web pages you will be competing with in a specific search engine. You can sign up for a free trial by going to www.wordtracker.com/free-trial.html.

> **Web Resource**
>
> **Don't Get Caught Overbidding**
> The biggest drain on your PPC budget is the amount of money you pay per click. The YSM Bid Tool at www.overture.com/d/USm/search/tools/bidtool/ can help keep your PPC budget under control. Just type in the keyword you want to use; YSM's overbid tool gives you not only the current maximum bid for that keyword, but also the actual ads from the companies that are targeting that word. Remember, you don't always need to be the no. 1 listing: A great selling title and description could outperform the no. 1 listing.

With these or comparable tools, you must then choose those search terms. Here are some tips:

- Focus on specific terms that are pertinent and specific to your market. Using broad-based terms such as *software* or *office supplies* could bring in a large unqualified audience that might or might not be looking for your particular product or service.
- If the primary search terms you want to use are outside the marketing department's PPC budget—that is, the bid amount for the term is too

high—build your list of search terms using secondary terms that reflect your product, service, or market niche. For example, instead of *software*, which is a very popular term and, therefore, very expensive, closely match your search term to your product or service: *accounting software*. Better yet, consider *accounts receivable accounting software*, *accounts payable software*, or *professional accounting software*. For the PPC campaign, you need 30 to 60 search terms. The composite traffic of many secondary terms could match or exceed the traffic of the most popular term for your market niche. In this way, you get the same traffic as the most popular and expensive terms (or more) while paying, on average, far less.

- In the major PPC search engines, your PPC listing should appear within the top three positions. The top three positions are the most important with Overture because they feed most major search engines and directories as sponsored listings, and appear at the top of the search results. And being above the fold on the search results page of Google's AdWords gives you the most visibility. (The marketing term *above the fold* refers to having your listing appear in the part of a Web page that's visible without scrolling.) Does that mean that if you're not in the top position, your site won't garner substantial traffic? No. If you must bid on a term, it isn't necessary to be in the first position to attract profitable traffic. Being second or third can be just as effective—and sometimes far less expensive.

> **Web Resource**
>
> **How Much Is a Click Worth?**
>
> At Compare Your Clicks (www.compareyourclicks.com), you run live comparisons of keyword bid prices at multiple pay-per-click search engines. Prices are displayed for the top six positions.

Writing Titles and Descriptions

After choosing the search terms, your marketing staff needs to write the titles and descriptions for the listings. This is an important step. The search terms must be mentioned in the titles and descriptions of the listings, but the message must stay simple—and yet be packed with benefits.

Here are some tips to use when writing those title and descriptions:

- Before attempting to write the first copy for your search terms' titles and descriptions, visit YSM and other search engines to check the competition for your terms. Your competition's titles and descriptions for the search terms you chose could be a great help to you in writing yours.

- PPC search engines don't accept superlatives. For example, at YSM, you aren't permitted to use words such as *best*, *most*, *least*, and *cheapest* (or comparable words that ends in *st*) in titles and descriptions. If you use them, your listing will be rejected automatically. Google has a similar policy.

- YSM and other PPC search services limit the number of characters that can be used in the titles and description of listings. But even more important is that the search engines that use your listings can and do cut off the length of the title and description in the search results of their search pages. Strive to make your selling point in the first few words of the title and description.

- Focus your titles and descriptions to qualify the visitor, while setting up expectations for what he or she will find at your site. Entice users to click your offer.

- A PPC campaign is not a "write once and forget it" type of marketing. The titles and descriptions for your PPC listings can and should be changed to reflect changes in your business, product, and service, or to improve your click-through rate.

Ensuring Relevancy

The URL that a PPC listing points to is the final—and most important—piece of a successful PPC campaign. It's crucial that your search terms be included not only in your listing titles and descriptions, but also in the Web pages where those listings direct the user. This will build confidence and credibility with potential customers, and it will help you get listed more easily on Overture and Google.

Web page relevancy to search terms is very important. One of the worst things an organization can do is mislead the visitor. You don't want to give the impression that you tricked the visitor into clicking your offer, especially after all the work that you put into designing, building, and optimizing your website.

Don't just point your pay-per-click advertisement to the website home page. If you own a pet supply website and your PPC search term is *dog food*, make sure your PPC URL points to the dog food section. You might also consider building specific relevant landing pages for these PPC ads. Landing pages are a great way to experiment with sales copy and track the success of your PPC campaign.

You must remember that your PPC listing has 1.54 seconds to grab a visitor's attention and get him or her to your site. Once there, you have about another 5 seconds to interest the user enough to lead him or her through a process of performing an action. (Whether your site's objective is to sell a service or a product, or whether you want the user to fill out a form or join a mailing list, the process is the same.) If you mislead the visitor, the chances of a repeat visit to your site are slim.

To list your site with YSM, you must carefully follow do's and don'ts for site relevancy. To avoid rejection of your submission, study the guidelines and don't attempt to list your search terms without preparing the targeted Web pages to send. Even if you don't use YSM, the rules are a good set of guidelines, no matter which search engine you use to make your PPC campaign a success.

An SEM Checklist

Here's a quick checklist to consult when considering how to list your site from the perspective of search-engine marketing:

- **Research all possible search terms**—Use free search tools at sites such as Good Keywords and Overture to find search terms that give you the results you need.
- **Focus on specific words**—Choose terms that are pertinent and specific to your market.
- **Take advantage of secondary terms**—Multiple secondary terms that really reflect your product, service, or market niche could give you better results than one primary search term.
- **Buy the right position**—Work to get your PPC listing within the top three positions at the major search engines. It isn't necessary to be in the first position to attract profitable traffic.
- **Include search terms in listing titles and descriptions**—Make sure that those important terms appear in the title and description you choose for a listing. Keep the message simple, yet packed with benefits.
- **Check out the competition**—How did your competition use the terms you chose? Use their efforts to generate your own ideas.
- **Avoid superlatives**—Listings get rejected if they use words such as *best*, *most*, and *cheapest*.
- **Count your characters**—PPC search services limit the number of characters in listing titles and descriptions. Cram your selling point into the first few words.

- **Qualify the visitor**—Aim your titles and descriptions to get the niche visitors you really want. Be sure to set up their expectations of what they'll find once they get to your site.
- **Make your pages relevant**—Include your search terms in the targeted Web page where the search engine user is directed from your listing. The 1.54-second countdown starts as soon as the visitor arrives.

Microsites

Microsites—or minisites, as they're sometimes called—are small websites (5 to 10 pages) used to promote a particular product or service, or even promotion or contest. Microsites have their own separate URL. They do not contain the full navigation of the home site; they are self-contained websites.

A microsite is not a landing page. A landing page is final-destination page connected to an email promotion or a search-engine marketing ad, and is a page on the full home site of an online storefront. A microsite can be a useful marketing tool. Suppose that you want to promote one particular product or line of products. You can use the microsite with its own navigation to better display and promote the need to buy a product or service. This gives you a more powerful tool to focus on a product or promotion and explain it in detail without the distractions of the other navigation on your home website.

Microsites can also be promoted and used to sign up people for sweepstakes and contests when you would need more than one page—beyond your normal product or service pages—to describe the award (usually your own product or service) and the rules of the contest or sweepstakes. Microsites are generally only temporary and are removed after a particular promotion has ended.

160 Characters (www.mobilefriendly.org/next.htm) is an example of a microsite that is used and updated with the latest news of the industry. Such a microsite is promoted separately—in search engines, for example—as an evolving-content page. Another example is a site for a financial services company. Suppose that you visited a website that contained a vast array of financial services, but you were interested only in car insurance. The home page of a large financial services company would have links and navigation to all its products and service.

But a microsite, where you can focus your offer clearly on one particular product without the possible confusion of other product offers—or even the same offer at a better price—can give you the flexibility to promote a special offer beyond your everyday storefront. That is, you can use microsites to test different offers and see which ones draw the best response.

Microsites also offer you the opportunity to have consumers view you as a specialist in a particular area, even if you offer a wide selection of products or service. This gives you a chance to promote to a more targeted audience that you couldn't with your main site. Going back to the financial services example, trying to be all things to all people doesn't help your unique selling position. But microsites can help.

When doing special discreet promotions, it might be better to use the microsite tool instead of squeezing all your promotions into the home page of your storefront. Show them you're a specialist in your field, that you understand the consumer's unique problem and have a unique solution. You can then gain their attention and trust before leading them into the core of your business offerings.

When you've drawn visitors to your site and have converted them into customers, the next challenge is to retain the customer your have worked so hard to attain. We cover that in the next chapter.

CHAPTER

15

Retaining Customers

In This Chapter

- The importance of customer retention
- How to build a house list
- How to create a successful email-marketing campaign
- How to create and use email newsletters
- Community used as a retention strategy

Too many online businesses think that when you've attracted visitors to your site and made the sale, the business is a roaring success. Not necessarily. Unless a company retains those hard-earned customers, there is a very good chance that it will eventually lose revenue and, more important, lose market share.

Although the Internet is largely filled with hundreds of millions of users, there is not an infinite supply of customers for your business. You need a retention plan as part of your marketing plan to grow your business not only with new customers, but also with those you already have. Besides, in terms of dollars and cents, it costs 10 times more to acquire a customer than to retain one. Let's look at the third letter in the concept of PARM: the basic retention strategies you should use in marketing your Yahoo! store.

The Importance of Retention

In the battle of attracting new customers to your site, we mustn't forget the value that existing customers hold for your Yahoo! store. Building an ongoing relationship with your existing customers enables you to leverage the funds spent on originally acquiring those customers.

That relationship is not just good customer service after the sale—it's good ongoing customer-relationship management. The bottom line is that you need to create a customer-retention strategy and a storefront that existing customers want to return to time and again. When Amazon was started, the management had a goal of retaining existing customers for 10 years. That was forward thinking. It showed that Amazon knew the concept of the lifetime value of a customer, and its intention to exploit it.

> **Free Info** Download the free informative article titled "Is Your Newsletter More Come On Than News?" at www.myecommercesuccess.com.

So where do you start? What marketing vehicles are good at customer retention? Here are the most important retention strategies that every e-commerce company should use:

- Build a house list
- Send promotional emails
- Develop email newsletters
- Use the community as retention

Now, let's go to the how-to's.

Building a House List

As you learned in Chapter 13, "Acquiring Customers (Part 1)," email marketing can successfully bring visitors to your Yahoo! store. This involves renting a list and sending your email promotion "cold." But email is also a powerful tool in retention marketing. You must first build an in-house list of existing customers or those who have asked to be in communications with your business.

A house list is important because those consumers on your list have already expressed interest in your business and the products or services you sell. They are receptive to your promotional messages.

Another important reason to use email in your customer-retention plans is that it's far less expensive than most marketing vehicles. Of all the businesses marketing through email in 2005, 61% was used for retention. But it does take work and marketing savvy. That's all well and good. But how do you build a house list?

Because you have a Yahoo! store, you already have the start of one: your current customers. The trick is to grow that list, not only to grab additional sales from your current customers, but to attract and convert prospects as well. You can do this by using regular and informative email communications, such as promotional emails, newsletters, and loyalty programs. More important, instead of renting an opt-in list at 25¢ to 50¢ per name, you get a list for free because the names in your house list are yours. In addition, surveys indicate that you should get a better response from your own house list than from a rented list.

Here are some ways to expand the house list you already have:

- **Get an offer**—Users will not hand over their email addresses unless there's something in it for them. Putting a sign-up box on your home page that just says "Sign up for our newsletter" is not going to cut it; you need to give your visitors a reason to want to be solicited. So you need something to entice them. The best way is to offer them something of value. If it's a newsletter that you are soliciting subscribers for, explain to them just what kind of news they will get.

  For example, you might say, "Sign up for our whitepaper and learn the top three reasons why investors fail." Or "Sign up for our newsletter and learn how make your garden bloom in color throughout all the seasons." Or "Sign up for our promotion emails and receive special discounts on our clothing accessories every month." You get the idea. Make sure you state that users who sign up for the free offer are placed on the mailing list. Not spelling it out could get you in trouble for sending unsolicited commercial email (a.k.a. spam). Spell out any terms in the privacy policy page.

- **Promote your email offers on your site**—Place a subscribe box on your home page (top right), and a way to subscribe on every page of your site. Including a small sign-up box on the home page is a poor way to attract subscribers. Instead, have a link to a page where you can better explain what's in it for subscribers if they sign up. Also, place the link on your home page—and all other Web pages on your storefront, enticing visitors to click on. As you should remember, this is one of the three important elements to have on your home page (unique selling position tagline, call to action, email capture). If you can't sell visitors, recruit them: Get their email addresses so you can market to them later.

- **Have your subscribers spread the news (pass-alongs)**—If they find your promotional emails of value, ask your subscribers to forward them to a friend. Better yet, send them to a page listed or linked in your email or newsletter where they can enter the email addresses of friends, family, and colleagues whom they feel would find your newsletter of value. Of course, you need to confirm the referred address via email, politely say that so-and-so thought they would be interested in a subscription, and then give them a chance to opt out before you include them in your house list. The last thing you want is to be accused of is spamming.

> **tip** **Promote Your Email Program On-Site**
>
> The promotion of your email program doesn't have to be in your main or secondary navigation. Your email promotion can look like a small banner ad on your Web pages touting the value of your newsletter, loyalty club, or promotional emails to whomever and from wherever they reach your Web page. Also, add an opportunity to subscribe at the end of your checkout process. If you require free registration for visitors to personalize their visits to your site, include an opt-in for your email promotion there, too.

- **Promote your newsletter on other websites**—Look around for websites that compliment and not necessarily compete for your business. Then, see if they'll do a co-registration deal with you. They might be willing to add your newsletter opt-in along with the newsletter that they offer during their newsletter-subscription process.

- **Advertise your newsletter to comparable audiences**—Newsletter advertising is far cheaper than banner ads—and newsletters get better results. By advertising in newsletters that match your audience, you not only save money, but your ad also is targeted. You can find a list of newsletters and e-zines to advertise in at www.newsletteraccess.com.

- **Promote your email promotions in meatspace**—You've spent a lot of time and money on your printed material (business cards, brochures, promotional flyers, letterhead), so promote your newsletter there and include the URL to the subscription page of your website. And if you exhibit at trade shows, give visitors to your booth a chance to sign up for your newsletter, loyalty program, or promotional emails.

The bottom line is that, by growing and using your house list, you can generate repeat visitors with periodic email mailings, get more links to search engines if you archive your content-rich newsletters on your site, and lower your acquisition cost per customer for far less than renting lists or buying banner ads.

Registration Page Basics

You might have a great offer that entices people to sign up for your house list, but if the process itself is too bulky or cumbersome, customers will quickly look for the door.

Here are some things to keep in mind for an effective registration page:

- **Explain the benefits and process of registration**—Don't expect visitors to your Yahoo! store to automatically sign up for your promotional emails based on a single phrase or one-line tagline. Explain the benefits of opting into your promotional program or newsletter, along with how the process works. Tell consumers what to expect and how long it will take to complete the form. The signup process should take less than a minute—any longer than that, and they're out the door.

- **Ask for permission**—Make clear your privacy policy and how you plan to use personal information that the subscriber gives you. Consumers today are skittish about giving personal information to strangers; be clear that you will not sell or loan their personal information to a third party. Also, don't automatically assume that every customer who buys from you wants to subscribe to your promotional email program or newsletter: Do not precheck the box at the end of your order process that says "Would you like to receive further mailings from us?" or "Send me offers and announcements from YourDomain.com." This will help keep your company out of the spam doghouse.

With the Campaigner email-marketing tool by GotMarketing, you can add a subscribe check box to your checkout process (see Figure 15.1). The great thing about Campaigner is that it's integrated with your Yahoo! store and can be accessed through the Store Manger via the Email Marketing link in the Promote column. All you have to do is sign up for a Campaigner account and then enable the Campaigner Customer Email Collection check box on the order form. This automatically adds the email address of any customer who opts into the Campaigner database. As a Yahoo! store owner, you can test-drive Campaigner free for 30 days and send up to 500 emails. After the trial period, you can sign up for a starter plan, which starts at $10 per month.

Finally, don't forget to create a privacy policy and post it on your site. Create a text link at the bottom of the home page—and every page of your site—so visitors can find it easily and review your policy.

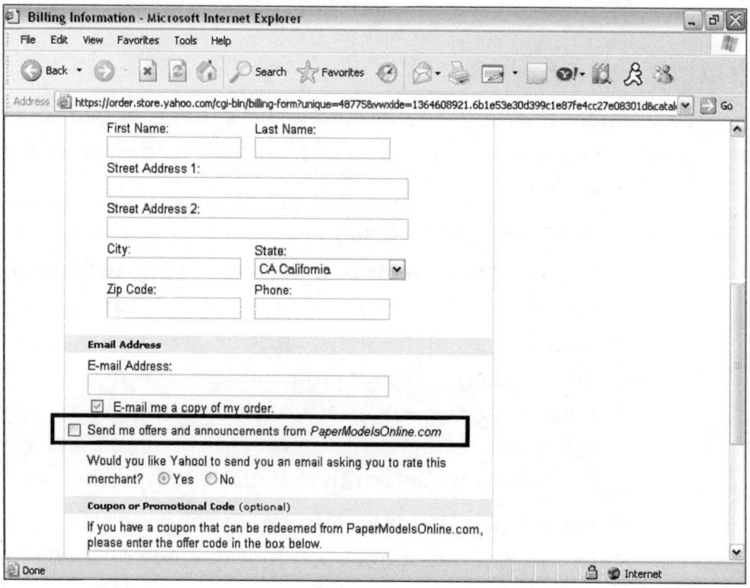

FIGURE 15.1

With the Campaigner email-marketing tool by GotMarketing, you can add a subscribe check box to your checkout process. Customers who opt in are automatically added to your email database.

- **Keep the form short**—Be considerate of the subscriber's time. A 2004 Jupiter Research study found that 42% of surveyed registration/subscription pages had 21 or more fields. That's way too much information to ask; you risk the subscriber abandoning your form. Ask for only minimal information, such as email address and name, to start building your house list. Later, if you offer something in return, such as a benefit, a free product or service, valuable information, or a contest or sweepstakes, you can ask more in-depth personal information to help you profile the subscriber for marketing purposes. When you do this and your form becomes longer, flash a light at the end of the tunnel—that is, tell them how long the form will take to complete and where they are in the process. Also, break up the form into small pages. This way, you can place page numbers on the top of each page to let subscribers where they are in the sign-up process and how many more steps are yet to come. Less is more.

> **tip** **Create a Privacy Policy the Easy Way**
>
> The Direct Marketing Association can create a free legal privacy policy for your company. Go to www.the-dma.org/privacy/creating.shtml and answer the questions that are on the page. At the end, a privacy policy is generated in HTML for your business; you can paste it directly into a Web page on your storefront.
>
> Here are some other websites that will create your privacy policy for you via wizard, for free:
>
> www.p3wiz.com
>
> www.privacyalliance.org/resources
>
> www.w3.org/P3P/validator.html

- **Collect personal information one bit at a time**—As in the previous tip, collect information one bit at a time. Don't get too nosey at first. Limit the requested information to five to seven questions, such as email address, first name, last name, and ZIP/postal code. Do not ask for phone numbers. Use polls and surveys to collect additional profile information incrementally on subscribers. Even if you keep required information to a minimum, you can ask one simple market-segmentation question to help qualify or segment subscribers.

- **Take advantage of form-fill standards**—When programming your form, take advantage of the current Web browser autocomplete function. For example, you can have a previously typed name drop into the Name field, making the registration process faster and more efficient for the subscriber.

- **Confirm ages**—Comply with the guidelines set by the Children's Online Privacy Protection Act of 1998 (COPPA), which prohibits companies from collecting data from children under 13—especially if your Yahoo! store attracts teenagers or children with the products you sell. Ask subscribers to confirm their age on your sign-up form, if it's appropriate.

Subscribe and Unsubscribe Tips

Whether you are using an email promotion campaign, a newsletter, or some other promotional method to build your house list, you must have an easy subscribe and unsubscribe process established for your email retention program. You have to make it easy for subscribers not only to opt into your email retention marketing program, but also to opt out. The law says so.

No matter which email retention strategy you use, you must avoid being accused of spamming your house list. You learned about the negative consequences of spamming in Chapter 13. Remember that on the Internet, bad news travels fast. An angry online customer has many ways to broadcast frustration to friends and strangers. On the Net, customers are in control, and they are more than willing to exercise it against anyone or any company that raises their ire.

The first step in the opt-in process is to send an email to subscribers confirming that they did indeed sign up for your promotional emails (called double opt-in). You can automate this process with an autoresponder email.

The confirmation email should do the following:

- Welcome the new subscriber and indicate what he or she has subscribed to
- Ask the new subscriber to confirm the subscription by replying to the welcome message or opting out with a response
- Provide subscribe and unsubscribe information at the end of the email message or newsletter
- A link to your company privacy policy at the end of your email

You can enable subscribers to opt out of your email promotions in three ways. The first way is to ask them to reply to the message with the words *unsubscribe* or *remove* in the subject line. This process poses a problem to your company because you have to read each email and manually unsubscribe them from your list. It also poses the problem that you might miss the email and not remove someone. Then, the next time the subscriber receives your email promotion, you will have an irate member of your house list on your hands—and you will not have complied with the CAN-SPAM Privacy Act.

The second way is to have a link inside your email that, when clicked on, automatically removes the subscriber's name from your house list. This takes some programming on your part, but it is one of the best ways to manage the unsubscribe process. If you would rather outsource this process to an established subscription-management company, check out Constant Contact, by Roving (www.roving.com), or Campaigner, by GotMarketing. You can access Campaigner right from the Store Manager via the Email Marketing link in the Promote column.

The best way to manage the subscribe and unsubscribe process is to use a special Web page on your site. Create a page on your website where recipients can unsubscribe by just clicking a URL in your email. As soon as they click the link, your server recognizes it as an unsubscribe action and presents them with a Web page stating that they have successfully unsubscribed from your list. This also gives you another chance to interact with subscribers at that page, perhaps to ask if they would like to subscribe to another list or join your new preferred shoppers club.

Steps to Email Marketing Success

Permission-based direct email beats all other direct-marketing vehicles because there are no production, paper, or postage costs. But it does take some work. That is, to create an ongoing successful email-marketing campaign, you need to constantly test it. It's important to test your promotional email and all its parts before you spend a lot of money on a potential campaign failure.

> **Web Resource**
>
> **Stay in the Know**
>
> Email Marketing Weekly (www.dmnews.com/cgi-bin/newslettersub.cgi) is a good resource for staying up-to-date on email marketing. It covers a full range of email-marketing issues from stories that appear over the week on www.dmnews.com, along with some original content.

You see, the Internet is the perfect direct-marketing medium, and those who were raised within the direct-marketing profession understand this. They also understand the importance of testing a direct-mail campaign before a full-blown launch.

Testing is the process of getting information about the marketplace from the marketplace—that is, discovering what the audience will really do, not what it says it will do. By testing multiple variables with small percentages of your list before you roll out your full email campaign, you can base the message decisions of your email campaign on results instead of opinion.

Here's how to test your email message in seven easy steps.

1. Test Your Subject Line

The subject line of your email message equates to an envelope. You must catch consumers' attention with this, or they'll send it to the trash file. Your subject line must immediately grab their attention and make them want to read the first few lines of your message.

The old adage in direct marketing is to hit the prospect with benefits and phrase those benefits in a personal statement, such as "How to get out of debt in 30 days" or "What stock brokers don't want you to know." The trick is to rephrase your subject line and test it in two or three different ways to see which one brings you the best response.

For example, "How to be debt-free in 30 days" and "7 quick and easy ways to pay off your debts now." For the test, try these iterations of the same statement with your test groups and see which one pulls the best.

Here's something to keep in mind when constructing those subject lines: Spam filters catch certain words, so avoid those words if you can. To find out more, go to www.grokdotcom.com/email-subject-lines.htm.

2. Test Your "From" Lines

Staying anonymous will quickly send your email to the dustbin. People want to know who is sending a message. Use your domain address in your "from" line. Or if you can, use the name of your company (XYZ Promotions), or even your real name and title (John Doe, CEO). In tests, the "name" part of the "from" line, the section that goes just before the sender's email address, indicates that this area is a very significant piece of real estate—maybe even more important than the subject line—to entice recipients to simply open the message.

3. Test Your Headlines

If the recipient has gotten this far in your email message, you have a few short seconds to keep his or her attention. The preview window of most email application programs is only two or three lines deep, meaning that you have fewer than three lines to keep the reader's attention.

What you say in the headline of the message body and the one or two lines that follow dictates whether the recipient will read the rest of your message. Your headline and the few lines of text that follow need to have punch. Sum up your entire offer and make the recipient read on. Your headline should be direct and personal, and should supply a benefit to the reader.

That leads to testing your offer.

4. Test Your Offer

This is obviously the intent of your email: to get recipients to buy or take some kind of action. Your objective is to test up to three versions of your message to a small percentage of different recipients on your list. If you're selling something, offer three different discounts to three different groups of recipients. For example, offer one test group a "Save $10" discount. If this represents a 10% discount off your product or service, test a different group with a "Save 10%" offer. You might even raise your price a bit and test a third group with "Buy One, Get One at Half-Price."

On the other hand, if you're trying to get your recipients to take some kind of action, such as join your preferred customers club to gather demographic information and interests for future marketing campaigns, test one group by offering a discount on the first purchase, test another with a contest, and test another with a free sample for signing up.

The information gathered from these test offers can help you focus on what kind of offer your recipients will respond to.

5. Test Your Response Options

Just because you send your offer electronically doesn't mean that your recipient wants to reply by same way. Give the recipient several different ways to take advantage of your offer. Besides the option of hitting the Reply button, give them the opportunity to respond via a toll-free telephone number, fax, link, or even snail mail. With Merchant Solutions Standard or Pro package, you can create track links to test response rates. Link Tracker enables you to assign special codes to each link to your store. These special links can be embedded into your email offer. You can use this to track how many visitors you're getting and how many sales arrived at your store via each specifically coded link.

To create a trackable link, follow these steps:

1. In Store Manager, click Create Links in the Promote column.
2. Enter a name for your link and click Create New Trackable Link For. The name is used only to help you identify the link; a unique link code is created. Another special link is created to show reports on how much traffic and revenue that particular link has generated.

Test each of these response mechanisms in your test messages to see which response medium they prefer. Never make assumptions about your target audience.

6. Test Text Versus HTML

More users than ever can read HTML email, but that doesn't mean they want it in their email box. If you choose to present your message in an HTML format, keep in mind that the HTML can be formatted in many ways. Test these to see which format brings the best results. But keep in mind that most users cruise the Net at 56K. This limits the size and type of HTML message you can send.

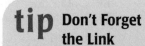

tip Don't Forget the Link

If you do send HTML, include a link to the URL where it resides in the top of your message, just in case the recipient cannot view it.

7. Test Your Links

If you are sending an HTML email, test what your audience will click on in response. Those pretty graphics that your designer has slaved over might look good to you, but if they can't elicit a click-through, it was a waste of time. Will recipients click on logos? Photos? Call-to-action text? Don't forget to flag links individually to determine where the click-throughs originated. With third-party email software, such as Constant Contact and Campaigner, you can track every single link on your email newsletter. You can generate reports to see how many and which readers clicked on which link.

Additional Email Tips

Those who succeed in email marketing have found the following to be of great importance, regardless of the seven easy steps just explained.

The time you send a message can affect the response to it. For example, messages sent on a Friday versus a Monday, or at lunchtime versus first thing in the morning, can pull dramatically different responses. Send all your test messages at the same time on the same day.

Also, test only *one* variable at a time. Change the subject line in one test, the message in another, or the "from" line in another. Also, designate one variable as a control—don't change it across all tests—and use it to measure the others.

Establish some success metrics. Will you be testing click-throughs, revenue per transaction, or new customer registration? Decide before you start your tests. When your test results are in, it's easy to check the click-through rates and close rates on your test program. Pick the variables that tested best, launch your full campaign, and watch the money roll in.

Finally, remember that testing never ceases; it's an ongoing process. What worked several weeks ago might not work now, so build a testing process into every email campaign. It will pay for itself many times over with a successful responsive campaign.

Succeeding with Email Newsletters

Mark Twain once said, "Climate is what we expect. Weather is what we get."

This also applies to your email promotions. The goal of any email-marketing strategy is to create a proper "climate" to sell your services and wares. Unfortunately, in many instances, all you get in return for your efforts is stormy weather.

The reason is this: If you're using your electronic newsletter as a primary way to sell your wares, not only will you be disappointed with the results, but your subscribers will inform you of their disappointment by using the Unsubscribe button. On the other hand, if you use your newsletter to build an ongoing relationship with your subscribers and create a climate for selling your product and services, subscribers will read it and you'll have a customer-retention vehicle like no other.

When subscribers sign up for your newsletter, they expect to get *news*, not offers. Pulling the old switcheroo on them will show your attempts at relationship building as they really are: a cheap way to promote your product or service.

So what's the difference between a promotional email and a newsletter? First, it's in the percentage; second, it's in the format.

News Versus Promotion

Let's consider percentage first. Your newsletter should have at least 80% to 90% of news consisting of links to third-party information, articles about the product or service you sell, and concerns of your prospects and customers. That is, your newsletter should contain information your subscribers can use, such as movie, book, or music reviews, or upcoming updates to the product they've purchased. You can also enhance your reputation—and make sales— through well-written articles in your product or service's subject area.

Customers and prospects are always looking for information that can help them either use or purchase the products and services they need. This is where you can shine as a helper and facilitator for your clients. The remainder of your newsletter should be about your company and its products or service. In other words, 80% to 90% of your newsletter should focus on your subscribers' needs—the rest can focus on yours.

Now on to format.

Format Considerations

How long should your newsletter be? If you have valuable information to include in your newsletter, don't be afraid of its length. If you provide valuable information that subscribers desire, they'll read every word. Here are the basic elements of an electronic newsletter. Use them when creating your company's email newsletter:

- **The welcome**—Thank your readers for subscribing and give a quick summary of what is contained in the current issue. And remember, you're speaking to one person at a time. Write as if you're speaking only to one subscriber, and keep the tone causal and personal.

- **News they can use**—Link to current news items about your product or service and market niche. If you're selling gaming software, for example, give brief news summaries of articles that review the latest games and the gaming industry; then link to them in your newsletter.

> **tip** **Clip Art Can Help Your Email Promotions**
>
> Microsoft's Small Business Center (www.microsoft.com/smallbusiness/resources/marketing/advertising_branding/how_clip_art_can_make_your_marketing_shine.mspx) has a great article on how to use clip art to make your email messages shine.

- **Customer focused news**—You might profile one of your customers in each newsletter and explain how your services or product helped him or her solve a problem. One-on-one interviews with industry experts are another way to spotlight your customer and the challenges your industry faces.
- **Feature article or tips**—Write a short useful feature—better yet, supply a series of tips that your customers can use. Think about packaging your message. People like to think in terms of numbers. Package your message in terms of "The 10 Tips for. . ." or "The 6 Secrets of. . ." or "The 7 Mistakes of. . .." Another way to package your content is in the form of "Did You Know. . ." or frequently asked questions.
- **Tell-a-friend**—Ask subscribers to tell a friend about your newsletter. If they like what they read, ask them to forward the newsletter to friends, family, and colleagues, and build in the referral code in your newsletter to do it. Don't assume they will think of it.
- **Subscribe and Unsubscribe**—Supply simple and easy instructions on how to unsubscribe and, for those who have had the newsletter forwarded by friends, family, or colleagues, how to subscribe.
- **Link to your website**—Provide multiple links in your newsletter to your website.

Some Additional Tips

Don't be afraid to learn from your competition. Subscribe to their newsletters. You'll pick up some competitive information, and you'll see how they use their newsletters to stay in touch with clients and prospects. Scan their newsletters to pick up ideas on content, writing style, personality, and tone.

There's even a revenue-generating opportunity with electronic newsletters. If your newsletter is unique and offers information or support that consumers can't get anywhere else, you can solicit paid subscriptions. You can also ask the manufacturers of your products to sponsor your newsletter—in effect, selling advertising space.

Don't be shy about asking visitors to your site to subscribe to your newsletter. Ask visitors to sign up when they first enter your website by placing your subscription offer on the home page (top right), and tell them what they'll receive as a subscriber. You also might want to offer an incentive to sign up, such as a discount coupon they can use on their first purchase, a free sample, or a demo of your product or service.

Remember that many of the popular email programs today can read an HTML-formatted email. When opened, an HTML-formatted email appears as a Web page instead of lines of simple ASCII text. That means you can display images, photographs, colors, and graphics in your email to make for a much richer experience for your reader.

Finally, and most important, keep your subscriber's privacy in mind. Building trust starts with building a good privacy policy. Make sure that your company has a privacy policy. Remember that building trust with your customer is a long-term prospect. You can easily lose that trust by sending promotions instead of news and mishandling the personal information you collect when consumers subscribe.

Using Community as Retention

Everyone has an opinion, and most people want to know that their opinions are taken seriously. Some enjoy helping other people; others want to learn more about a subject, issue, or product. These desires cause people to gravitate to online communities. As word gets out that serious discussions are going on at your Web store, and if you can promote those discussions on your site, shoppers will come back on a regular basis to see what's discussed next. This is using *community* as a retention strategy.

In addition, adding community elements can be a key driver for users when making a purchasing decision. Word-of-mouth—hearing from other users, not from your organization—is the best reason for a new user to buy from you. Keep in mind that a community works best when there's something to talk about. Establish a content area on your site about your product or service. Expanding your site in this way accomplishes two objectives:

- It provides grist for the conversational mill.
- It increases your search-engine ranking by generating additional content for searches matched with your keywords. This content should include archived issues of your email newsletter. Search engines looking for keywords even read PDFs.

tip A Bonus to Community Interaction

Sometimes, there's a bonus attached to this interaction with your site visitors: Some customers might actually end up taking over some of your product support role by helping other customers. Such interactions should be monitored, of course, and sometimes you have to mitigate wrong answers, but existing customers who use the product constantly sometimes come up with better solutions (and faster) than you might.

Discussion Boards

One use of community elements on your storefront is the discussion board. Discussion boards and forums (or message boards, as they are sometimes called) provide a bulletin board of threaded discussions. They start with a series of subjects or questions that readers can post their comments or answers to. Later, readers read the posts and add their two cents to the thread of postings, either to the original subject or in response to a reader's posting.

Visitors to your site are allowed to read all posts. But if they want to participate in the discussion, they usually need to register and get a username and password. When they register, you can collect some demographic and interest information for marketing uses.

Chat Rooms

Live chat rooms are another type of community element. This is the stickiest interactive community tool of all. Having a live chat room on your website can keep visitors on your site for hours at a time. That's a lot of face time for one Web page. During this time, you might place offers on the chat discussion page pitching your products or service. You might even join in the chat about your product or product category, identifying yourself as the merchant and offering to answer any questions about your company and its products.

As with discussion boards, you don't need to set up a resource-demanding chat room on your server or your hosting company's server. You can use one of many free chat services on the Net by providing a link from your site to the chat services server. As mentioned before, one such service is Delphi (www.delphi.com). Another is FreeChat (www.sonic.net/~nbs/unix/www/freechat/). You can download the free chat software from these sites and install it on

> **warning**
> **Chat Room Downside**
>
> Chat rooms have a downside: Unlike discussion boards, where you can read all the messages posted there and remove any that are deemed unfit for your board, chat rooms are open free-for-alls. To supervise them would take a staff of people monitoring them 24 hours a day. To solve this problem, you can open the chat room at certain times of the day when monitoring is available.

> **warning**
> **Hello? Is Anybody There?**
>
> Nothing kills a chat-room tool like people dropping by and asking, "Is anybody there?" and getting no response. That is why a chat moderator should always be present when your chat room is open.

your server. Users of your chat room do not need to download any software; they can use the chat room through their Web browser.

Discussion Lists

Although discussion boards and chat rooms require shoppers to visit your site, there are other ways to build a community with shoppers that do not require a site visit but that build loyalty and keep your Web store in their mind. One of the best and least expensive ways to build community is to use of an email discussion list.

A discussion list is a discussion board via email. Subscribers to your discussion list regularly receive emails containing comments that are "echoed" to every other subscriber on the list. Every subscriber on the list receives every post to the list. All posts to the list are done via an email message sent to the list. In a typical discussion list, the listserver software enables a member to send a message to the list address and then broadcasts or echoes that message to all the list members, all within a few minutes.

A well-executed discussion list can gain wide visibility and a very good reputation for your business and for the products or services you sell. Members of a popular discussion list could number in the thousands and offer a great opportunity to sell your product or service.

You don't need to place a program on your site; you can use one of several free services on the Net. One is Yahoo! Groups (www.groups.yahoo.com), which enables you to set up your own private discussion list for your shoppers. Consumers can send and receive emails, schedule meetings, share files and photos, or have private group chats.

> **tip** **Drop Your Programmer—Install Programs Yourself**
>
> A multitude of free CGI scripts is readily available on the Web. One such site is Matt's Script archive. He has guest books, counters, discussion boards, and forums—even search engines for your site. Check them out at www.worldwidemart.com/scripts.

Three types of discussion lists exist:

- Unmoderated discussion lists
- Discussion list digests
- Moderated discussion lists

An unmoderated discussion list sends all messages received to all members of the list. If the number of members on the list is small and the members are not very active, this is not a problem. But if it's a large list with active members, it could generate hundreds of messages a day and swamp the users of the list.

One solution is to create a list digest. The digest collects all the messages sent to the list, bundles them, and emails them in one email to the list members. The digest can be either daily or weekly.

Another way to cut down on the number of emails to the list is to have a moderated discussion list. The free listserver services provide what's called unmoderated discussion lists. That means that all posts that are sent to the list appear without any review. If you want to control what is said on the list or the number of posts sent to the list, you must bring the listserver software in-house.

Web Marketing Today (www.wilsonweb.com/reviews/free-lists.htm) has a good review of free mailing list programs. It explains the main features, pointing out differences and advantages of each listserver.

The next chapter discusses some ways to earn money from the shoppers on your site and how server logs can be used to increase the effectiveness of your marketing program.

CHAPTER 16

Monetizing

In This Chapter

- Creating home pages that sell
- Avoiding abandoned shopping carts
- Increasing revenue in additional ways
- Avoiding credit card fraud

One of the prime purposes of your marketing plan is to generate revenue for your Yahoo! business. In this chapter, we discuss ways of generating revenue from your Yahoo! store, and how to avoid fraudulent orders that threaten to reduce your revenue.

Creating Home Pages That Sell

It's obvious that the prime function of your Yahoo! store is to generate sales. The generation of that revenue starts on your home page. Because the home page is the most important piece of real estate on your site, you need to create a home page that *sells*.

Remember these important keys when creating a home page that sells:

- **Add personality and simplicity**—Your page should have a personality. Like a good book cover, it should draw shoppers into your site, giving them a taste of what's to come and sense of something beneath the surface. A good book cover has a simple but enticing tagline that explains its version of a unique selling position. It has a graphic on the cover that tell the reader the book's unique tagline in pictures as well as words. Brief copy explains more of what the book is about on the back cover—maybe a testimonial or two and something about the author that adds credibility to the product. A good book cover conveys a lot in a small amount of space and tempts you to open it and read further. Your home page should do the same.

- **Use a simple but powerful tagline**—As we have said many times before, a home page has three important jobs. First, it briefly explains your unique selling position with an effective tagline. Second, it gives an immediate call to action and asks for the sale. Third, it contains some kind of email-capture mechanism that entices shoppers to give you their email address—this could be newsletter enrollment, special offers, downloads, a contest, and so on. If you can't sell them, recruit them.

- **Sell, don't entertain**—Your Yahoo! store is there to sell shoppers, not entertain them. Drop the spinning graphics, Flash movies, and splash pages. Stay away from animations, 3D graphics, image maps, and background sound files—they only interfere with asking for the sale.

- **Put your home page on a diet**—Be careful of page bloat. Your entire home page should be no larger than 45K—including graphics. It should be only a page. You want your home page to load fast, get your message across, and close a sale right then and there, if possible.

- **Use simple navigation**—Keep your navigation simple and easy to understand, sparse in words and links. Keep the *Rule of Seven* in mind: No more than seven navigation links for your primary navigation. Any secondary links, such as Privacy Policy and Contact Us, should be text links at the bottom of each page.

Your home page is important and is there to sell. Make sure that's what it does for your Yahoo! store.

> **tip** **Mystery Meat Navigation**
>
> Don't get cute with your navigation graphics. Vincent Flanders, who owns Web Pages That Suck, defines Mystery Meat Navigation like this: "One popular, but horrible, design technique is based on JavaScript rollovers. It's horrible because you can't just look at the links and know where they will take you. You have to mouse over the links to find out your destination—and that's wasted effort which will probably alienate your visitor."

Shoppus Interruptus: Losing the Sale

As you are finding out, succeeding with your Yahoo! business is no easy task. First, you build your Yahoo! store; then you have to drive customers to it, merchandise your store to entice shoppers to buy your product or service, and, finally, make the sale.

You're home-free, right? Not necessarily. The curse of all shopping sites is the abandoned shopping cart. Recent studies have found that up to 75% of all online shopping carts are abandoned before the sale is completed. Imagine this: You walk unto your local grocery store and see dozens of shopping carts filled with groceries abandoned in the shopping aisles. If you were the manager of that grocery store, you would have a heart attack. But that's what it's like every day at most online stores.

All that work building, marketing, and managing your Yahoo! store, and then failing to close most of the sale. So how can you reduce the number of shopping carts that are abandoned at your storefront?

You have little choice of shopping-cart software for your Yahoo! store. Yahoo! provides it, and, as shopping carts go, it's very good. But you can do some things to help reduce the abandonment rate of shopping carts.

The most important thing to do in this case is to give shoppers all the information they need up front so that they are not surprised with unexpected costs, information, or procedures during the checkout process. Building that customer relationship by offering a good shopping experience before the sale will help reduce abandoned shopping carts during the sale.

Here's how:

- **Ensure fast-loading pages**—Keep page bloat in mind. Sell, don't entertain, your shoppers.

- **Make it easy to navigate**—Organize your storefront based on what the customer wants, not how your business is organized. Remember, shoppers don't give a hoot about you or your company—only what you can do for them. Focus on helping customers understand what you are selling and leading them to make a purchase.

- **Streamline checkout**—Keep the distance between the desire to purchase and the purchase itself at a minimum of steps. A shopper should be able to place an order with you and arrive at checkout within two to three mouse clicks. If not, the shopper might become frustrated and leave your site.

- **Give clear information and instructions**—Make your product or service offering easy to understand. Explain all shipping and handling costs, along with any other costs necessary to complete the sale, before shoppers enter the checkout process. Have this information on the customer service pages of your storefront.

- **Tell the customer whether the product is in stock**—Don't wait until the customer reaches checkout to say that the desired product is not in stock.

- **Offer a "save" option**—If the shopping cart is abandoned, provide a page or pop-up window that appears before the shopper leaves your storefront, offering a way to save the sale. For example, offer a special discount, an add-on product, or free shipping if the shopper returns to the shopping cart to complete the order.

- **Specify shipping costs**—Let your customers know how much shipping will cost before the checkout process—don't surprise them. Add a shipping calculator on the product page. The UPS OnLine Tools enable you to display rates, services, and time in transit on your checkout pages.

- **Include your shipping and return policy**—You can provide a link or include your shipping and return policy on every product page.

- **Include your contact information**—Customers might have questions before they place an order. Providing a phone number or even a live chat enable customers to get their questions answered immediately. You do not want customers to hesitate before placing an order.

- **Testimonials and product reviews**—Build consumer confidence by providing feedback from other shoppers. Customers love to hear feedback and reviews from third-party sources.
- **Product guarantees**—If you offer low-price or money-back guarantees, state this in your checkout process or product pages. Some customers might be comparison shopping and will know that you will meet or beat any advertised price.

Keep these tips in mind to reduce the rate of shopping cart abandonment at your Yahoo! store.

Other Ways to Increase Revenue

Besides earning sales, you can generate revenue in your Yahoo! store in other ways. Consider these tried-and-true ideas to be found money. First, use your everyday email communications to generate revenue.

When shoppers opt into your email newsletter, special promotions, contests, coupons, or preferred shopper club, add a special offer with the email confirmation. Special offers should be included in every autoresponder with a link to a special landing page—or, better yet, a microsite.

Don't forget the customer service emails that you send to clarify or confirm an order—or even when notifying the customer that an order has shipped. This is a perfect time to try to add onto the sale or generate a new order. Thank the customer for the order and, as a thank-you, include a special offer. This gives shoppers another reason to make a purchase.

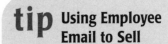

tip Using Employee Email to Sell

Put a link to a special offer from your Yahoo! store at the bottom of every employee email that goes out. Again, link to a special landing page or a microsite.

Another idea using employee email is to allow employees to send exclusive offers to friends and family with special rates and discounts. This could be a good way to move overstock or outdated items in your inventory. IBM offers end-of-life products at excellent discounts to family members of employees. You also could offer special discounts during an employee-appreciation month; employees are consumers, too.

If you advertise open positions on your website, when resumes come in, respond to them with a special offer. Use an autoresponder thanking candidates for their interest in the job offering and include a special discount or coupon for your product or service. Offer them a special 10% discount to thank them for applying to your company.

Besides using email, you can sell noncompetitive products and services that complement your offerings. If you have a travel site, make a deal with a travel-accessory site and bundle your service with its product in return for a percentage of the sale. Carrying this idea further, join the affiliate programs of companies that complement what you sell. You know your shopping audience and the target market that is attracted to your storefront. Go to www.associateprograms.com (see Figure 16.1) and review the many different affiliate programs that are offered there. You should be able to find several that fit your target audience.

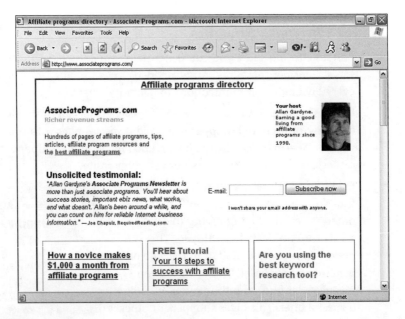

FIGURE 16.1
Associate-Programs.com lists hundreds of affiliate programs in dozens of categories.

Finally, if you have a large amount of traffic at your storefront and have a highly specialized and targeted audience, you might be able to sell advertising or sponsorship space on your storefront.

Avoiding Fraud

Any person experienced in e-commerce knows that building an online business takes a lot of work. Nothing can be worse than seeing all your hard work lost through credit card fraud.

Before the onset of e-commerce, credit card companies preferred not to give merchant accounts to companies that were deemed mail order/telephone order (MOTO) companies. Trying to get any cooperation or help from Visa or

MasterCard was like trying to get blood from a stone. American Express was better: They took the side of the merchant first and the cardholder second. Not so with the other cards. If a MasterCard or Visa card holder had a problem with a mail order company, that company was deemed guilty until proven innocent, and the business had little or no recourse in getting its money—or even its product—back.

Times have changed. Today, Visa and MasterCard actively promote the use of their cards online. And for good reason: There has never been a recorded incident of an individual having a credit card stolen while being securely transmitted over the Net. In fact, there is more of a risk having your credit card number stolen offline than online. Although policies are in place to protect the credit card holder, the credit card companies have neglected to protect the merchants from the consumers. Unfortunately, there *still* is no protection. You bear the responsibility of protecting yourself. The merchant pays—not the customer.

But why doesn't your bank protect you against fraud? Because your merchant agreement with them says it can't. It's that MOTO thing again. Transactions by merchants on the Net fall under the heading of MOTO. Most credit card merchant account agreements leave you, the merchant, 100% liable for fraud committed at your website. And that's not all. You're also required to pay the $15 to $25 charge (the chargeback fee) that the bank hits you with when the charge on the customer's stolen card is reversed by his or her bank.

That's not a pretty prospect. And knowing that it's pretty much guaranteed that someone will try to defraud you sooner or later darkens the picture even further.

> **warning**
> **Avoid Customer Chargebacks with a Passion**
>
> If you accrue too many chargebacks, your merchant account can be terminated. After one is terminated, it's nearly impossible to get another merchant account. Settle customer complaints before they charge back their cards.

Protecting Your Business from Credit Card Fraud

So how do you protect yourself? By following these steps. Each one in itself might not be a red flag, but if you see more than a few, your fraud antennae should go up:

- Don't assume that just verifying a credit card (getting an authorization number) is sufficient fraud protection. The verification process simply checks that the card has not been reported stolen and that it has sufficient free credit available to fund the purchase.

- Your first level of fraud protection is the *Address Verification Service* (AVS). But it has its limitations. AVS compares the billing address of the customer with the records held by the card issuer. If the card number and billing address match, AVS gives it a thumbs up. The problem is, the card could still be stolen and a thief can ask that the order be shipped to another address. If you don't use AVS, make sure the customer's billing address matches the shipping address. If it does not, find out why the customer wants the products shipped to another address.

> **warning**
>
> **AVS Warning**
>
> AVS works only for addresses in the United States. If you sell software or information that can be downloaded instantly, AVS provides no protection. All a thief has to do is obtain a valid credit card number that corresponds to a stolen credit card number, and your instant buy becomes an instant fraud!

- Another way to check to see if the customer information is valid is to compare the billing address to the phone numbers given. Do this by visiting www.Anywho.com (see Figure 16.2). With Anywho.com you can do a search for an address using their reverse phone number lookup.

FIGURE 16.2
With Anywho.com, you can do a search for an address using reverse phone number lookup.

- Place notices, buttons, and images on your order forms and your website content to let consumers know that fraudulent orders will be punished to the fullest extent of the law.
- Look at the products being ordered. Does this match similar frauds you caught in the past? Look at the product mix. Does it make sense? We discovered that most orders for US Robotics modems were fraud orders. We guessed it was a very popular modem and could easily be resold at swap meets. Be wary of big orders, especially for brand-name items or peculiar ones, such as three MP3 players at once.
- If the customer demands overnight delivery, this can be a sign of a fraudulent order. Because the scam artist isn't paying for it, he or she doesn't care how much it costs—and wants to get it in a hurry.
- Look at the email address that's provided. Most thieves use a free email address to hide their identity. With fraudulent orders, the customer's email address is often one of the free email services such as Hotmail, GMail, MSN, or Yahoo!.
- Another clue is a suspicious billing address, such as 123 Main Street. You can check to see if an address is real by using `<a href=http://maps.yahoo.com>Yahoo! Maps</a>`. An address that includes a P.O. Box also could be a red flag.
- Finally, if someone places a valuable order and asks that it be left at the front door, be suspicious. This could be a sign that a thief is using an innocent person's house as a drop-off point. If an order is for a high-priced item or one that you don't want to pay to replace, request that it be signed for.

If you suspect fraud, take these actions:

- Call the customer. Use the phone numbers you requested and collected from him. When you contact him, don't automatically assume that you're dealing with a thief. The customer could have entered incorrect information, and you don't want to offend him and lose the sale. In general, though, a thief will not want to have a long conversation with you. If the phone number is wrong, try to contact the customer via email for a valid phone number. Be very suspicious about this, though: Most people usually don't give out wrong phone numbers unless they mistyped them.
- If the billing address doesn't match or is incorrect, ask the customer to give it to you again. If the area code doesn't match the billing address's city, ask why.

- Ask the customer for the name and phone number of the establishment that issued the card. Both are usually printed on the back. If the customer cannot supply it, this is a sign that he doesn't physically have the card—he has just a stolen number.

If you still feel uncomfortable with an order, even after talking to the customer, ask for payment in advance. And if you're hit with a fraudulent order, document all contacts. This will give you greater protection and a better chance of getting your money or product back. Keep all voice mails and emails, along with caller ID, to prove your case. Ask for a signature to further protect yourself in these cases.

Remember, it takes a lot of orders to replace just one order lost to fraud. So it's better to pass on the ones that you're not 100% certain about. Follow these tips and protect your business—no one else will do it for you.

As you've seen, there's more than one way to make money from your Yahoo! store. In the next chapter, we show you how to mine the server logs for marketing data and use in your marketing plan.

CHAPTER

17

Monitoring Site Sales and Performance

In This Chapter

- Mining your server logs for marketing information
- Using Yahoo! store's site stats
- Deconstructing a statcounter report

Site logs are a great tool to optimize your advertising and promotion campaigns, better improve your site navigation, know your visitor-to-purchase frequency, track where visitors are coming from, and improve the value proposition on your home page. In this chapter, we show you how to use this valuable marketing tool and the software to do it with.

But first, let's examine how to mine that gold from your site logs.

Mining Your Server Logs

If you're not a member of the IT cabal, the phrase *server logs* could bring a blank look to your face. Not to worry. We explain this mysterious data-mining tool and how to use it to better market your Yahoo! store.

Let's start at the top, with server logs. Every Web server keeps track of the number and type of hits your site receives and where they come from. The information is all there, but it's buried in that black box of the Web server that hosts your Yahoo! store. To grasp this data and make sense of it, you need the Rosetta Stone of a Web log analysis programs: a Web analytical and statistics tool.

A site log analysis program can provide some important information. First, it gives you a set of general reports about the traffic to your site, including the number of page views, visits, and unique visitors for any time period you choose. The general reports also give the average visits per day, average page views per day, average page views per unique visitor, and average visitor length. Visits can be tracked by IP addresses, domain names, and cookies.

Second, these reports can tell you where your visitors are coming from, including their geographical location, what type of browser was used, what pages were most commonly used to enter your site, and what visits were referred by which search engine and from other URLs.

Third, the reports can tell you on what page visitors entered your site and on what page they left.

That's all well and good, but how can you use this data for marketing purposes?

Armed with this kind of information, you can discover how well your advertising and promotion campaign is doing and whether it's worth the return on investment (ROI), what Web pages (that means information) seem to be of most interest to site visitors, how well (or not so well) visitors navigated your website, and what the ratio is of visitors to purchases at your site (that is, how well you're pitching your product or service and what your close ratio is).

Let's consider this market intelligence one at a time.

Advertising and Promotion

You're spending money on banner ads, keywords, search-engine placement, newsletter advertising, email marketing—even offline advertising vehicles such as magazine, newspapers, radio, and TV. As a businessman once said, "I know that half of my advertising budget is wasted, but I don't know which half." Not so on the Web. Using your log reports and assigning unique landing pages for each advertising program, you can determine right away whether a particular form of advertising is pulling traffic to your site. The log reports can even give you a way to compare one type of advertising vehicle against another, to see which one works best. This way, you can find out what half of your adverting budget is wasted and target all of it to advertising and promotion vehicles that yield the best results.

Improving Your Value Proposition

Your visitors don't always enter your site through your home page. Other entry points (landing pages) include pages listed in search-engine results such as Google, pages bookmarked by visitors from earlier visits, and pages sent to others as referrals to your site. Why is this important? Because your visitors are telling you what pages they find to be of most value. Your server reports list the most popular entry pages on your site. So, here's a hint: Look these pages over and see why they are so popular. Then, apply that information to your home page. Your visitors are telling you in no uncertain terms how you should frame your value proposition, and that should be prominently displayed on your home page.

Finally, the pages from which your visitors exit your site are just as important as the pages through which they enter it. Here, your visitors are telling you that either they've either found all they need to know or they found that the page—and, thus, your site—is no longer worth visiting. Review those pages and see why they are driving visitors from your site.

Optimizing Your Navigation

Your site logs can help you track your visitors around your site (with a click trail). They tell you whether visitors navigated your site using your search box, links on your master navigation bar, hyperlinks, or the sublinks on page columns. Why is this so important? Think of your website as a physical store.

There's a reason the most popular products sold in a store are in the back: Visitors have to pass other merchandise that they might not have thought of buying. This is called merchandising. Understanding your visitor's traffic patterns can give you the opportunity to present merchandise to them in the context of their visit. The traffic logs (click trails) can also help you identify bottlenecks or confusion in your site-navigation structure that might be frustrating visitors and driving them from your site.

Calculating Your Close Ratio

One of the most important pieces of data that a server report can provide relates to your close ratio. This is the ratio between the number of site visitors and actual sales. Your server report can tell you how many times an average consumer visits your site before making the first purchase. How many times before making a second purchase? Or a third? Taking these ratios as a benchmark, you can use the information that the server reports generate to improve your advertising campaigns, value proposition, and navigation structure, to enrich your visitor-to-purchase ratio.

Using Yahoo! Site Stats Resources

Store Editor and Web Hosting statistics are completely different, and each has its own data set. You need to view the appropriate statistics for the method you are using to create your pages. If you are using a combination of both Store Editor and Web Hosting, you need to mine both sets of stats.

Both stats packages are Web based, so you can view your stats with just your browser. The advantage of using the Web Hosting side is that you can download the raw log files for use with a third-party analysis tool, for more advance statistical reporting or have it automated. You can also use a workaround for advanced statistical reporting by using a third-party online stats tool if you are using Store Editor (discussed later).

Web Hosting has its own statistics section, called Site Statistics, under the Hosting Control Panel (see Figure 17.1). Site Statistics pulls information from log files that track traffic only to your Web Hosting account. If you do not use Web Hosting, you will not see any statistics. These statistics do not apply to traffic from the Store Editor or Catalog Manager products. With Web Hosting, you can download raw log files to use with your own Web statistics software, such as WebLog Expert (www.weblogexpert.com) (see Figure 17.2), WebTrends (www.webtrends.com), and LiveSTATS by DeepMetrix (www.deepmetrix.com).

CHAPTER 17 Monitoring Site Sales and Performance   253

FIGURE 17.1
You can view Web Hosting statistics in the Web Hosting Control Panel.

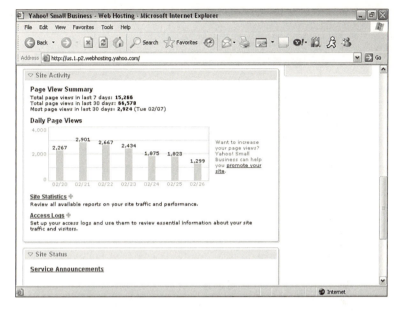

FIGURE 17.2
WebLog Expert is a great third-party tool for analyzing your access log.

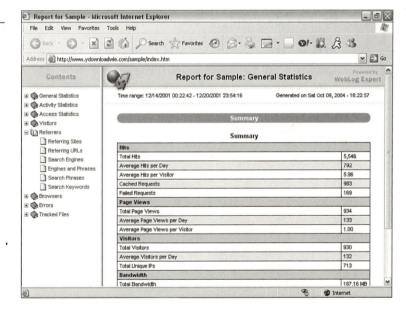

> **Yahoo! Talk**
>
> Site Statistics is Yahoo!'s Web Hosting statistics program.

In contrast, the statistics maintained in Store Manger under the Statistics column apply only to traffic on the Store Editor Web pages and sales of products in Catalog Manager. When a visitor goes to a Store Editor page, the stats gets recorded in at least three places in Store Manager's Statistics section: Reports, Page Views, and Click Trails. When a visitor makes a purchase, the sale is recorded in at least two places in Store Manager's Statistics section: Sales and Reports.

Viewing Web Hosting Site Statistics

Site statistics provide basic Web statistics supplied by Yahoo!, including these (see Figure 17.3):

- **Page views**—How many visits for each page
- **Visitor profiles**—Which operating systems, browser, and screen resolution visitors are using
- **Referrers**—Whether a visitor clicked on a link from another website or came from a search engine, and what keywords were used

To view Web Hosting statistics, follow these steps:

1. From the Manage My Services control panel, click the Web Hosting Control Panel link.
2. Scroll down until you see the Site Statistics link, and click the link.

FIGURE 17.3
Site Statistics is Yahoo!'s built-in statistics program for Web Hosting.

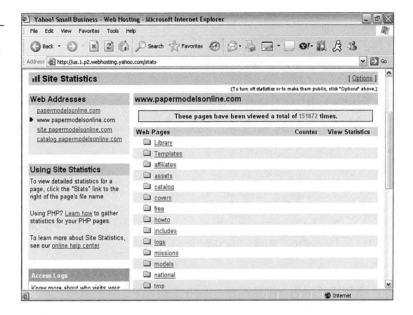

Configuring and Downloading Access Log Files

Downloading access log files and analyzing them with a more robust statistics-analyzer program, such as WebLog Expert, can give you more in-depth detail on how your site is performing. Before you can start downloading log files, you need to turn them on. As a default, the Yahoo! store has access log files turned off. You must turn them on and configure access log setup. You can select how many recent logs you want to keep; whether you want to roll access logs daily, weekly, or monthly; and which time zone you are in.

To configure access log files, follow these steps:

1. From the Manage My Services control panel, click the Web Hosting Control Panel link.
2. Scroll down until you see the Access Log Files link, and click the link.
3. Configure the settings under the Access Log Setup column.

To download access log files, follow these steps:

1. From the Manage My Services control panel, click the Web Hosting Control Panel link.

> **warning**
> You can keep only up to 28 log files. Therefore, make sure you download the files before the system overwrites the old files with the new ones.

2. Scroll down until you see the Access Log Files link, and click the link.
3. Click the View Access Log link under the Access Log Setup column. From here, you can download each log file.

Viewing Store Editor Statistics

If you are using the Store Editor and Catalog Manager, you can view your statistics in Store Manger.

To view Store Editor statistics, follow these steps:

1. From the Manage My Services control panel, click the Store Manager Control Panel link.
2. In the Statistics column, you can view statistics on page views, sales references, and searches (see Figure 17.4).

If you are using Store Editor, you will not be able to download access log files for more detailed statistics. Although you can get basic statistics, we recommend using a third-party online stats solution. This is a great workaround for users of Store Editor.

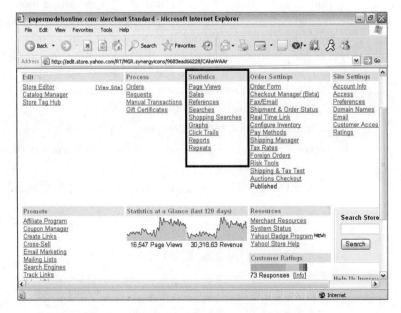

FIGURE 17.4
If you are using the Store Editor and Catalog Manager, you can view built-in statistics in the Statistics column in Store Manager.

Using Third-Party Online Service for Detailed Statistics (Workaround for Store Editor Users)

Store Editor users can get more in-depth statistical reporting by using a third-party online stats service. This is a workaround because there are no access log files for you to download and analyze when using Store Editor. Instead of having your statistics sent to Yahoo!'s access log files, as with Web Hosting, your store statistics are sent to the third-party online stats server access logs.

When you sign up for an account, you simply add a piece of code to your RTML template. Every time someone visits a Web page, the Web tracker code sends important information to your third-party online Web stats log. The system automatically generates charts, graphs, and statistics to make analyzing your traffic easier.

The difference with this online stats service is that you do not need to install software on your machine or be restricted to using just Yahoo!'s stats reports; the Web-analysis software is installed on their server. However, you might need to consult with an RTML programmer to add the code to your RTML template.

Statscounter (www.statscounter.com) and Google Analytics (www.google.com/analytics/) are two free online stats counter services you can use. You can sign up for an account on their websites. Google Analytics (see Figure 17.5) and Statscounter (see Figure 17.6) both provide more detailed statistics than the built-in Yahoo! stats.

Let's deconstruct an example of a server analysis report to understand what makes them tick.

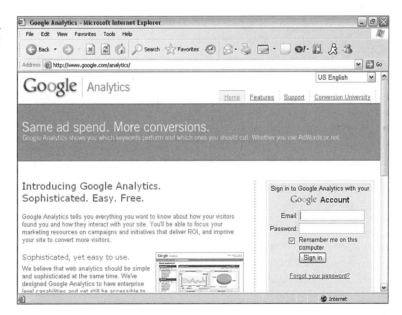

FIGURE 17.5
Google Analytics is a free online stats service provided by Google.

FIGURE 17.6

Statscounter is a free online stats service. You can install an invisible counter on each of your Web pages.

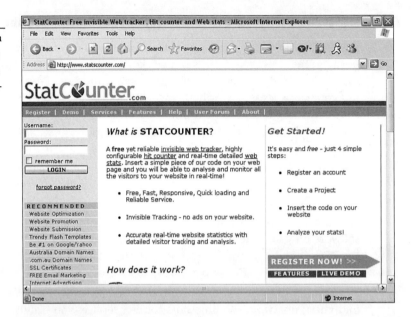

Deconstructing a Statscounter Report

Here are some of the statistics you can view with Statscounter reports:

- **General statistics**—Page views, visitors, bandwidth
- **Activity statistics for page views, visitors, and bandwidth**—Daily, by hour of day, by day of week, by month
- **Access statistics**—Pages, files, images, directories, entry pages, exit pages, paths, file types
- **Visitor statistics**—Host, top-level domains, countries, U.S. states, cities, organizations
- **Referrers statistics**—Referring sites, referring URLs, search engines, engines and phrases, search phrases, search keywords
- **Browsers statistics**—Browsers, operating systems, spiders
- **Error statistics**—Types, 404 errors

Let's take a look at some of the statistics provided and discuss why they are important to analyze:

- **Visitors**—Monitoring visitor statistics can tell you whether your traffic is increasing or decreasing (see Figure 17.7). These statistics can give you in insight into how well your marketing campaign is doing. For example, if you are doing a TV or print advertisement, you will want to monitor whether your visitor rate has increased during that particular marketing campaign. You cannot track these types of advertisements as you can with banner click-through, so this is one of the best ways to monitor this type of advertisement campaign.

- **Page views**—Page views (see Figure 17.8) are a great way to see which product pages are popular and which ones need additional exposure. For example, you might find that certain pages receive more traffic than expected. This could be the result of search-engine placement or an interest that you never thought existed. You can use this data to make changes to the page, such as adding products on that page or creating menu links to lead them to other product pages. Page views are also a great way to monitor advertising campaigns. You can create new pages specifically for each campaign and then use the page-view data for that particular page to see how much traffic that campaign produced.

- **Search engines**—If you are serious about generating search-engine traffic, these reports are a must. With the search-engine reports, you can see which search engines are sending visitors and how much traffic they're generating (see Figure 17.9). You can also get a breakdown of the keywords that visitors typed in to get to your site from each search engine. With these reports, you can determine which keywords or keyword phrases that you are targeting are getting picked up by the search engine. You can use this to adjust your keyword content on your Web pages.

- **Entry and exit pages**—Not all traffic starts at your home page (see Figure 17.10). Search engines and other sites linking to your site can send traffic to any of your Web pages. Figuring out why those pages are your entry pages can help you duplicate the tactic on your other pages. You will also want to determine why those are your exit pages. Figure out why people are leaving your site and from which pages. The page might load too slowly, you might not have a call to action, the sales copy might not be good enough, and so on. Fixing these issues can dramatically increase sales.

- **Geographic location**—If you are selling products internationally, this is a great report to see if you are getting traffic in other countries (see Figure 17. 11). If you are selling only in the United States, you can view statistics by state and even city.

- **Referrer**—You can get a list of all domains and even the exact URL of where your traffic is coming from (see Figure 17.12). This helps in determining how well your link-exchange program is going or why others sites are linking and sending you traffic. You can also use this information to see if your banner-advertisement campaign is sending you traffic.

These are some of the report statistics you will use the most. Make sure you explore all the specific reports to see if the information holds any value for you.

FIGURE 17.7

Visitor reports show how many people are coming to your site.

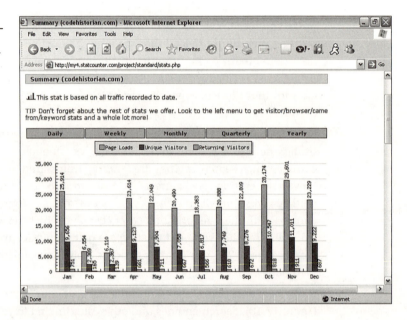

FIGURE 17.8
Page view reports show how many times each page is being requested.

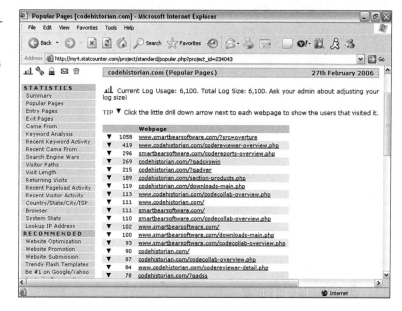

FIGURE 17.9
Search-engine reports show which search engines are sending you traffic and what keywords or keyword phrases are used.

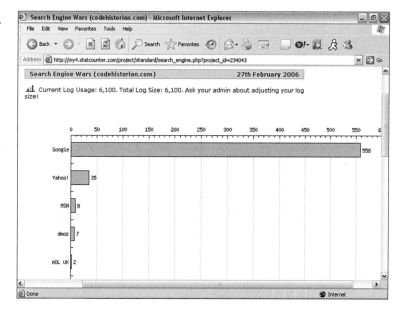

FIGURE 17.10
Entry and exit reports show which pages people are landing on to enter your site and which pages they are exiting from.

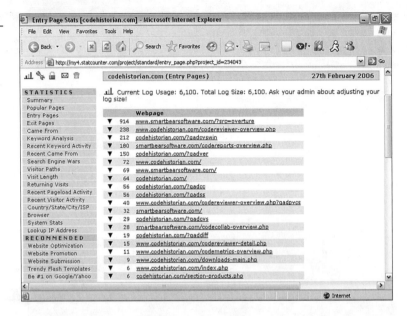

FIGURE 17.11
Geographic location reports can be of assistance if customer location is important to you.

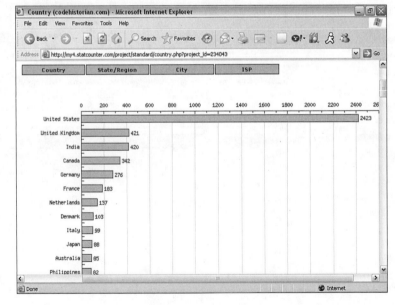

FIGURE 17.12

With referrer reports, you can view a list of other websites that are sending traffic to your site.

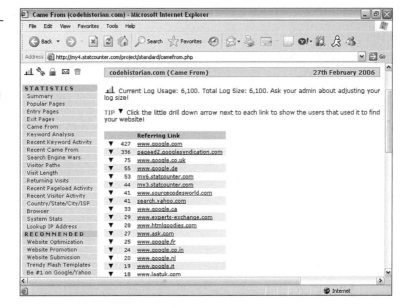

Your Web server reports and the statistics they provide are a valuable tool to fine-tune your marketing program and give you a window into what is happening at your Yahoo! store. In the next chapter, we cover the lost stepchild of marketing—public relations—and how you can use it to market your Yahoo! store.

CHAPTER 18

Public Relations

In This Chapter

- What public relations (PR) is
- PR's importance to your business
- How to create a proper online press room
- How to write a press release and where to distribute it

They say that a jungle is just a rainforest with poor public relations, and a squirrel is a rat with good public relations. Ask yourself this: Is your online business a jungle or a squirrel?

Like it or not, perception *is* reality in the online world. Where else can a guy in a garage build a website that has the look and feel of a multimillion-dollar corporation? And if done right, you can get a million dollars' worth of free publicity without spending a dime on advertising. In this chapter, we show how you can augment your ad dollars and gain the benefits of PR right from your own website.

What Is Public Relations?

As we've seen, there's quite a zoo of marketing animals to use to promote your Yahoo! store. But what is the difference between advertising, promotion, publicity, media relations, and *public relations*? How do they stand apart from each other?

Here's a common story from the PR industry that can help clarify the difference.

Once upon a time, the circus came to town. To drum up business, the circus promoters put up posters around the city that read, "The Circus Is Coming to Town." Okay, so they weren't great on copy writing. At any rate, we call that advertising. On the day the circus opened, posters announcing the circus were put on an elephant and paraded through town. Animals are great at capturing attention. That's promotion. At one point, the elephant ran amuck and thundered through the mayor's flower garden. That's called publicity. And if you can get the press to publish the story on page one, that's media relations.

If you are able to get the mayor to smile about the incident, *that's public relations!*

The Importance of the Press Release

Public relations, or PR, is usually an afterthought at most e-business websites today. Now, every business wants and needs free publicity, but sprinkling a few press releases or links to news articles on a Web page does not make public relations. PR is one of the most misunderstood and, at the same time, most valuable marketing tools an e-business can have. And one of the most important elements of this tool is the online *press release* and the *press room*. A proper online press room—often the forgotten stepchild of e-business—can be a source of important publicity and a resource for journalists.

But online PR is fraught with misconceptions. The biggest misconception consists of writing an ill-conceived press release of little interest but to the CEO, and emailing or faxing it to as many editors and reporters as one can think of. This misconception is followed closely behind by the next: Editors and reporters will actually write stories about you from these releases. PR professionals know better. Press releases do little for your business anymore because the "publish and pray—send and forget" strategy of old no longer works. In addition, bombarding journalists with press releases can actually harm the reputation of your company with editors and reporters.

Does that mean you give up on writing them? Of course not. If press releases are conceived well and sent out as a part of a comprehensive promotional program, they have their uses.

We look at that a bit later.

The Online Press Room

Before you compose that press release and click the Send button, put yourself in a journalist's place. Here's someone who is swamped by hundreds of releases a week and is trying to hit a deadline for a story. The journalist needs fast, accurate, succinct information, in a place that's easy to locate on the Net. If the journalist is writing about a company, the first place he'll turn to is not the stack of press releases that most often go ignored, but to the Web. Journalists start by either visiting a target company's website or turning to the search engines to look for businesses that manufacture, distribute, or sell the product or service they are writing about.

Your company now must give serious thought to how journalists can quickly and easily access the information they need from your website. This demonstrates the necessity of an easily navigable site with a clearly labeled press room (see Figure 18.1) that quickly satisfies the journalist's need for basic information.

FIGURE 18.1

Intel has a good example of a press room designed for journalists.

Constructing Your Online Press Room

So what makes up an online press room? First, a press room is like an online *press kit*. Online press kits are really no different than the printed kind. If you visit a booth at a trade show and identify yourself as someone with the press, any established business should be able to hand you a press kit. When you design a separate press room for your website, imitating what's in a professional press kit will ensure that you touch on all the necessary bases. After all, this is what journalists and reporters are looking for.

This is what a reporter wants from your online press room:

- In clear concise language, and not in business jargon, describe your company and what makes its products or services unique. Tell what impact your product or service has on your industry, and what problem it solves. Here's your chance to describe your unique selling position again. This is where you sell the sizzle, not the steak—the benefits, not the features, of your product or service. Don't claim that you're going to be the next Amazon or Microsoft, but make an effort to distinguish yourself from your competition.

- If you have images or photographs of your product—or even a downloadable demo—provide links to those files in the press kit, along with links to any plug-in required to view them.

- List the key people in management, and detail their professional and business background. State what position they hold in the company and why they are qualified for that position.

- Give a press contact. This is very important and most often forgotten. Choose your best company spokesperson, one that can tell a compelling story about your company. Give the press a *direct line* and *specific email address* to contact that person.

- Ask if journalists would like to receive future notices about your company and products, and give a choice of *how* they'd like to be contacted—email, fax, telephone? Get their permission up front to make sure any future releases will end up on their desk—not in their wastebasket.

- Finally, list all your latest press releases and media mentions in order, with the most recent first.

> **warning**
>
> **A PR No-No**
>
> Never make reporters register to enter your press room. If you do so, you can count the time they stay on your page in milliseconds. Sure, you run the risk of making your press kit available to others than the press—including your competition. But that's the nature of the Net. When you create an online presence for your company, you open your kimono for the entire world to see.

Constructing the Press Release

Writing a press release is more art than science. And to be read, it must be done right. The biggest challenge is to know what journalists consider genuine news and what they consider fluff. Being so close to your e-business, you can easily lose perspective: What you see as earthshaking news to you will get the automatic delete from journalists.

Issuing too much company fluff as news will eventually result in your future news releases being ignored—sort of like the boy who cried "Wolf!" too often. Make your release newsworthy by solving a current problem or filling a current need. Pinpoint what that need or problem is, and write the release from that perspective.

Along with making your press release newsworthy (see Figure 18.2), you need to keep the following in mind when writing your release.

FIGURE 18.2

Press Release Writing.com has samples of proper press releases you can use.

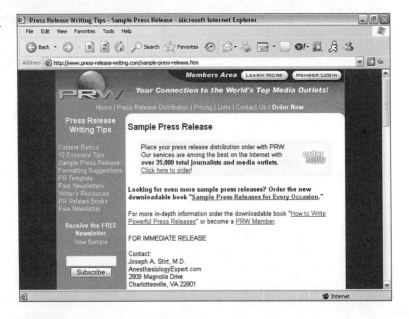

Web Resource

Free Press Release Template

Press Release Writing.com offers a free press release template to help write your press releases correctly. For a small fee, you can download the book, *Sample Press Releases for Every Occasion*, and get attention with your press releases. You can find this at www.press-release-writing.com/press-release-template.htm.

- **Create an unmistakable opening**—The first line of your press release should read "FOR IMMEDIATE RELEASE," in all caps. This lets the reporters know that the news is authorized for publication on the date they receive it.

- **Write a headline that gets straight to the point**—Write a headline using a combination of lowercase and capital letters, keeping your headline to 10 words or less. Remember, what you say here determines whether the reader will read the rest of the release. It's the 1.54 seconds again.

- **Create a strong leading paragraph**—The first part of your lead

tip Keep It Short

Keep your press releases short if you want them read. Journalists are always pressed for time, and a lengthy diatribe will not motivate them to read your release. Keep your release less than one page in length—about 500 words maximum.

paragraph should include the city it was released from or where the event took place, the newswire it was released over, and the date of the release. It would look like this: "DENVER - (BUSINESS WIRE) - Jan. 31, 2002." All releases must include a date because reporters do not always use releases immediately. Your lead paragraph should then answer the who, what, where, when, why, and how of the event. The lead paragraph is really an abstract or summary of the whole release.

- **Give the journalist reading the release the reason why it's important to his or her readers**—Here's where you give a detailed explanation from the reader's perspective. Add all background information, quotes from objective or third-party sources, comparisons with competitors, and so on. If you're sending your release inside the text of an email message, format it in the style of the most common email reader. Stay away from HTML tags, tabs, or columns; text-based email programs do not read these well.

- **Include a brief company summary**—Mention your company expertise in your niche, your location, years in business, and so on. Keep it short. Don't include your annual report.

- **Include complete contact information**—Give a contact name, an email address, and your URL. The contact name you supply should be someone who's available and capable of answering questions from the press.

- **Close the release**—Close with the characters "-30-" or "###," which are style conventions that let reporters know they have reached the end of the release.

> **tip PR Do's and Don'ts**
>
> PR do's:
>
> - Do make your press releases short and to the point.
> - Do include all necessary contact information.
> - Do check spelling and grammar in your release. Do it twice, just to be sure.
> - Do keep typefaces large, legible, and readable for both email and faxes.
> - Do write a clear and meaningful subject line that reflects the contents of your release.
>
> PR don'ts:
>
> - Don't write unclear press releases. If it doesn't make sense to the reader, it will not be used.
> - Don't send a release to a publication without knowing the audience or what the publication is all about.
> - Don't send attached files. Don't send a word-processing document or a zipped file that the contact needs to download, unzip, read into his word processor, determine the compatibility for, print, review, and so on.

The ultimate question is this: Have you designed a press room for a journalist working on deadline to easily find the needed answers on your site? If so, your little stepchild has become a full-fledged member of your marketing and promotion family.

Where to Send Your Press Release

When you have your press release written, you need to tell the world. So where do you send it? Here are websites to consider.

First, there's PR Web (www.prweb.com). One nice thing about PR Web is that it offers free posting. The following charge either a posting fee per release or an annual fee to use their press release distribution service:

- **PR Newswire** (www.prnewswire.com)—Requires an annual fee for posting
- **Business Wire** (www.businesswire.com)—Requires an annual fee
- **URLwire** (www.urlwire.com)—Posts on demand and charges per posting, but does not have an annual fee
- **Internet News Bureau** (www.newsbureau.com/services)—Charges per posting, but does not have an annual fee
- **Xpress Press** (www.xpresspress.com)—Charges per posting, but does not have an annual fee

Let PR help you promote your business and use this lost stepchild to increase the visibility and credibility of your Yahoo! store.

Outsourcing Your Public Relations

If you don't have time to craft that press release or build relationships with the media, consider hiring a public relations firm. Not only can such a firm handle writing your press releases, but most likely, it will already have relationships with the media (news reporters, newspapers, news stations, and journalists). Those established personal relationships can mean instant media coverage with just a phone call.

If your target market is local, use a local firm that specializes in your area. In contrast, if your target market is nationwide, use a public relations firm that specializes in national coverage. A good public relations firm should be able to write, send, and follow up on a press release for about $500.

In the next chapter, we cover customer service—how to, what to, and when to do it.

Part V

Operating Your Yahoo! Business

19 Customer Service

20 Warehousing and Inventory Control

21 Financial Planning

CHAPTER 19

Customer Service

In This Chapter

- How to service the customer before the sale
- How to service the customer during the sale
- How to service the customer after the sale
- How to deal with product returns
- How to handle disgruntled customers

A company's customer service permeates every stage of the buying process, not just when customers have order status questions or lodge a complaint. In addition, online customer service requires electronic assistance that can guide customers to a purchase. In the online world, shoppers can be easily frustrated by bad site design or the inability to find the right information to make a purchase decision.

To create a world-class customer service experience, you must respond to customers in a personalized, timely manner through the use of customer-service technology before, during, and after the sale. In brief, it's not customer service management, but *customer relationship management*.

So how do you build good customer service into your Web store? Easy. Walk a mile in your customer's shoes. Ask yourself, "What kinds of service would I expect before, during, and after a sale?" In this chapter, we look at the best approaches to make your Yahoo! store shine when servicing your shoppers.

Service Starts Before the Sale

A well-designed storefront that *sells* instead of entertains is the first step in providing customer service before the sale. Here, we consider some of the most important elements of your site that are geared to lead a shopper to a buying decision.

First, there should be no more than two to three clicks from the product offering to checkout. Don't give a long song and dance about a product without having a Buy button prominently displayed. This is important to keep in mind when you customize your Yahoo! store because you might get carried away with the freedom of customizing your page design.

Second, give some thought to your Order Confirmation page, which usually ends the checkout process. Most storefronts lead buyers through the purchase process—and then push them out the door! Amazon's Order Confirmation page is a good example of one that is useful: It is also a recycling page of sorts that gives buyers some additional cross-selling offers, a chance to comment, a way to review their account, and a history of current and past orders. In effect, Amazon's page actually pulls buyers back into the storefront to entice them to buy some more. Have more than just an Exit button on your Order Confirmation page. Be creative. What other choices can you give the shopper—who is in a buying mood—to purchase again, right then and there?

Third, have a comprehensive set of Customer Care FAQs (frequently asked questions) on your storefront. As explained before, this is your chance to remove as many objections to buying your product, or buying from you, as you can. Customer Care FAQs list the most common answers to customer service questions. They not only list customer service policies, but they also delve into the most common customer service problems and how to solve them. Link to your FAQs from your home page: A well-written FAQ will be one of your most popular pages, so make it easy to find. Link the answers to your questions to other pages on your site, where appropriate, such as a map to your offices or links to the products mentioned in your answers.

Finally, offer a First-Time Visitor orientation. Picture this: A first-time visitor comes to your website. This visitor came with a shopping list in hand and wants to make a purchase. What can you do to make this shopper feel comfortable enough to buy from you?

Here's how:

Create a First-Time Visitor icon and place it very visibly on your home page. This is a great way to welcome new visitors and give them a feeling that help is just a mouse click away. The icon brings them to a First-Time Visitor page that contains a brief description of the customer service they can expect when they buy from your web store. RM Carspares (www.rmcarspares.co.uk/docs/first.html) has a good example of a First-Time Visitor page (see Figure 19.1).

FIGURE 19.1
RM Carspares invites the first-time visitor with a User's Guide to the site.

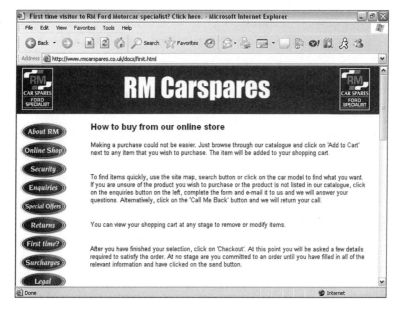

For instance, you might provide your customer service email address, toll-free customer service phone number, fax number, and customer service hours. Include your customer satisfaction guarantees and return policies. Tell shoppers how their order will be handled—how fast their order will ship, how you will confirm their order, when the order will be shipped, and how to track the order after it has shipped. Also provide a link to your FAQs about your products and services, and tell shoppers that you have a secure site where they can use their credit card without fear.

Finally, direct shoppers to the fastest way to place an order on your site, such as a list of specials and popular items for first-time customers, or the product or service directory page of your Web store. If executed properly, your first-time visitors will get a nice warm and fuzzy feeling about your Web store and will feel secure enough to make that first purchase.

Service During the Sale

Servicing the customer during the buying process is just common sense. You want to remove as many sales objections as you can to allow the shopper to make a buying decision. Two of the best ways to make a customer comfortable with a purchase at the point of sale is to provide real-time stock status and shipping time information.

Provide a link to shipping information on every product page. Consider creating a pop-up window of shipping rates and estimated delivery time. This way, the customer does not leave the product page. If you plan to use UPS Online Tools, your customers can receive real-time shipping rates. These rates can be enabled in the shopping cart as well; buyers do not need to start the checkout process to see this information.

If a customer knows the stocking status of a product and when it will ship, you eliminate many of your customer service problems. Amazon does a very good job of informing the potential customer of what books are in stock and within what time frame they will ship. Keep in mind that what you promise on, you must deliver. So if you find that a product offered by a customer is not in stock or if shipping of the item will be delayed, be sure to contact the customer immediately and estimate when the product will be shipped. With the Yahoo! store, you can set up Inventory Management to let your customers know whether the product is in stock or how many products are left. In Chapter 20, "Warehousing and Inventory Control," we show you step by step how to set up your Inventory Management settings.

Sometimes, stock status and shipping time estimates are not enough, and the customer needs additional information at the point of purchase to make the sale. This is where live customer care becomes important.

You can offer free live customer support using ICQ at www.icq.com/download/, Yahoo Instant Messaging at messenger.yahoo.com, or AOL's Instant Messenger service at www.aol.com/aim/. Shoppers can download the free desktop application and communicate with you in real time if they have a question.

A number of new technologies enable you to place live customer support right on your website so that customers can click to get in touch with a real live human by phone or by online chat. Services such as LivePerson (see Figure 19.2), at www.liveperson.com, offer a pop-up chat box that gives instant customer contact with a real person.

FIGURE 19.2
With just a click of a button, LivePerson opens a small chat window on your site where customers can chat with a customer service agent and ask questions.

Live chat can be a great tool for immediate online customer service. But to do it right, keep these steps in mind from Jack Aaronson, the CEO of the Aaronson Group:

- Anticipate and script as many user scenarios (use actual cases) as possible. This avoids encountering a problem for which no canned response really fits.
- Write all responses in the brand, voice, and style of your company. Otherwise, the user feels as if he's talking to a robot.

- Make sure all of your customer service reps (CSRs) read the information input by the user and review the log before responding to the user. If CSRs ask the same questions repeatedly, it ruins the chat event.
- Make sure the CSRs understand the brand and voice of your company. This gives them a better idea of how to answer questions when there are no canned responses. As a corollary, empower CSRs to type their own responses instead of restricting them to the canned responses.
- Implement a QA service so a team reviews chat logs. This will hopefully provide insight on what use cases should exist and what CSRs do wrong.

These are the basic, minimal steps to creating an effective live chat feature on your website.

Service After the Sale

You might say that service after the sale is where the rubber hits the road. You've spent a lot of time, money, and energy getting the sale. Now you have to keep it.

Online customers are a skittish bunch. No matter how comfortable you've made them in buying from your Web store, after they press that Buy button, they still want to be secure in the fact that their order has actually been received and that their product has been shipped.

To soothe customer concerns about an order and eliminate many email messages to your customer service department, be sure that you send a real-time instant order confirmation to the customer as soon as the order is placed. The order confirmation message should include an order number, what they bought, where it will be shipped, and the total amount of the order, including all shipping and handling charges and applicable taxes. The great news is that, with the Yahoo! store, this process is automated for you if enabled. After the order is placed, the customer receives the confirmation email immediately.

To enable automated order-confirmation emails, follow these steps:

1. In Store Manager, click the Shipment and Order Status link in the Order Settings column.
2. Enter a valid email address to appear as the sender of your order-confirmation emails in the Order Confirmation Email text box. Entering an email address enables the automated confirmation emails.
3. Click the Update button.

After the order has shipped, another email confirmation should be sent with relevant shipping information and order status. If you cannot ship within the time promised on your site, send an intermediate email to keep the customer informed of the status of the order and when it might ship. If you are using UPS Online Tools, you can insert a tracking number into the shipping status email. Customers can then track their own packages. This reduces phone calls and emails asking, "Where is my order?"

After the order has been shipped and enough time has elapsed for the customer to receive it, send another email asking if the order was received and whether there were any problems with the order. This proactive approach to customer service will pay off in spades. It shows that you do care about your customers and that you are willing and able to correct any problem they might have had. In addition, if they respond to your follow-up email, some customers might write you a good testimonial that—with their permission—you can print on your Web site. You can also provide a link and ask them to rate and review your store. Yahoo! store includes a merchant rating system: Users can rate merchants on a scale of one to five stars.

Finally, despite the best efforts of your customer service strategies, some customers will be disappointed in the product they bought and want to return it. It's important that you have a no-hassle return policy. Remember, your prime goal is to keep the customers you have, so you will have to weigh the return of a product or a refund on a service in light of how valuable your customer is to keep.

Sometimes, returns are a blessing in disguise. Okay, not blessings, but they're useful for your business. Most times, customers will give you reasons for the return, and this information is good feedback on a particular product or the manner in which you sell from your site. Collecting all the returns data and adding it to your customer service requests will help you identify merchandising problems and opportunities.

Merchants should also review refund and return policies from other sites and use the policies that seem the best fit. An iron-clad refund and return policy can save a lot of

> **tip — What Are They Saying About You?**
>
> It's a good idea to periodically monitor consumer-generated media. Use PubSub (www.pubsub.com), Bloglines (www.bloglines.com), Google Groups (groups.google.com), and Technorati (www.technorati.com), among others. You can also receive alerts in the form of emails and text messaging by setting up Yahoo! alerts (alerts.yahoo.com). All you have to do is enter keywords such as your name or company name. When news containing those keywords hits the Internet, an alert is sent to you immediately.

headaches of chargebacks and returns for bogus reasons. You should have your policies in place so you can refer to them, and then decide on a case-by-case basis how flexible you want to be. This allows you to decide whether a refund will net you a loyal returning customer or avoid unreasonable buyers.

Follow-Up After the Sale

A good tool for acquiring input regarding your business, product, and customer service is an after-sale survey. Wait a few days after customers have received your product or service, and then email a customer-satisfaction survey. The elements of the survey should include the following and should be just check boxes and/or radial buttons:

- How did you hear about our company?
- Were you pleased with your product?
- Would you purchase from us again?
- Would you recommend us to others?
- Was ordering from us convenient?
- How was our customer service?
- Did you receive your product on time?
- Can we improve in these areas?
- Overall rating?

At the very end of the email survey, provide a comment box for additional comments. You can also take this opportunity to say thank you to the customer by including a discount code. This encourages repeat customers.

You might also want to add some kind of an incentive to make the customer want to fill out the survey—possibly free shipping on their next order, a coupon, or a free gift.

Many Happy Returns

Product returns are a problem for all retail establishments. But for an online storefront, it can be much more involved because of the nature of an online business. Let's face it: Returns are a fact of life in any retail environment.

It's important that you list your terms of sale and your return policy and procedures on your site. Remember that shoppers don't like surprises. If you're sure they understand the terms of their purchase before they click the Buy Now button, you can pre-empt some of your returns. Tell shoppers under what conditions they can return a product. How many days or weeks do they have to decide to return it? Will they get a refund or a credit? Who pays the shipping back to you? You or them? If the product is defective, who is responsible for replacing it? You or the manufacturer?

Be clear and specific, and list all details about your return policy on your website.

Handling Disgruntled Customers

The old adage goes, "A satisfied customer tells no one. A dissatisfied customer tells 10 of his friends." And on the Net, a dissatisfied customer can tell thousands of other consumers about a bad shopping experience. But, as with product returns, customer complaints—if used correctly—can be a valuable resource that you can turn to your advantage. They can give you valuable insight into problems with your selling process. Accept each complaint for what it is: a chance to learn. And if you can solve the problem to a customer's satisfaction, that customer might even evangelize your company.

First, answer every complaint promptly and politely. Before answering with a solution to a customer's complaint, be sure that you understand the problem and be as specific as possible in your replies. If the customer is frustrated and complaining, expect the tone of his or her message to be angry and confrontational. That doesn't mean you should be. Respect your frustrated customers, and reply to them in an empathetic tone.

> **tip** **Protecting Against Return Abusers**
>
> The Return Exchange (www.returnexchange.com/) offers a weapon to combat repetitive product returns. It compiles a database of potential return abusers from data supplied by multiple stores and companies.
>
> The compiled data is analyzed, and return/exchange abusers are identified. The Return Exchange notifies participating retailers in a process similar to credit card authorization. The POS system identifies potential abusers. The retailer can then take whatever action it deems appropriate.

> **tip** **Pay Your Customers to Complain**
>
> Even negative feedback is useful in running your business. Sometimes, it's better than positive feedback. Run a "Complaint Contest" to elicit feedback on your site and service.

But don't stop there.

If you've not received a reply, follow up with the customer to make sure you have addressed his or her concerns. This additional email will show the complaining customer that you are willing to come to a mutually agreeable solution to the problem. If a customer sees that you are willing to work with him or her, this will go a long way toward resolving the issue.

Just remember that every complaint, no matter how illogical, should receive a reply. Your best efforts could turn a complaining customer into one of your best customers.

In summary, remember that good service is a promise you make to your customers. Don't make promises you can't keep. In the next chapter, we cover the hiring and staffing of your Yahoo! store.

CHAPTER

20

Warehousing and Inventory Control

In This Chapter

- How to set up your warehouse
- Rules of inventory control
- How to do just-in-time delivery
- Packaging tips

How many products you carry and how much stocked inventory you need determine how much storage or warehouse space you require. Will you use your house, find an offsite warehouse, or outsource your warehousing needs? Be sure to include the added expenses in your business plan. Your products are not only a space hog, but they involve an extra cost for storage. Inventory control becomes important—and not only for space concerns. Your inventory is your cash, your working capital. If it's all tied up in a slow-moving inventory, it impacts the operation of your entire business.

In the retail world, every square inch of shelf space is accounted for. For a product to stay on the shelves, it has to produce a certain amount of revenue. If not, most likely, it will go on clearance and disappear from the store forever. Unless you have room to spare, you don't want your products to sit idle, especially if you are paying for warehousing space. Move it or lose it! Every day that goes by, each item will cost you more. Why, you ask? Because you're paying to store it.

Setting Up Your Warehouse

Each warehouse layout is different and depends on your type of product, space, and process. Chapter 11, "High-Volume Product Store," explored Neeps, Inc., in detail to see how it set up its current warehouse. With more than 10 years of experience under its belt, Neeps has found a process that is efficient and effective. If you are planning on setting up your own warehouse, reread that chapter.

> **tip** Don't be afraid to ask other warehouse facilities or online stores about how they set up their warehouse. You'll be surprised at how helpful others will be. Learn from their mistakes and successes. Setting up your warehouse incorrectly can be costly, so this will save you a lot of agony.

Here are some considerations when warehousing your products at home and offsite:

- **Space**—How much space do you need? Is there room for growth?
- **Location**—Where will you place your products? In your garage, spare bedroom, closet, basement, attic, storage shed, self-storage facility, home office, rented space, or elsewhere?
- **Security**—How valuable is your merchandise? Will you need an alarm system or lock? Your warehouse might or might not have an alarm system built in.

- **Insurance**—Will you need additional insurance to cover your merchandise?
- **Loading**—Will it be easy to load and unload your products? If you are using your garage as your warehouse, you can just back up the car and unload. If you are using one of the rooms in the house, you mostly likely will need some type of dolly.
- **Loading ramp**—Does your warehouse have a loading ramp for your trucks? A loading ramp can be helpful especially if you are storing and shipping hundreds or thousands of products daily.
- **Shelves and racks**—How many shelves and racks will you need?

Getting Help

Are you planning to hire help to stock, manage, and ship your products? If so, you need a clear and easy-to-follow process of fulfilling your orders. Your process should be easy enough that a seasonal or temporary employee can begin work immediately. Your product information should also have a location code. Just because you know by memory where all the products are located does not mean that your employee will. Having a step-by-step order-fulfillment process reduces the amount of training your new employees will need. A good check-in and check-out procedure will also reduce the amount of spoilage, missing, not shipped and stolen inventory. Warehousing positions tend to have high turnover rates.

Inventory Control

Merchant Solutions has an inventory-management system that lets you set stock levels for your products. You can let your customers know whether your product is currently in stock. Setting inventory levels helps you avoid having to call a customer to let say that the desired product is not available.

Two methods are available if you choose to enable the Inventory Management feature: Real-time Inventory and Database Inventory. Real-time Inventory (available only with Merchant Standard and Professional package) enables you to check an external inventory file that's hosted on your own server or a third-party server. This is a necessity if you are using a third-party backend management system such as OrderMotion. Database Inventory is Yahoo!'s built-in inventory-management system. All you have to do is set inventory levels for each product in Catalog Manager. Every time an order is placed, the inventory amount is reduced by the amount in the order. You can also set up inventory level notification when an inventory level reaches a specific threshold.

You can let customers know whether the product is in stock in two ways. You can either display how many products are left or display a Yes or No (see Figure 20.1).

> **Yahoo! Talk**
> Database Inventory is Yahoo!'s built-in inventory-management system. You can use this system to set real-time inventory levels.

FIGURE 20.1
When Inventory Management is enabled, you can display the available units of a particular product when the customer adds an item to the shopping cart.

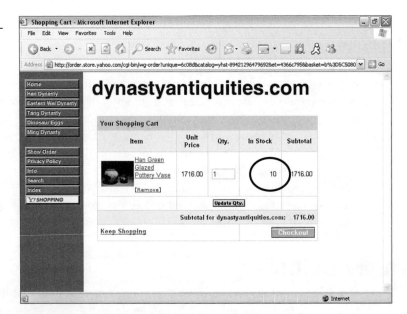

Setting Up Inventory Management

If you need to keep track of your inventory and let customers know whether your products are in stock, you need to enable and configure Inventory Management:

1. In Store Manager, click Configure Inventory under Order Settings.
2. Three inventory option choices are presented: None, Real-Time Inventory, and Database Inventory. Real-Time Inventory uses an inventory script that runs on your own server. For this example, we use Database Inventory because it can be configured using Merchant

Solutions. After you select Database Inventory and click the Modify Settings button, the page refreshes with additional configuration options.

Two additional sections appear when you select Database Inventory:

- **Alerts**—Send email alerts, set alert thresholds, and set the time and frequency of the alert emails.
- **Settings**—Allow the customer to see the availability or quantity of the product, set the default inventory quantity, and set whether the quantity can exceed availability. If you select No for the Quantity Can Exceed Availability setting, the following message is displayed: "None: Requested quantity not available for some items at this time."

When you have configured all your settings, you must input the inventory level for each of your product.

Yahoo! Talk Real-Time Inventory allows store owners to use a third-party order-management system such as OrderMotion.

Setting Inventory Levels

Setting inventory levels and alerts ensures that you will be notified if an inventory level reaches a certain threshold. This will give you adequate time to fulfill product inventory levels:

1. Click the Inventory link under Process in Store Manager.
2. Click the Edit button. The page refreshes and a Quantity field box appears for each item.
3. Enter the current inventory level for each item and click the Save button (see Figure 20.2).

FIGURE 20.2

You can enter current inventory levels in the Quantity field box.

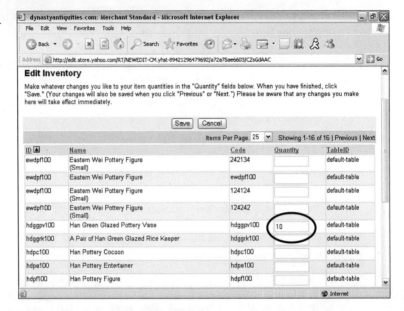

Setting Inventory Levels for Product Options

Inventory levels can be set for product options, but each option requires a unique code. For example, if you are selling T-shirts that are available in three different sizes, each size requires its own unique code. After you assign each option a code, the product option is displayed in the inventory listing. If you do not assign a code for each option, you can set only an inventory level for the product, not the options.

Here's how to assign a unique code to product options:

1. From the Store Manager, click the Catalog Manager link in the Edit column.

2. From Catalog Manger, click the Manage Your Items link. A list of your products is displayed. You can view up to 100 products at a time.

3. Click the product link you would like to add option codes to.

4. Scroll down until you see the Options field. You must define your options before you can enter your option codes. After you have defined your options, click the Enter Individual Items Code link underneath the Options field box (see Figure 20.3).

5. A page appears with blank code field boxes next to your specified options (see Figure 20.4). Select the corresponding option from the drop-down menu. The drop-down menu defaults to the first product option

CHAPTER 20 Warehousing and Inventory Control   291

defined in the items page. After you enter your new options code, click the *Save and Continue* button.

When you have completed entering the options code, you can go back to the Inventory page in Catalog Manager and enter the inventory level.

FIGURE 20.3
To enter options codes, click the Enter Individual Items Code link underneath the Options field box.

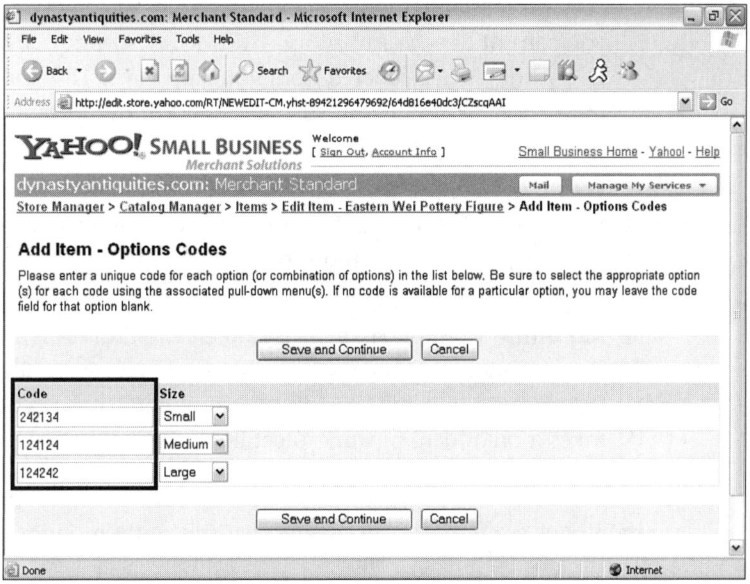

FIGURE 20.4
Enter product option codes in the blank fields next to each option.

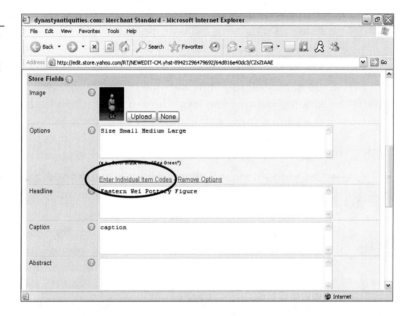

Your inventory-management procedure depends on the number of products you offer, the size of your company, and the volume of products you are selling.

Here's a list of things to consider when planning your inventory-management procedures:

- **Identification**—How will you identify each product? Will it be by name, SKU number, bar code, price, or your own unique code? If possible, use the product name as part of the identifier. Doing so enables you to immediately identify the product without having to look it up.
- **Documentation**—Make sure the procedures are well documented. This ensures that new employees have a reference and can repeat the same procedures. Include procedures for such issues as shipping, product holds, handling returns, damaged products, return-to-sender, invalid mailing addresses, lost mail, and order documentation.
- **Training**—If more than one person is helping you, make sure that everyone is properly trained using the documented procedures.
- **Accountability**—If you have employees, make sure they are accountable for their mistakes. If they do make mistakes, make sure they are quickly rectified, or have another training session with that employee. Also, have a procedure to quickly communicate with customers so they know what to expect. An apology often is needed as well.
- **Tracking**—Will you be able to track which item was shipped to which customer? Having good documentation and a tracking system gives you control of your inventory. This includes what has been received and what is back-ordered from your suppliers. This can be a great deal of work, especially if you carry products from multiple suppliers.
- **Re-evaluate**—Take a look at your procedures periodically. Make sure your processes are still effective, and determine whether any improvements can be made. Ask your assistants or employees whether they have any recommendations or changes on how the processes can be streamlined or improved.
- **Monitor**—Monitor the processes to ensure that all the steps are followed. Any missteps can cause the whole process to fail, thus making the tracking of inventory impossible. When things get out of control, it takes a great deal of work to get back on track—and it can be costly.

If you rely on a third party to stock and ship your products, make sure the company has enough of your inventory. Constantly monitor current inventory

Just-in-Time Delivery: Saving Money on Storage

If you manage your inventory correctly, you can save money on storage and storage space. Unless you have to purchase products in bulk to get a certain price break, you don't want to carry hundreds or thousands of the same product, only to move a few per month. Not only will your money be tied up in that product, but so will your warehousing space. Although the cost per product might be more, consider the cost of warehousing: The added cost per product could be cheaper than the cost to warehouse the product.

See if your supplier will be willing to drop-ship the products direct to the customer. Drop-shipping saves warehousing space and up-front inventory cost. If you decide to have items drop-shipped, consider using a more advanced backend system, such as OrderMotion (www.ordermotion.com), which automatically sends fulfillment notifications direct to the drop shipper.

> **tip** Instead of going direct to OrderMotion, you can reduce your startup cost and monthly cost by using Solid Cactus Complete Commerce (www.solidcactus.com), powered by OrderMotion. Complete Commerce is also fully customized for use with the Yahoo! store. For more information, visit www.myecommercesuccess.com.

> **warning**
> If you are both drop-shipping and shipping your own products, consider the extra shipping cost. If a customer orders a product that needs to be shipped by you and another product that needs to be shipped by the drop-shipper, you will need to ship two packages.

Using UPS Online Tools to Streamline Your Shipping Process

If you haven't selected a shipping partner yet, you might want to consider using UPS (United Parcel Service). UPS OnLine Tools is integrated with the Yahoo! store. This means a more streamlined shipping process by processing your shipments directly from your store's Order Manager.

Integration benefits include these:

- **Address validation**—No need to worry about customers entering incorrect city, state, and ZIP information. If customers make a mistake, the system alerts them with an error message. This avoids costly returns and delays in shipping.
- **UPS tracking**—Customers can track their shipment up to the minute right from the order status page. You can also create a Track Package search box on your website (see Figure 20.5). This reduces excessive inquiries of "Where is my order?" because the UPS tracking number is automatically inserted into each order.
- **UPS rates**—Customers can compare and select the shipping service that best fits their needs and budget.
- **UPS time in transit**—During the checkout process, a display shows the number of days in transit for each of your UPS shipping services within the United States.
- **Print labels**—You can print shipping labels right from the order screen with your own printer. No need to go down to the UPS Store—you can just schedule a UPS pickup.
- **UPS branding**—A "We ship via UPS" message is displayed during checkout and upon order confirmation. UPS's reliable service should make your customers feel secure about receiving their products.
- **Added handling fees**—You can add a handling fee on top of the UPS actual shipping fee by combining shipping rules. One rule uses the UPS Real-Time rates; the other adds a fee that you determine to every order. This not only covers the cost of packaging, but it also creates a buffer to cover the expenses of resending costs, or selecting faster and more expensive shipment options when you can't charge the customer for additional or multiple shipping. The extra dollar or two can also be a small profit center.

For additional information, visit http://promotions.yahoo.com/ups/static/merchant_center.html.

Web Resource For additional information and how to set up the UPS OnLine Tools, visit www.myecommercesuccess.com.

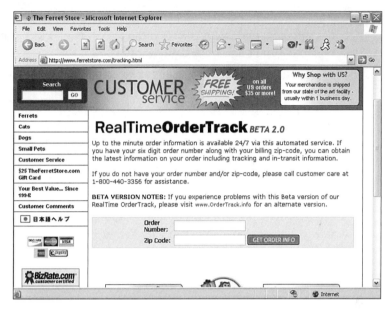

FIGURE 20.5
Allow customers to track their own shipments by creating an order status page. This reduces excessive inquiries of "Where is my order?"

Packaging Tips

Picking the right box: Pick a box with enough room to add cushioning material. Depending on the size of your products, you will most likely need a variety of different-sized boxes. Check with your shipping provider to see whether it offers free packaging material. If so, this will surely reduce the cost of shipping your products. If not, buy some boxes.

Choosing the right box also reduces the shipping cost. Depending on which shipping provider and method of shipping you use, most likely the size of the box will be part of the calculation when determining shipping cost. The bigger the box, the heavier it is, and the more wrap or packing peanuts you will need, the more it will cost.

Cushioning: Place cushioning around your items. Close and shake the box to see whether you have enough cushioning material around your items. Add newsprint (newspaper paper that has never been printed on—the ink on newspapers makes a real mess of things) and bubble-wrap if you hear the product shift.

If your items are fragile, consider double-cushioning your items and adding "Fragile" labels. For example, you might want to bubble-wrap your item and then add Styrofoam around it to keep it from shifting. Remember, a broken item has a domino effect: Not only will the product be returned, but you also will have to reship the item, delay the shipping time, lose revenue on additional shipping, and lose revenue on the broken item if it cannot be returned or replaced—and anger your customer, to boot.

Sealing your package: Use special packaging tape to seal your box. Choose clear or brown tape. Make sure all the seams and openings are taped. Don't use string or twine because the loose material can get caught in the mail-processing equipment. Place words on the shipping box such as "Fragile," "Electronics," "This Side Up," "Glass," or create other labels that might help with special handling.

Now that we've covered warehousing your product and managing your inventory using the Merchant Solutions resources, it's time to talk about money. In the next chapter, we cover the basic accounting statements that you will need to adequately and effectively run your Yahoo! business.

CHAPTER
21

Financial Planning

In This Chapter

- How to create a proforma
- How to create an income statement
- How to create a cash flow statement
- How to create a balance sheet

If you're going to make the transition from a part-time business to one that will become a primary source of income, you need to have a good idea of what money you'll need, where it goes, and how it's spent. You need a clear picture of your financial position at any one point in time.

To do that, you need a proforma (a projection of your revenue and expenses) and what's called in the accounting trade the Big 3 financial statements (income, cash flow, and balance sheets). The financial planning you do for your business is just as important as your business plan. If you have done your homework, the financial documents you have prepared can help you assess the ongoing operation of your business and the business assumptions you've made.

> **tip** **Don't Get Spreadsheetitis**
>
> Today's spreadsheet software makes it too easy to create multiple variations of financial documents. In the case of financial projections, less is more.

Include four comprehensive reports in your financial plan:

- Pro forma
- Income statement
- Cash flow statement
- Balance sheet

We cover the hows and whys of these as we move through this chapter. But before you do this, you must perform one important exercise: create your financial assumptions. For a more comprehensive understanding of financial statements, see *Write a Business Plan in No Time* (Que Publishing, 2005), by Frank Fiore.

The Proforma

A proforma is nothing but a projection of the assumptions you make of your business's expected revenue and expenses. Because you don't know for sure the number of sales you will make or the expenses you will incur until they happen, your proforma acts as a blueprint—or let's say, blue-sky projection—of your business one, two, or three years in the future.

But if it's all projections, what use is it?

The proforma can give you a clear view of the financial viability of your business. The proforma shows where your money has come from and where it could be spent over a specific period of time, usually on an annual basis—January through December—or your tax year. It also acts as a guide that you can check against as your business develops during the year, and it allows you to revise your assumptions on a monthly basis to better match the reality of your business.

As your business year progresses, your proforma comes closer to reality and becomes a very important window on the performance of your Yahoo! store and the initial projections you created.

Where to Start

Always begin your financial assumption with projected sales because this number drives all others. When you have your sales projections, describe your cost of goods. This is the costs that go into making your product, or what it costs to acquire the product from your supplier, distributor, or wholesaler. For example, if you make and sell wooden toys, the cost of goods would be the cost of the wood, nails, and paint—the material—needed to build the wooden toys.

Next are your expense assumptions. These include all the expenses that your company will incur on a regular basis, including rent, postage, shipping costs, personnel, equipment, telephone service, and marketing expenses, to name a few.

> **warning**
>
> **Be Realistic with Projections**
>
> A good rule of thumb to keep in mind is to overstate your expenses and understate your revenues. This will give you a conservative proforma and one that could be closer to reality.

Let's take a look at a basic proforma:

- **Gross income**—This is the gross sales from revenue from your products or services. It includes all the income generated by the business and its sources.
- **Cost of goods sold**—This is the actual cost of the products, materials, or ingredients you purchase or manufacture for resale.
- **Gross profit or gross revenue**—This is the difference between your gross income and your cost of goods sold. Gross profit can be expressed in dollars, as a percentage, or both. As a percentage, the gross profit is always stated as a percentage of revenue. For example, if you sell a product for $10 and it costs you $9 to make, your gross profit is $1, or 10%.

- **Expenses**—These include your start-up expenses and ongoing operating expense, as well as all overhead and labor expenses of the operations of the business. In other words, they include fixed expenses that must be paid at the same rate, regardless of the volume of business (including rent, utilities, salaries, and wages), and variable expenses, which change based on the amount of business you do (including advertising, sales commissions, freight, and supplies).
- **Total expenses**—The total of all expenses.
- **Net profit (or loss)**—Gross profit or gross revenue minus total expenses before taxes.

Here's a simple format to use when creating your proforma. Use a spreadsheet program, such as Microsoft Excel, to enter your line items and quantitative numbers.

Proforma

Income

1. Gross sales
2. Cost of sales
3. Gross profit (1 minus 2)

Expenses

1. Variable expenses
    a. Advertising
    b. Freight
    c. Shipping costs
    d. Credit card costs
    e. Parts and supplies
    f. Sales salaries
    g. Postage
    h. Legal and accounting fees
2. Fixed expenses
    a. Insurance
    b. Licenses and permits
    c. Office salaries
    d. Rent
    e. Utilities
    f. Fixed salaries and wages, and tax withholdings
    g. Phone service
    h. Equipment lease

Total expenses

Income from operations

(Gross sales minus expenses)

Income before income taxes (called IBIT)

This is just a simple statement. Your proforma could be different and could have many more line items, depending upon the complexity of your business. And if you plan to offer health insurance or other benefits, you need to enter that expense as a line item in your proforma.

After you've determined and described your business assumptions in your proforma, it's time to create the Big 3 of your financial plan:

- Income statement
- Cash flow statement
- Balance sheet

Organizing Your Financial Statements

At first, you might be intimidated by the task of forecasting the finances of your business. But in reality, it's not so bad if you plan well. Valid financial projections consist of making educated guesses of how much money you'll take in and how much you'll need to spend. Then, use these estimates to calculate whether your business will be profitable.

Let's look at the income statement first.

> **tip** **Know the Credit Card Costs**
>
> A company that does not take and process credit cards in today's business environment is a company that is running on only one cylinder of eight cylinders. But setting up a merchant account to accept and process credit cards presents a series of costs that you need to reflect in your income statement.
>
> The costs of accepting and processing credit cards can include some or all of the following:
>
> - **Set-up fees**—These are the cost to you for the bank setting up your account.
> - **Sizable deposit**—If you are a new business, the bank might require a deposit up to six months of projected credit card sales.
> - **Discount rate**—This is the personate of the sale that the bank will charge for processing the credit card. This "discount" rate can be between 1% and 5% of your sale.
> - **Transaction fees**—This is another fee added per credit card charge processed.
> - **Monthly statement fee.**
> - **Minimum processing fee**—Some banks charge a minimum processing fee if the transaction fee is too low.
> - **Chargebacks**—This is the fee a bank charges if a customer disputes a charge and the bank refunds the money.
>
> The discount rate and fees, and the set-up costs go under "Credit Card Expenses" on your proforma.

Creating Your Income Statement

Your income statement is synopses of revenue, expenses, and profits of your proforma statement. The income statement gives you a quick bird's-eye view of the expected performance of your business.

A simple income statement looks like this.

	Year 1	Year 2	Year 3
Sales of . . .			
Other sales			
Total sales			
Cost of goods			
Gross profit			
Variable expenses			
Fixed expenses			
Net income			

But many businesses forget one financial statement, which can tank even the most successful-looking business in a proforma or income statement: a company's cash flow statement. Projected profits don't guarantee money in the bank.

Creating Your Cash Flow Statement

Even if your proforma tells you that your business will become profitable, unfortunately, those projections can't tell you if you will have enough cash on hand at any given time to cover your monthly expenses, or even to pay for your inventory or materials to offer the products or services you sell.

That's the purpose of a cash flow statement, one of the most critical tools for the evaluation of your business. It tells you how much money you must have on hand or available to draw on to stay in business while you are becoming profitable. Many a company has failed because of a lack of cash flow. A company might show a profit, but its cash is tied up in inventory and others that owe them money on sales. A necessary amount of working capital is critical to a company's success.

As with the income statement, the numbers and projections from your proforma flow into the cash flow statement. You begin your cash flow statement with the money you have on hand and the money that is available for you to draw on. For example, this includes the amount of money you have in the bank, the cash available on your credit cards, or a business loan or personal credit line from your bank.

The cash flow statement doesn't have to be long or involved. It should cover only the key elements of your cash flow projections.

When you've determined the cash resources you have on hand or available to you, make a list of expenses, including any expenses incurred when manufacturing a product for sale. Then, subtract the expenses from the total cash available. The result is a net cash flow—positive or negative. If the net cash flow is negative, you need to increase the cash available for the business, even if your proforma and income statement show profit.

Here's what a simple cash flow statement includes:

1. Start with a beginning cash balance of your business in Month 1. As mentioned before, this is the total of cash on hand plus the monetary resources you can draw on.
2. Then, add the cash receipts from sales or the revenue generated for the month from all sources. The total of the beginning cash balance and cash receipts from sales gives you your total cash available.
3. Then, subtract your monthly expenses and all accounts payable (the money you owe suppliers for inventory or manufacturing materials). This gives you a total cash disbursements figure.
4. Subtract the total cash disbursements from the total cash available. You end up with your net cash from operations for the month.
5. You then carry this net cash from operations to the next month, and that becomes your new beginning cash balance.
6. From here, you create the next month of your cash flow statement. Create all following months the same way.

A simple cash flow statement or projection looks like this.

	Month 1	Month 2	Month 3
Beginning cash balance			
Cash receipts from sales			
Total cash available			
Cash disbursements			
Total cash disbursements			
Net cash from operations			

A profitable income statement might make you smile, but if you run out of cash to operate your business, you might have to close your doors.

Creating Your Balance Sheet

As with the income statement and cash flow statement, the balance sheet uses the information from your proforma projections.

A balance sheet consists of three basic parts:

- Company assets
- Company liabilities
- Equity of the company

Company assets means anything a business owns that has a monetary value, such as cash on hand; receivables (customers and vendors that owe your company money); the value of a company's inventory on hand; other inventory items, such as office and shipping supplies or manufacturing supplies; and any prepaid expenses or deposits. Prepaid expenses are those that are fully paid for in advance, such as insurance premiums and maintenance contracts. Deposits are funds that are paid but that a company fully expects to have returned after a period of time, such as deposits on equipment rentals. Also included in the company assets are long-term assets, or fixed assets, such as manufacturing equipment, and long-term investments in financial instruments that cannot be readily converted to cash.

Company liabilities are monies owed to vendors and creditors. These include accounts payable, accrued liabilities (accrued expenses that not been paid out yet, such as salaries and overhead), and city, state, and federal taxes. Other long-term liabilities include bonds payable that are due at the end of the year, mortgages or loans, and any amount still owned on long-term debts such as notes.

A company's equity is equal to the company's net worth. After the assets and liabilities have been entered into the balance sheet, you can compute the equity of your company. You arrive at this number by subtracting company liabilities from your company assets. This number is important to investors because this is how they calculate the amount they will invest in your business.

A simple balance sheet looks like this.

Current	Year 1	Year 2	Year 3
Assets			
Cash			
Receivables			
Inventory			
Prepays			
Fixed assets			
Total assets			
Liabilities			
Payables			
Taxes			
Notes			
Bonds			
Other debts			
Total liabilities			
Company equity			
Total assets minus total liabilities			

Quick Steps to Creating Your Financials

Answer the questions that follow, and you're on your way to a set of useful financials.

Creating your proforma:

- What are your gross sales from revenue from your products or services per month? Include all the income generated by the business and its sources.
- What is your cost of goods sold per month? This is the actual cost of the products, materials, or ingredients you purchase or manufacture for resale.
- What is your gross profit or gross revenue per month? This is the difference between your gross income and your cost of goods sold. Gross profit can be expressed in dollars, as a percentage, or both. As a percentage, the gross profit is always stated as a percentage of revenue.

- What are your variable expenses per month? Variable expenses are those that change based on the amount of business you do, such as advertising, sales commissions, freight, and supplies.
- What are your fixed expenses per month? Fixed expenses are paid at the same rate, regardless of the volume of business, such as rent, utilities, salaries, and wages.
- What are your total expenses per month? These include both fixed and variable expenses.
- What is your net profit or loss per month? This includes gross profit or gross revenue minus total expenses before taxes.

Creating your income statement:

- What are your total sales for each year?
- Do you have revenue from other types of sales? If so, add them into your income.
- What is your cost of goods sold for each year?
- What is the gross profit for each year?
- What are your variable expenses for each year?
- What are your fixed expenses for each year?
- What is your net income for each year?

Creating your cash flow statement:

- What is the beginning cash balance for the month?
- What are the cash receipts from sales for the month?
- What is the total cash available? Add the beginning cash balance to cash receipts from sales.
- What are the different cash disbursements for the month? This includes the monthly expenses and all accounts payable (the money you owe suppliers for inventory or manufacturing materials).
- What are the total cash disbursements for the month?
- What is the net cash from operations? Subtract the total cash disbursements from the total cash available to get the net cash from operations for the month.
- Carry the net cash from operations to the next month. That becomes your new beginning cash balance.

Creating your balance sheet:

- What are your company assets? Include all cash, receivables, inventory, prepays, and fixed assets.
- What are your total company assets?
- What are your company liabilities? These include all payables, taxes, notes, bonds, and other debts.
- What are your total company liabilities?
- What is the equity of your company? This is your total assets minus your total liabilities.

A good set of financials offers you a valuable window into the operations of your business and can be a great planning tool to reach the objectives and goals of your Yahoo! store. In the next chapter, we look at the process of finding and hiring a staff for your business, and the duties required of them to successfully run your Yahoo! store.

Part VI

Manning Your Yahoo! Business

22 Finding and Hiring

CHAPTER

22

Finding and Hiring

In This Chapter

- Assigning and understanding staff duties
- Independent contractors versus employees
- Where to find and hire employees
- How to keep good employees
- How to get free help

Sooner or later, your online business will grow to a point that you need to hire additional help. You're starting to spend too much of your time doing administrative tasks, such as packaging, shipping, and customer support, when you should be spending your time managing and growing your business. Store owners sometimes find themselves getting burned out by trying to handle every aspect of their business themselves (accounting, shipping, packaging, customer support, inventory control, marketing, and so on).

Knowing when to call in the cavalry not only will save your sanity, but also will enable you to concentrate on growing and operating your business.

Ask yourself these questions before you start the hiring process:

- Do I need full-time, part-time, or intermittent help?
- Do I need specific help, such as in accounting, or someone who can do a variety of task (answer phones, run errands, process orders, and so on)?
- Is physical location important? Do I need that person to come to my location, or can that person work from home or offsite? And do I have the space for that person to work in my home?

In this chapter, we cover everything from where to find help to staff duties.

Assigning and Understanding Staff Duties

So who does what? Understanding what is involved with operating an online store not only helps you assign tasks, but it also assists you in hiring help. The following is a list of typical duties of running an online store. Also, don't forget to check out Appendix A, "Launching Your Yahoo! Business Quick Start Guide."

- **Customer support**—This means making sure all support telephone calls and emails are answered promptly. Customers usually contact you for more information about a product, the delivery of a product, support for a product, or the return of the product.
- **Order processing**—When you receive the order, the order credit card needs to be verified and processed. A packaging slip also needs to be printed for fulfillment.
- **Fulfillment**—Products must be packaged and shipped. This includes printing any labels, adding cushioning, and either taking the packages to the shipment location or arranging a pickup.

- **Marketing**—This includes creating, managing, and monitoring advertising campaigns. It includes pay per click (PPC), banner advertising, affiliate marketing, link exchanges, search-engine placement, print advertisements, and more.
- **Inventory management**—Monitor and fulfill inventory levels. When a product reaches a certain threshold, you must contact the vendor to order additional products.
- **Vendor management**—Depending on how many vendors you use, managing all of them can be very time consuming. Not only do you have to monitor your inventory levels, but you also need to monitor their inventory levels. Ordering multiple products from multiple vendors can be confusing.
- **Website updates**—Content is king! Keeping your site fresh with new content, products, and specials gets your customers to return to your site. You need to constantly update your website. Updates also include content writing, adding new products, testing new sales copy, developing promotional items, and contributing to your blog or product reviews.
- **Graphic design**—Business cards, banners, postcards, email newsletters, flyers, Web graphics, and product photos should all designed and developed by a graphic designer.
- **Accounting**—You need to know how much is going out and how much is going in. Accounting duties include credit card processing, credit card refunds, invoice payments, deposit verification from merchant accounts, and employee salary payments.

Understanding every single aspect of operating your business will help you figure out if the duty should be outsourced or brought internal. It will also help you write job descriptions when placing ads.

Outsourcing

The first thing you need to consider is outsourcing. Should you hire an employee or outsource the service? Both methods have their pros and cons. You will find that not all positions can be outsourced. For example, if you need help packing and shipping and your inventory is stored at your location, you need to hire someone unless you plan to outsource your storage as well.

Outsourcing can even be less expensive than hiring an employee. Some outsourcing companies do not have monthly fees; they charge only when a service or transaction is done on your behalf. The per-service or transaction fee can easily be calculated to determine what your bottom-line profit margin or ROI will be per order. Outsourcing services are usually handled by a company and not an individual. Therefore, a team of people usually service your needs. This way, you don't have to worry about coverage if someone is sick or goes on leave.

Nowadays, every aspect of your business can be outsourced. The question is whether it should be done and whether it makes financial sense. Speak to other online stores to see what portions of their business are outsourced and whether they recommend a particular company. YStore Forums (http://newforums.ystoretools.com) is a great resource to chat with other Yahoo! store merchants.

Independent Contractor Versus Employee

Should you hire an employee or independent contractor? Hiring a company employee requires you to provide benefits and pay employee income taxes, Social Security taxes, and Medicare taxes that could amount to almost 35% of an employee's wages. If you contract out the work to an independent contractor, you can just file a federal income tax form (Form 1099) at the end of the year; it will be the independent contractor's responsibility to pay taxes and seek benefits.

Who is an independent contractor? According to the IRS, a general rule is that you, the payer, have the right to control or direct only the result of the work done by an independent contractor, not the means and methods of accomplishing the result. You cannot tell independent contractors when they can work or not work. If you incorrectly classify an employee as an independent contractor, you can be held liable for employment taxes for that worker, plus a penalty.

For additional information, visit www.irs.gov and search for the article "Independent Contractor vs. Employees."

The Hiring Process

There are six essential steps in the hiring process. The process can take days, weeks, or even months, depending on how fast you can review the resumes, schedule the interviews, and make your final decision:

1. **Define the position**—Write a detailed job description and list of duties. Establish the salary range for the position.

2. **Post job listing**—Contact local newspapers or online websites to place a job vacancy ad. Your local Craig's List (www.**craigslist**.org) is great and free.

3. **Accept and review resumes**—Accept resumes either via email or by mail. Have a check off list of requirements to filter qualified applicants. Be prepared. Depending on your job market, you could receive more than 450 applications per week. In addition, there are rules regarding applications. You must keep *all* applications for a minimum of one year. Check with your local employee office.

4. **Schedule and interview candidates**—Call applicants to schedule an appointment for an in-office interview. You can also conduct a phone interview to further filter applicants.

5. **Screen applicants**—Perform background checks and verify references. Use a personal reference when hiring—someone who can vouch for the potential employee. If you don't know whom you're hiring, get what's called a credit and criminal background check. You can do this through your county office administration or, even more easily, online. The cost is roughly $49, and the benefit is worth every dollar. You will need permission from applicants, so get them to sign a release/permission form that includes social security number and other information necessary to perform the check.

6. **Make an offer**—When you select the top candidate, you can either call or send the applicant an offer letter. List the proposed salary and benefits.

Hiring the Right Person

Hiring the right person for the job can sometimes be a crapshoot. The right person will help you grow and run your business smoothly, and the wrong person will be a thorn in your side, just slowing you down. Although websites and newspapers can help you find people who are actively looking for employment, the best candidate might already have a job and isn't actively looking. That's when networking comes in. Ask friends, family, community business members, and even your employees to recommend or keep their eye open for someone. That diamond in the rough might want a change but is not actively seeking employment. Great jobs are nearly always filled through referrals.

Where to Find and Hire Employees

To find employees, you can place an ad in the local newspaper or use online job sites. Depending on which site you use, you might pay a fee to post a job listing.

For local print listings, contact your local newspaper. These sites are currently the hot job destination websites. The sites not only have a national reach, but they also can be narrowed by city:

- Yahoo! HotJobs (www.hotjobs.com)
- Monster (www.monster.com)
- Craigslist (www.craigslist.org)
- CareerBuilder (www.careerbuilder.com)

Posting your job listing on any of these online websites will get you plenty of resumes.

Interviewing Candidates

After you review the sea of resumes from your job listing, it's time to select a few candidates and start the interview process. You can either begin with a telephone interview or schedule an in-person interview. An initial phone interview is best to filter applicants who either exaggerated on their resume or were not very clear about the specific qualifications you were looking for. Some applicants might not even know exactly what the job entails. The initial phone interview helps you screen applicants so that you don't waste your time or theirs.

When you schedule an interview, you will want to develop a set of interview questions. Having a standard set of questions helps you compare apples to apples. You can always have the applicants elaborate on each question, but this helps give you a starting point.

> **Web Resource**
>
> **Developing Interview Questions**
>
> Monster (www.interview.monster.com) has a list of the top common interview questions. Although it's geared toward the interviewee, you can use the list to get ideas for your own questions.

After you interview all the candidates and make your final decision, don't wait to long to make an offer. The longer you wait, the more likely it is that person will accept an offer from another company. Snatch up your new talent as quickly as possible. Contact candidates in writing, by letter, or, better, via email.

Screening Backgrounds and Checking References

Before making an offer, prescreen your applicants by performing background and reference checks. You want to make sure that no part of the resume or interview answers was fabricated.

Benefits of prescreening applicants include the following:

- Discourages applicants who are hiding something
- Saves time, resources, and money recruiting, hiring, and training
- Reduces the chance of injury to employees
- Reduces employee theft
- Reduces employment turnover
- Reduces insurance premiums
- Protects against negligent-hiring lawsuits
- Eliminates uncertainties in the hiring process

You can perform employment background checks by using services such as Verified Person, at www.verifiedperson.com (see Figure 22.1).

Its services include the following:

- Social Security number verification
- State and county criminal search
- Nationwide criminal search
- Federal criminal search
- Ongoing criminal screening
- Enhanced sex offender search
- Education verification
- Employment verification
- Professional license verification
- Pre-employment credit history
- Motor vehicle records
- Reference checks
- Workers' compensation
- U.S. government terrorist watch list search

- Drug screening
- International criminal searches

Pricing varies, depending on how much information you need to verify.

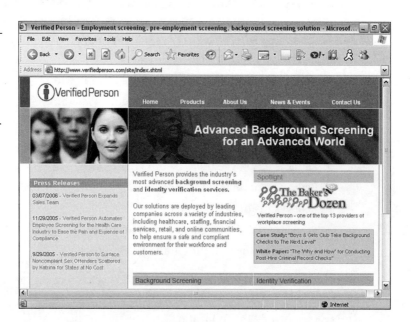

FIGURE 22.1
Verified Person performs employment background checks. Services include SSN verification, criminal records search, employment verification, and drug screening.

Hiring Family and Friends

Asking your friends and family to pitch in is great, especially if you need them only periodically. But be aware that hiring loved ones can be tricky—or worse. Remember, you're running a real business, and sometimes, you need to make business decisions. As they say in mobster movies, "It's only business." Your business decisions and choices are not personal, but your family and friends might not see it that way. Let's take a look at some of the advantages and disadvantages of hiring family and friends.

Advantages of hiring family:

- Family members and close friends might be more committed than the average employee: They might see your business as an extension of the family and want to see it grow.
- They will often work nights and weekends, if necessary.
- You know them well and are familiar with their capabilities and shortcomings.

- You trust them with the most important and delicate elements of the business, including cash and inventory.

Disadvantages of hiring family:

- Other employees might feel that there is nepotism, especially if friends or family are given a higher position or increased pay.
- Family could take advantage of their status because they know it will be hard to fire them.
- Family issues could be brought into the workplace. The line between your personal life and professional life might become blurred.
- Your close relationships with your family and friends might turn sour if business becomes personal.

Make sure that the person you hire actually has the skill set to perform the duties. Have a detailed job description so there are no misunderstandings or surprises. If possible, have friends and family members work under managers who are not related to them.

How Much Should I Pay?: Setting Pay Levels

Setting your pay scale too low will not attract the experienced applicants you are looking for. Setting your pay scale too high might give you an expectation the person cannot achieve. The more important a person is to the ongoing success of the organization, the more the person should be paid. Employees usually fall into four main categories: indispensable, valuable, average, and replaceable. Placing each employee into one of these categories will help you determine where they should fall in the pay range. Remember that any employee can rise from one category into the next over time. As a result of improved performance, this will earn them an increase in salary. You can measure these milestones through quarterly or yearly performance reviews.

Yahoo! HotJobs (www.salary.hotjobs.com) has a free salary wizard that shows you what the salary ranges are for almost every position. You can even drill down to your particular city (see Figure 22.2). The data is collected from thousands of HR departments at employers of all sizes, industries, and geographies, to show you the base, median, and high salary range.

Another great way to find out what other employers are paying for similar positions is to visit online jobs sites and search for the same position. Most often, employers will display their pay range for that position.

FIGURE 22.2

Yahoo! HotJobs (www.salary.hotjobs.com) has a free salary wizard that shows you the salary ranges for almost every position.

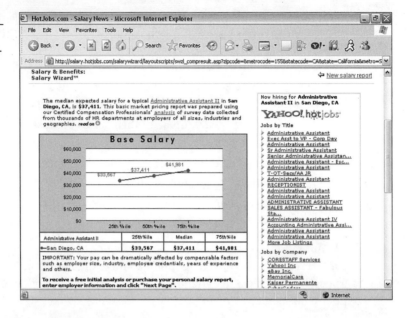

Getting Part-Time Help

If you need help only a few days a week or even a few hours a week, you need to hire someone on a part-time basis. Hiring someone part-time also eliminates major benefit expenses. Students and stay-at-home parents are excellent candidates for part-time employment. They usually have other commitments during the day, such as kids and school, but they also want to make a little extra money for other expenses.

Local community and college newspapers usually have part-time employment sections. Also, ask neighbors and friends to see if they know anyone who is seeking part-time employment. High school and college kids are great for this—they're flexible, intelligent, and inexpensive.

Getting Free Help

Free help? Sound too good to be true? Yes, you can get free help by hiring college interns. College students are always looking for internships for school credit and real work experience. Contact your local colleges to place an ad. Most colleges will even put you in direct contact with the professors who teach the type of job duties the interns will be performing. The professors will usually recommend or advertise the position for you personally. It's a win-win for you and the student. Students in the fields of business, information technology, and marketing, among others, often make excellent interns.

> **tip** **Motivating Unpaid Interns and Volunteers**
>
> When the position does not involve money, offering employee discounts, free meals, and other gifts will help motivate and retain your employees.

> **warning**
>
> **Be Flexible: Retain Those Interns**
>
> Because of school and possible other part-time jobs, intern schedules are very sporadic. Being flexible and willing to adjust will help you retain those interns. With every new school semester or quarter, their school schedule will change.

Keeping Good Employees

High employee turnover is one of the leading factors in the failure of many small businesses. Are you doing everything you can to keep your talented employee pool? Besides for the obvious reasons of higher salary and better benefits, employees leave for different reasons. Money isn't everything. Improving the work environment and offering little incentives as an appreciation for work well done goes a long way.

Here are a few tips for keeping good employees:

- **Offer office perks**—Provide free snacks and soda. You can even bring in baked goods and breakfast bagels once in a while.
- **Schedule Friday lunches**—Buy lunch for the office. This costs only an extra $4 to $6 per employee, and it's a great way to start the weekend and to say thank you for the hard work during the week. It's also a good way to get everyone together to talk about what's going right and what's going wrong each week. It's great for brainstorming.
- **Be flexible**—With family schedules and other commitments, some employees need a flexible schedule. For some, it's not about the money, but the time. Keeping their at-home life happy translates into a happy

workplace. If you're flexible, your employees will bend over backward to go the extra mile.

- **Provide comfort**—Give your employees comfortable chairs and good lighting. Imagine spending all day sitting in an uncomfortable chair: It could be worse than sitting on an airplane. This will also reduce worker's compensation.
- **Listen to your employees**—Listening to their ideas and points of view will help them feel like they are part of the team. Who knows? An employee might come up with that winning strategy. (It often happens!)
- **Offer incentives**—Develop one-time incentive programs and goals, either individual based or project based. This will give your employees a sense of ownership and pride.
- **Reduce employee friction**—Keep your ears to the ground. Employee friction can cause stress and tension in the whole office. Reduce friction by attacking the issues head on and early. Gossip can kill your company.
- **Focus job duties**—Create job duties that are a good match for employees. Some companies encourage their employees to apply for other positions within the company if they don't like theirs or want a new challenge. This way, you keep your employees within the same company. This can be a great value because these people are already familiar with the company and process.
- **Foster trust**—Build trust between employees and management. Management should be approachable. New ideas and issues will never float to the top if employees don't feel that they can speak to their management team.
- **Talk to your employees**—Stop them in the hall and ask how they are doing. Show them you care how they are doing.
- **Encourage growth**—Make room for your talent to grow. Continuously challenge employees and let them strive for advancement. Other top reasons for people leaving their jobs are that they are not challenged, there is no room for growth, and they are bored with what they are doing.

Remember, it costs less to offer little incentives than it does to find, hire, and train a new employee.

If you follow the advice and instructions we have provided here for your Yahoo! store, you will be well on your way to succeeding with your Yahoo! business.

Appendixes

A Launching Your Yahoo! Business Quick Start Guide

B Business Plan Elements

C Important Resources on the Web

Launching Your Yahoo! Business Quick Start Guide

If you have not yet set up a Yahoo! store with Merchant Solutions, this quick start guide will help you through the process. For further details, refer to the book *Launching Your Yahoo! Business* (Que, 2006). Each step refers to a chapter within that book.

Step 1: Register your domain name and sign up for a Yahoo! Merchant Solutions account.

To sign up for a Merchant Solutions account, go to www.smallbusiness.yahoo.com/merchant. You can choose from three packages. The starter package starts at $39.95. You can also save 25% for three months, plus enjoy a waived setup fee on new Yahoo! Web hosting and e-commerce accounts by visiting www.myecommerce-success.com to receive your discount code.

- Registering your domain name: Chapter 4
- Selecting a Merchant Solutions package: Chapter 8

Step 2: Explore the Manage My Services control panel.

From here, you can go to the Store Manager to work on your store; the Web Hosting Control Panel to view stats, manage files, and view recent backups; the Domain Control Panel to manage advance DNS settings and subdomains; and the Email Control Panel to manage and create email accounts.

- Manage My Services control panel: Chapter 9

Step 3: Set up the capability to accept payments online. Sign up for a merchant account or use your existing merchant account.

A merchant account is required to accept all major credit cards, including Visa, Master Card, American Express, and Discover. With Merchant Solutions, you can choose to apply for Paymentech (www.paymentech.com)—Yahoo! Merchant Solutions' preferred provider—or any other compatible First Data Merchant Services (FDMS) merchant account (see www.fdms.com).

You can also use PayPal as your online payment-processing service if you do not want to use a merchant account.

- Setting up your merchant account: Chapter 10
- Signing up with Paymentech: Chapter 10
- Using your own merchant account: Chapter 10

Step 4: Organize and add products to your store.

Catalog Manager is a built-in tool that enables you to manage your inventory of products, including pricing and product descriptions about each item. You can enter your products one by one using Store Editor or Catalog Manager.

> **note** If you will be using the Database Upload feature to upload your products in bulk, refer to Chapter 6, "Yahoo! Store Features and Advanced Techniques."

- Adding products: Chapter 9
- Adding products with Store Editor: Chapter 9
- Adding products with Catalog Manager: Chapter 9

Step 5: Customize your store layout and navigation.

Customize your store layout and design by configuring colors, typeface, image dimensions, page layout, button properties, and page properties.

- Customizing your store: Chapter 9

> **note** If you plan to customize your site by using RTML templates instead of the default Store Editor, refer to Chapter 5, "Customizing Your Yahoo! Store."

Step 6: Configure your backend systems and operations.

After you select a shipping company and your shipping methods, you need to configure those options for the order form. You also need to set up your tax tables. Will you charge tax for orders that originate from your state only? You must configure the tax tables before you publish your store. You can also set up Inventory Management to notify customers if your product is in stock. You can also set thresholds to alert you when a product reaches a certain number.

- Setting up shipping options: Chapter 10
- Setting up tax tables: Chapter 10
- Setting up order notifications: Chapter 10
- Setting up Inventory Management: Chapter 10

Step 7: Publish your site; open your store for business.

When you've finished configuring your backend system, adding your products, and customizing your store layout and navigation, you're ready to publish your site and open for business!

- Publishing your site: Chapter 9
- Publishing your order settings: Chapter 10

APPENDIX B

Business Plan Elements

What comes out of a business plan depends on what goes into it. A successful implementation of a business idea starts with a solid and well-organized plan. For more on how to write a proper business plan, see *Write a Business Plan in No Time* (Que, 2005), by Frank Fiore.

Your plan must clearly communicate who you are, what you do, what your product or service is, what consumer or business need it solves, how you plan to implement your business, what markets you will service, and how much money or how many resources you will need to execute your plan.

So let's take a look at the essential questions that every business plan must answer to help you succeed in your new endeavor.

Who Is Your Business?

Be clear on who you are in your business plan. Why? Well, for example, if you're going to seek funding for your business idea, investors and bankers will surely want to know who they are dealing with. They will want to know about your experience, your skills, and your role in the business you chose. In addition, they will want to know who will supply the business experience and expertise you lack, and your plans on how to acquire that extra talent.

Finally, what is your business? What is your legal structure? Is it a sole proprietorship? A partnership? A corporation?

What Does It Sell?

The purpose of a business is to sell something: a product, a service, or information. In any case, your business plan must explain in detail what kind of product or service you plan to sell. What is it? What makes it unique? How does it compare with your competition? Does the competition dominate your market niche? If so, can a newcomer break into the market? How do you plan to compete? Do you have a competitive advantage? Is your product as good as your competition? Is it better? Why?

You must also look ahead. When you're established in the marketplace, can a new company easily undercut your prices or your earnings with a newer product or service? Do you have a barrier to competition? If so, what is it?

Why Is It a Business? What Need Does It Solve?

You must clearly explain how your product meets a consumer need. To do that, you must identify your target customers and explain how your product or service will meet their needs. Who are you targeting? Consumers? Retailers? Wholesalers? The government? Is your product practical? Will it fill a need? What need?

You also need to identify where or how you will be acquiring your product. Who are your suppliers? And who are your backup suppliers if your primary ones fail to deliver? If you are manufacturing your own product, who is supplying your parts?

Finally, where will your business be located? What physical location will be necessary? Office space? Retail space? Warehouse space? Will there be a combination of some sort? Are you starting a home-based business? If so, do you have space in your home? Where will you locate it? What about your community's CC&Rs? Are there conditions and restrictions on what you can use your home for? Will they allow for a home business such as yours?

What Is the Implementation Plan?

A business plan will do you little good if you don't have a strategy to implement it. How many months of zero revenue will be needed to start up your business? Do you have a phased plan for development, complete with what you want to accomplish, by when and what must take place before each phase happens? What are your major decision points? What milestones do you want to hit, and by when? What actions do you need to take to meet those milestones?

Your implementation plan and your proforma provide a yardstick for measuring how well your plan is being executed. Investors and bankers who are funding your idea with venture capitol or loans will want to see an implementation plan and how well you're hitting your targets. Are your target goals realistic? Does your plan support your belief that the goals are achievable?

In summary, an implementation plan lays out your company's objectives, the tasks or actions necessary to reach those objectives, a timescale of events or actions, and a way to monitor your progress.

Where Is Your Business and What Markets/Customers Will It Service?

Who will buy your product? What are the demographics of your target market? Where do your customers live, work, and shop? Do they shop online? What online areas do they frequent? Then, back up your findings with real data from private, public, or government sources, such as census information, databases, and industry information. What is the potential size of your market? How big of a piece of the market can you garnish of your business? How do you feel you can serve this market? Why?

How Will You Market Your Business and Your Product or Service?

What are your plans for marketing your business? Are they realistic and based upon your proposed marketing budget in your financials? What is your overall marketing strategy? How will your choice of marketing vehicle help you reach your target market? What advertising media will you use? Print? TV? Radio? The Internet? Some combination of these? Will you use direct mail or telemarketing to reach potential customers? How will you use public relations in your marketing mix? Will you also include trade shows, seminars, and workshops in your marketing plan? How will you use them? Where and when?

How your business plan answers these questions is critical to the success of your company.

How Much Money Will You Need to Get Your Business Started and Running?

What is your source of funds and resources? Will you need financing? What kind? Equity? Debt? A combination of both? How much will your business need to reach the break-even point? How much will you need to meet your sales and revenue projections? What personal resources will you contribute to the business? If you're seeking a loan from a bank, your friendly banker will want to know what kind of financial risk you're personally taking.

What about human resources? Who will you need to hire and how much will they cost? What technical resources will you need? Where will you buy them? How much will they cost? Will you need some conventional or special business insurance? What is it? What will it cost?

Pulling It Together: The Business Plan Elements

The structure of a business plan is not random: It has a logical progression of thought. The marketing plan comes after the information on your product or service, but before your implementation and financial information. As for the other parts, the order in which they appear in your plan depends upon the best way you feel you can communicate and sell your business concept.

Certain parts of a standard business plan might not apply to your business. But all plans should answer two basic questions:

- Is this a product or service that people will buy?
- Are you the right person to make your idea a success?

Organizing your plan in a way that answers these questions will determine how successful your plan will be in garnishing resources and support.

Let's look at the basic elements that make up a business plan:

- Your executive summary
- Your company mission and objectives
- An overview of your company

- A description of your product or service
- Your management team
- Your marketplace
- Your marketing strategy
- Your competition
- The risks and opportunities of your business
- Your implementation plan
- Your capital requirements
- Your financial plan
- Any supporting exhibits

The executive summary is probably the most important section of your plan. Why? Because it's the first thing that is read *but* the last thing you write. That's because it is a short summary of all the most important parts of your business plan—it's meant to sell your idea to the reader. If you can grab readers' interest, they will be more likely to read the details of your plan.

Because this is a summary, you have to wait until you've written all the parts of your business plan before you write the executive summary. But remember, an executive summary is just that: a *summary*, not a Foreword. In effect, it's your entire plan in a nutshell.

The sections of your plan that deal with your company itself are the company mission and objectives, the company overview, and the management team sections. The company mission and objective details your company mission and vision statements. It describes what your business will do and why. It also lays out a vision of your company and where it wants to be in the future. The company overview provides a description of your company—start-up, existing company, legal form, and so on—and its goals and objectives. The management team section lists the key personnel—executives and key management and staff—that you propose to use to manage and operate your company.

The focus of what you intend to sell and how you will sell it is in the product or service description section of your plan. Here, you describe not only what you intend to sell, but also what human needs it fulfills. In other words, this section describes your product and service in detail and explains your unique selling position. Hand in hand with your product or service description is an analysis of the marketplace you will sell within and the marketing strategy you will use to market your product or service. Finally, the section on distribution channels explains the distribution or sales channels you will use to sell your product.

A Pollyanna approach to a business plan will not garner much interest or support. Yes, there are opportunities now and in the future that will help your business succeed. But to ignore the risks is to invite disaster. There are companies in your marketplace that will compete with your business. Every business faces risks from them and those of the everyday operations of a company. Sections in your business plan on competition and risks and opportunities must list and deal with these.

A business plan is not only a selling document, but a planning one, too. It represents a roadmap that your company plans to follow to implement your business idea. That's the purpose of the implementation plan. This plan describes step by step how you plan to carry out your business plan.

The last few sections of your business plan deal with money and resources. They list the capital requirements you need to launch and operate your company to reach a break-even point, and they describe a financial plan that provides a proforma (or assumptions) of revenue, expenses, profit, and loss.

Finally, you can include supporting exhibits in your plan. This can include your company or competitor's brochures, proposed advertising and promotion materials, industry studies, maps and photos of locations, magazine pieces or other articles, lists of equipment owned or to be purchased, copies of leases and contracts, letters of support from future customers, and other materials that support the assumptions of your plan. This section also includes the resumes of your management team, board of directors, and advisors.

APPENDIX C

Important Resources on the Web

This appendix provides a list of Net-based resources that will broaden your understanding of e-commerce and provide valuable information to help you succeed in your online business. These e-business resources will help your growing enterprise compete by using sound business practices, establishing business and marketing relationships, building product and service quality programs, and entering international markets.

The resources listed here take a variety of formats. Many are standard Web addresses, whereas others are mailing lists. To subscribe to the mailing lists, simply send an email to the address listed, unless instructed otherwise.

Yahoo! Store Resources

Need help with your Yahoo! store? These websites offers Yahoo! store–specific resources, from video training to expert RTML development.

Yahoo! Merchant Solutions

smallbusiness.yahoo.com

Ready to get started with your Yahoo! store? Yahoo! Merchant Solutions has three packages to choose from. You can also register your domain name during the sign-up process.

My E-Commerce Success

www.mycommercesuccess.com

MyEcommerceSuccess.com offers comprehensive Yahoo! store resources, including training videos, articles, development companies, books, seminars, newsletters, and e-marketing strategies.

Solid Cactus

www.solidcactus.com

As Yahoo!'s premier development partner, Solid Cactus has developed hundreds of Yahoo! stores.

Y-Times Publications

www.ytimes.com

This publisher produces books on Yahoo! stores and RTML.

Y Store Forums

www.ystoreforums.com

The forum is a community to educate and assist with all aspects of operating a Yahoo! store.

Monitus

www.monitus.com

This Yahoo! store consulting and development firm also offers Yahoo! store seminars.

OrderMotion

www.ordermotion.com

Here, you'll find a real-time backend order-management solution.

Deconstructing Yahoo! Store Participants

In Chapters 9–11, we deconstructed three separate websites: a digital product store, a manufactured product store, and a high-volume store. Don't forget to refer to these sites when reading the chapters.

WriteExpress: Digital Product Store

www.writeexpress.com

WriteExpress offers letters and templates for Microsoft Office; software for writing novels, drafting wills and legal documents, and using correct grammar; and a variety of related writing software and e-books.

Neeps, Inc.: High-Volume Product Store

www.theferretstore.com

Neeps currently carries more than 5,400 pet-related products. It sells everything from dog products to exotic pet products for animals such as ferrets.

Pacific Pillows: Manufactured Product Store

www.pacificpillows.com

Pacific Pillows carries luxurious pillows, down comforters, and bedding that you find at luxury hotels such as the Ritz-Carlton, Marriott, Hilton, DoubleTree, and Hyatt Hotel.

Email Discussion Lists

Chat with other website and store owners. Email discussion boards are a great way to help and get help from others with experience.

E-Tailer's Digest

www.etailersdigest.com/subscribe.htm

E-Tailer's Digest is a resource for retail on the Net, published in a moderated digest form every Monday, Wednesday, and Friday. The E-Tailer's Digest topics include subjects that pertain to retailing.

FrankelBiz

www.robfrankel.com/frankelbiz/form.html

FrankelBiz is the Web's only listserv devoted exclusively to doing business on the Web instead of just talking about it. List members exchange reciprocal discounts, offer business leads, and do business with one another. Sponsors offer products and services at discounts to members.

GB Internet Marketing

www.digitalnation.co.uk/subscribe.htm

The GB Internet Marketing discussion list deals with all aspects of Internet marketing related to the United Kingdom.

GLOBAL_PROMOTE

www.join-global_promote@gs4.revnet.com

This list is a forum for the discussion of issues relating to sales and marketing in the worldwide Internet marketplace.

The List of Marketing Lists

www.nsns.com/MouseTracks/tloml.html

This is a comprehensive directory of marketing discussion lists.

IESSlist

www.majordomo@ix.entrepreneurs.net

Internet Entrepreneurs Support Service (IESS) is a discussion group for entrepreneurs and businesses doing business on the Internet.

The Best Internet Marketing Forums

www.ozemedia.com/forums.htm

If you want to rapidly increase and enhance your online presence, you should become an active member of forums or discussion boards. The best ones are great places to spread the gospel, in a quiet way, about your service or product.

Retailer-News

www.retailernews.com

The Retailer News Digest mailing list is a moderated discussion list for retail business owners, managers, and salespeople.

SMBIZ

mail.abanet.org/archives/smbiz.html

The Small Business discussion list is for all small business owners, workers, marketers, and developers. To subscribe, send the message `subscribe`.

E-Business Publications

Stay up-to-date with the industry with these e-business publications. These websites offer a wealth of information, from e-commerce technologies to buying trends.

American Demographics Magazine

www.demographics.com

This is the online reproduction of the print version of *American Demographics* magazine. Here, you'll find the best demographic information online, a necessity for any good marketing plan.

Boardwatch Magazine

www.boardwatch.internet.com

This is a guide to Internet access and the World Wide Web.

CLICKZ

www.clickz.com

This column is published each business day; it includes an eclectic mixture of online marketing news, opinions, and interviews.

CNET

www.cnet.com

In addition to carrying all the latest technical news online, CNET publishes a weekly summary that provides links to all the major Internet stories from the previous week.

Entrepreneur Magazine

www.entrepreneurmag.com

You'll find a wide range of articles and suggestions for starting, managing, and maintaining a small business.

Fast Company

www.fastcompany.com

This site contains plenty of articles about emerging businesses. The site is well organized and expansive, and it covers up-to-date issues for today's entrepreneur.

INC. Online

www.inc.com

This is an award-winning Web magazine for growing companies.

Interactive Week

www.interactive-week.com

This site covers a variety of aspects of the Internet and interactive technology.

Net Magazine

www.netmag.co.uk

This is a popular European Internet magazine.

The Small Business Journal

www.tsbj.com

The Small Business Journal magazine has tons of small business articles and information.

Web Commerce Today

www.wilsonweb.com/wct

This is a monthly email newsletter about selling products directly over the Internet.

Wired Magazine

www.wired.com

This is an Internet culture and business magazine.

E-Commerce Times

www.ecommercetimes.com

E-Commerce Times offers industry strategies for online merchants and provides daily news, articles, and research.

Internet Retailer

www.internetretailer.com

This publication also offers industry strategies for online merchants, and provides daily news, articles, and research.

Search Engine Watch

www.searchenginewatch.com

This is a good source for search-engine marketing news and articles.

Employment Websites

Need to hire full-time, part-time, or even seasonal help? Employment websites are a great way to find your next employee. Unlike traditional print advertising, your posting can be seen by thousands of prospective employees immediately.

Yahoo! HotJobs

www.hotjobs.com

Monster

www.monster.com

Craigslist

www.craigslist.org

CareerBuilder

www.careerbuilder.com

Press Release Distribution Services

Posting your press releases to these newswire distribution services increases your chances of getting exposure on major news websites and in publications.

PRWeb

www.prweb.com

PRWeb offers free posting.

PR Newswire

www.prnewswire.com

PR Newswire requires an annual fee for posting.

Business Wire

www.businesswire.com

Business Wire requires an annual fee.

URLwire

www.urlwire.com

URLwire posts on demand and charges per posting, but does not have an annual fee.

Internet News Bureau

www.newsbureau.com/services

Internet News Bureau charges per posting but does not have an annual fee.

Xpress Press

www.xpresspress.com

Xpress Press charges per posting but does not have an annual fee.

Mailing List Resources

Looking for an email list–management service, or need to rent an opt-in list to advertise your products and services? These websites will help you do just that.

GOT Campaigner

Campaigner can help you grow your customer base, increase sales, create repeat customers, and measure the return on investment (ROI) of each direct emailing campaign.

Constant Contact

www.constantcontact.com

This do-it-yourself email-marketing service enables you to manage your email list and create email newsletters.

infoUSA Prospecting Lists

infoUSA is the premier provider of business and consumer mailing lists, sales leads, and databases. infoUSA is the only company that compiles business and consumer data under one roof.

Financial Resources

If you're looking for financing to help your business, these financial resources will help you calculate your budget needs and obtain current interest rates.

Business Owners Idea Cafe

www.businessownersideacafe.com/financing/budget_calculator.html

You can find a simple, free budget calculator at the Business Owners Idea Cafe.

Interest Rate Monitor

www.bankrate.com/brm/rate/cc_home.asp

Bank Rate Monitor lists a lot of frequently updated information on which banks and credit card companies are offering the best rates.

Web Analysis Tools and Services

Advanced online statistics-reporting tools and services can help you determine which products and pages are getting exposure and which ones are not. They also provide detailed customer behaviors and buying trends.

WebTrends

www.webtrends.com

Here, you'll find enterprise-class Web analytics and marketing performance-management solutions.

LiveSTATS by DeepMetrix

www.deepmetrix.com

This site has Web Analytics tools and solutions.

Statscounter

www.statscounter.com

This is a free real-time online-based Web analysis service.

Google Analytics

www.google.com/analytics/

This free, real-time, online-based Web analysis service is integrated with Google AdWords.

General Resources

Don't forget to visit these other helpful resources, which offer a range of services and resources to help you succeed with your Yahoo! business.

Domain Name Availability

www.networksolutions.com

This service checks the availability of a domain name.

Emarketer

www.emarketer.com

This site aims to be the definitive online-marketing resource. It includes news, statistics, and step-by-step guides to succeeding online. A weekly newsletter also is available.

Incorporation and Trademarks

www.corpcreations.com

This site offers incorporation and trademark services online (for all 50 states plus offshore).

NUA Internet Surveys

www.nua.ie/surveys/moreinfo.html

NUA publishes a weekly email newsletter that summarizes all the latest Internet surveys and statistics. This newsletter is an invaluable resource if you want to know who's online and what they're buying.

Wilson Web

www.wilsonweb.com

This site contains a wealth of links to articles relating to every aspect of Web commerce. Much of the information is free, although some areas are accessible to paying subscribers only.

Delphi Forums

www.delphiforums.com

Delphi Forums is one of the largest discussion boards on the Net, with more than 500,000 individual discussion forums to participate in.

Yahoo! Groups

www.groups.yahoo.com

Yahoo! Groups is a good resource for finding discussion boards that relate to your product or service. This is also one the easiest ways for companies to communicate with prospects and customers on the Internet.

Lsoft

www.lsoft.com/lists/listref.html

Lsoft has the CataList, the official catalog of LISTSERV lists on the Net. CataList has tens of thousands of public discussion lists that you can subscribe to.

Blogger.com

www.blogger.com

You can use a free blogging tool at www.blogger.com. This popular application can get your blog up and running in minutes.

MyISPFinder

www.myispfinder.org

MyISPFinder can help you find and choose an ISP in your state.

Merchant Accounts

These companies specialize in merchant accounts for online merchants; all are compatible with First Data Merchant Services (FDMS):

- 1st American Card Service: www.1stamericancardservice.com
- Card Service International: www.cardservice.com
- Chase Merchant Services: www.chasemerchantservices.com
- Wells Fargo Merchant Services: www.wellsfargo.com
- First Bank: www.fbol.com
- Bank of Hawaii: www.boh.com
- Express Merchant Processing Solutions: www.empsebiz.com
- First Interstate Bank: www.firstinterstatebank.com
- Paymentech: www.paymentech.com

Nolo

www.nolo.com

The Nolo website is a great resource for information on the different forms of business entities and how to form them.

Direct Marketing Association

www.the-dma.org/privacy/privacypolicygenerator.shtml

This site has a free legal privacy policy generator.

AdSlogans.com

www.adslogans.com

This tagline database service can help you create your own unique slogan.

Instalogo

www.instalogo.com

You can create your own logo online with this service.

The Logo Loft

www.thelogoloft.com

This site has an affordable custom logo design service.

United States Small Business Association (SBA)

www.sba.gov

This is a government-sponsored website to help small business. You can get free consulting from retired professionals in your area.

Index

Symbols

1160 Characters, 217

A

Aaronson Group, 279
Aaronson, Jack, 279
abandoned shopping cards, 241-243
Abbey, Craig, 155
About Us pages, e-commerce sites, 49
above the fold, designing websites, 120
access log files, configuring and downloading, 255-256
accounting, Neeps, 168
ACOA, 9
Add to Cart button, 72-73
adding
   multiple revenue streams, 34-35
   products to your store, 326
Address Verification Service (AVS), 246
adjusting variables, 63
AdSlogans.com, 184, 347
advanced searches, 78-80
advertising, 9, 190-191
   banner ads, 192
   contextual advertising, 193
   e-zines, 193
   mining server logs, 251
   Net advertising, 191-192
   newsletters, 193
   Tell a Friend links, 119
advertising income, 35
advertisements, competitors ads, 126
advisors, Learning Fountain, 31
AdWords, 214
affiliate marketing, 154, 172
Amazon.com, 34, 59
American Demographics, 339
American Express, 245
Analysis stage, 62
angel investors, 25
aquiring PARM, 178
assigning staff duties, 312-313
AssociatePrograms.com, 244
automated payment processing, 167
avoiding fraud, 244-245
AVS (Address Verification Service), 246

B

back-end systems
   configuring, 327
   Neeps, 166-167
   Pacific Pillows, 151

background checks, 317-318
balance sheet statements, creating, 304-307
banks, borrowing from, 25
banner ads, 126, 192
　credibility, Pacific Pillows, 148-149
benefits of selling online, 144
best-selling item display, 81, 84
Bestsellers feature, 100-104, 111
Better Business Bureau, 52
Big 5, branding, 185
bin location systems, setting up, 167-171
BizCheck, 184
Blogger.com, 346
bloglines, 281
blogs, 33
borrowing from a bank, 25
branding, 8-9, 180-182
　with Big, 51, 85
　tips for online branding, 183-185
　USP, 180
breadcrumbs, 77-78, 145-146
　enabling built-in breadcrumbs, 94-97
　fonts, 96
　search engine features, 86
Building Brands, 182
Business Control Page, 34
business identity, choosing, 12-13
Business Owners Idea Café, 24, 343

business plans, 7-12, 329
　competition, 20-21
　funding, 332
　how will you marketing your product, 331
　implementation plan, 331
　implementing, 22-23
　pulling it together, 332-334
　what does it sell, 330
　what does it solve, 330
　where is your business and who will it serve, 331
　who is your business, 329
Business Wire, 272, 342
Business.com, 21
businesses
　managing, 21-22
　positioning, 179
　　branding. See branding
　underpromising and overdelivering, 182-183
Buy Now button, 119
buying motivations, 18

C

C corporations, 16
calculating close ratios, 252
call to action (CTA), 190
Campaigner, (Got Marketing), 152, 224, 227
CAN-SPAM Privacy Act, 195-197
capital, 7, 10, 23
　financing your business, 24-25
　start-up costs, 23-24
Capital Resource Library, 25
CareerBuilder, 316, 341

Cascading Style Sheets (CSS), 99-100
cash flow statements, creating, 302-306
Catalog Manager, 291
catalog pages, e-commerce sites, 53
Catalog Request feature, 107-108
categorized site maps, search engine features, 86-87
CC&R's (covenants, conditions, and restrictions), 14
CGI scripts, 236
change page name to text, search engine features, 86
chargebacks, 245
Chase, Larry, 183
chat rooms, 33, 235
Checkout Manager, customizing pages, 121
checkout pages, customizing, 120-121
Children's Online Privacy Protection Act (COPPA), 226
choosing business identity, 12-13
CI Seek, 20
Click to Enlarge Image, 72-74, 97-98
click-through, 191
CLICKZ, 339
close ratios, calculating, 252
CNET, 339
Color Combos, 140
Colors, 118
Combo Tester, 140

commerce, 29
  e-commerce sites, 34-35
Commission Junction, 54
communities, 29
  e-commerce sites, 33-34
  retaining customers, 234-237
community message boards, 173
community pages, e-commerce sites, 54
company assets, 304
company liabilities, 304
Compare Your Clicks, 214
competition, 20-21
  testing design effectiveness, 140
Competitive Intelligence Resource Index, 20
competitors, advertisements, 126
"Complaint Contest," 283
configuring
  access log files, 255-256
  back-end systems and operations, 327
confirmation emails, 226, 280
Constant Contact, 227, 343
consumer opinions, 32
contact information, 51, 242
contact pages, e-commerce sites, 51
content, 29
  e-commerce sites, 29-32
  managing content flow, 122
  search engines, 37
  web pages, storyboarding, 44

content copy, formatting, 122
content flow, 141
content overload, avoiding, 125
content pages, e-commerce sites, 54
context providers, Learning Fountain, 32
contextual advertising, 193
converting currency, 32
COPPA (Children's Online Privacy Protection Act), 226
copy, words that sell, 127-128
Corporate Creations, 345
corporations, 16
CPA (cost per action), 192
CPC (cost per click), 192
CPM (cost per thousand impressions), 192
CPS (cost per sale), 192
CPT (cost per transaction), 192
Craigslist, 316, 341
credibility, 123-124
  Pacific Pillows, 148-149
credit card fraud, 244-245
  protecting yourself from, 245-248
credit cards, 301
cross-selling, 81, 84, 110-112
CSR (customer service reps), 280
CSS (Cascading Style Sheets), 99-100
CTA (call to action), 190

currency, 32
cushioning, 295
custom contact forms, 73, 77
custom option displays, 73, 76
Customer Care FAQs, 276
customer feedback, 140
customer motivations, 19-20
customer relationship management, 276
customer service, 276
  after the sale, 280-281
  before the sale, 276-278
  disgruntled customers, 283-284
  during the sale, 278-280
  follow-up after the sales, 282
  outsourcing, 151
  returns, 282-283
customer service reps (CSR), 280
customers
  acquiring. See search engine marketing
  keeping, 121
  repeat customers, creating, 172
  retaining. See retaining customers
  types of, 19
customizing
  checkout pages, 120-121
  store layout and navigation, 327
  Yahoo! Stores, 61-63
    adjusting variables and inserting custom HTML headers and footers, 63
    deciding to do it yourself or hire an expert, 68-69

inserting custom HTML headers and footers, 64-65
reasons for, 58-61
with RTML, 66-68
with web hosting, 65-66

D

Database Inventory, 287-288
Database Upload feature, 87-91
DeepMetrix, 252, 344
Delphi, 235
Delphi Forums, 345
descriptions, writing, 214-215
design pitfalls, 124-125
  competitors, 126
  content overload, 125
  don't make visitors think, 124
  graphic overload, 127
  navigation, 126
  plug-ins, 127
  shopping car abandonment, 125
design stage, 62
designing
  above the fold, 120
  e-commerce sites. *See* e-commerce sites websites
    considering what visitors see, 119
    WriteExpress, 138-140
developers, hiring, 150
digital products, 132-133
  cons of selling, 136
  file size limits, 134
  PDF files, 136
  pros of selling, 136
  selling Mac and PC platform file formats, 136
  uploading, 134-135

Direct Marketing Association, 52, 346
  privacy policies, 225
directories, getting listed at, 205-206
discounts, 173
  packaged deals, 148
discussion boards, 33, 235
discussion lists, 33, 236-237
disgruntled customers, 283-284
Disney, storyboards, 42
DMnews, 199
domain names, registering, 325
downloading access log files, 255-256
drop-ship notification, 167
drop-shipping, 158, 293
Dun & Bradstreet, 21
dynamic cascading menus, 77, 80
dynamic pagination, 77-79

E

e-business, 12
e-business publications, 339-340
e-commerce site development versus website development, 28-29
e-commerce sites, 29
  commerce, 34-35
  community, 33-34
  content, 29-32
  pages, 46-47
    About Us pages, 49
    community pages, 54
    contact pages, 51
    content pages, 54
    FAQ pages, 49-51
    home pages, 47-49

online press rooms, 53-54
privacy policies, 51-52
product or services catalog pages, 53
shipping information, 52-53
site maps, 54-55
E-Commerce Times, 341
E-Tailer's Digest, 337
e-zines, 193
eBay, marketing strategies, 153
Eisenberg, Bryan, 45
Eisenstein, Sergei, 42
email
  confirmation emails, 226, 281
  house lists, creating, 221-223
  increasing revenue, 243
  opt-in email, 194
  promoting email programs, 222
email discussion lists, 337-339
email forms, 107-108
email marketing, 172, 194-197, 227-231
  opt-in email lists, 197-199
  testing headlines, 228-229
  testing "from" lines, 228
  testing links, 230
  testing offers, 229
  testing response options, 229-230
  testing subject lines, 228
  testing text versus HTML, 230
Email Marketing Weekly, 227
email newletter subscriptions, 82

email newsletters, 152, 231-234
  format considerations, 232-233
  news versus promotions, 232
Emarketer, 344
emotional selling proposition (ESP), 182
emphasis with color, 118
employees
  finding, 316
  free help, 321
  hiring. See hiring
  interviewing candidates, 316
  keeping good employees, 321-322
  outsourcing, 313-314
  part-time help, 320
  pay levels, setting, 319-320
  versus independent contractors, 314
  warehouses, 287
employing family and friends, 21
employment websites, 341
enabling built-in breadcrumbs, 94-97
Entrepreneur, 339
entry pages, 259
equity investors, funding through, 25
equity of companies, 304
ESP (emotional selling proposition), 182
establishing legal identities, 14-16
Evaluation stage, 62
exit pages, 259
external style sheets, 99

F

family
  employing, 2
  hiring, 318-319
FAQ pages, 183
  e-commerce sites, 49-51
Fast Company, 340
FDMS (First Data Merchant Services), 326, 346
feedback, 29, 140, 283
  consumer opinions, 32
Feedback stage, 62
FerretStore.com, 126
file size limits, digital products, 134
financial planning, 298
  credit cards, 301
  proforma, 298-299
    creating, 299-306
financial resources, 343
financial statements, 301
  balance sheet statements, creating, 304-307
  cash flow statements, creating, 302-306
  income statements, creating, 302, 306
financing. See capital, 24
finding
  employees, 316
  free help, 321
First Data Merchant Services (FDMS), 326, 346
First-Time Visitor orientation, 277
Flanders, Vincent, 181, 241
flowcharts, 43-44
focus groups, 140
fonts, breadcrumbs, 96
footers, inserting custom HTML footers, 63-65

formatting content copy, 122
forms
  free forms, 107-108
  shipment status forms, 114-116
forums, 33
FrankelBiz, 338
fraud
  avoiding, 244-245
  protecting yourself from, 245-248
free forms, 107-108
FreeChat, 235
friends
  employing, 21
  hiring, 318-319
"from" lines, testing, 228
FTC, 52
full-time business, 5-6
funding, 10
  through equity investors, 25

G

GB Internet Marketing, 338
Gechnorati, 281
geographic locations, statistics, 259
Gerstner, Louis, 12
GLOBAL_PROMOTE, 338
goals of marketing, 189-190
Good Keywords, 213
Google AdWords, 344
Google Analytics, 257, 344
Google Groups, 281
GOT Campaigner, 343
Got Marketing, 224
  Campaigner, 152

graphics
  avoiding graphic overload, 127
  Secure Shopping graphic, 82, 85
guarantees, product guarantees, 123

H

header tags, 207
headers, inserting custom HTML headers, 63-65
headlines, 114
  testing, 228-229
hiring, 312
  assigning and understanding staff duties, 312-313
  developers, 150
  employees, 6
  family and friends, 318-319
  finding employees, 316
  interviewing candidates, 316
  part-time help, 320
  references, 317-318
  the right person, 315
  screening backgrounds, 3, 17-318
hiring process, 314-315
home pages
  creating home pages that sell, 240-241
  e-commerce sites, 47-49
Honig, Marvin, 184
Hoover's Business Links, 20
house lists
  creating, 221-223
  registration pages, 223-226
  subscribing and unsubscribing, 226-227

HTML
  inserting custom headers and footers, 63-65
  versus text, 230

I

ICQ, 279
identities
  business identity, choosing, 12-13
  legal identities, 14-16
IESS (Internet Entrepreneurs Support Service), 338
image alt tags, search engine features, 86
IMAGE operators, 98
images
  Click to Enlarge, 97-98
  uploading multiple images at once, 91
implementing business plans, 22-23, 331
impressions, 191
improving value proposition, 251
Inc. Online, 340
income, 35
income statements, creating, 302, 306
increasing revenue, 244
  email, 243
independent contractors versus employees, 314
informers, Learning Fountain, 31
infoUSA, 343
inserting HTML headers and footers, 63-65
Instalogo, 179, 347
Intel, online press rooms, 268

interactive communities, building, 33-34
Interactive Week, 340
Interest Rate Monitor, 343
internal marketing, 199-201
Internet Entrepreneurs Support Service (IESS), 338
Internet News Bureau, 272, 342
Internet resources. *See* Appendix C
Internet Retailer, 341
interns, 321
interviewing candidates, 316
inventory, 286
  drop-shipping, 293
  real-time inventory checking, 167
  saving money on storage, 293
  tracking, 292
inventory control, 287-288
  Inventory Management, 287-289
  setting inventory levels, 289-292
inventory levels, setting, 289-290
  for product options, 290-292
Inventory Management, 287-289
inventory-management procedures, 292

J

JavaScript rollovers, 241

K

keyword-rich content, 207
keywords, taglines, 181

L

Launch stage, 62
Learning Community, 33
Learning Fountain, 29-32
legal identity, establishing, 14-16
Liabilities, 304
licenses, 14
limited liability company (LLC), 14
Lindstrom, Martin, 183
LineCheck, 184
link anchor text, 207
link farms, 210
link popularity, 207-210
links, 230
List of Marketing Lists, 338
live support, 159
LivePerson, 279
LiveSTATS, 344, 252
LLC (limited liability company), 14-16
location of navigation, 126
Logitech, 50
The Logo Loft, 347
logos, 179
logs
   access log files, configuring and downloading, 255-256
   server logs, mining. See mining server logs
losing sales, 241-243
Lsoft, 345

M

Mac platform file formats, 136
"The Magical Number Seven, Plus or Minus Two: Some Limits on Our Capacity for Processing Information," 43
Mail Abuse Prevention System, 197
mail order/telephone order (MOTO) companies, 244
mailing list resources, 342-343
Manage My Services control panel, 326
management, 9-10
managing
   businesses, 21-22
   content flow, 122
marketing, 9, 141. See also advertising
   advertising, 190-191
   buying motivations, 18
   email marketing. See email marketing
   goals, 189-190
   house lists, creating, 221-223
   internal marketing, 199-201
   permission marketing, 195-197
   search engine marketing. See search engine marketing
   target markets. See target markets
   watering-hole marketing, 188-189
marketing features, 81
   cross-selling, 81, 84
   email newsletter subscriptions, 82
   multiple product image views, 81-83
   random best-selling item display, 81, 84
   randomly displayed testimonials, 82
   Recently Viewed Items section, 82, 85
   Secure Shopping graphic, 82, 85
   Send This Page to a Friend, 81-82
   shopping cart cookie tester, 82
   You Save display, 81-83
marketing plans, 17-18
marketing savvy, 188
marketing strategies, 152
   affiliate marketing, 154
   eBay, 153
   email newsletters, 152
   Neeps, 171-172
   pay-per-click marketing, 153-154
   print marketing, 154
   television commercial marketing, 154
Martin Lindstrom, 182
MasterCard, 245
Matt's Script, 236
media relations, 266
menus
   dynamic cascading menus, 77, 80
   text-based menus, search engine features, 86
merchandising, 182
merchant accounts, 346
   signing up for, 326
message boards, 173
metatags, 207
   search engine features, 86

Michelin, 184
microsites, 217-218
Microsoft's Small Business Center, 232
Mike's Marketing Tools, 180
Miller, George, 43
mining server logs, 250-252
monetizing PARM, 178
Monitus, 336
Monster, 316, 341
motivations
   buying motivations, 18
   customer motivations, 19-20
MOTO (mail order/telephone order) companies, 244
Moveable Type, 34
multiple breadcrumbs, 77-79
   search engine features, 86
multiple-product Add to Cart, 73-75
MyEcommerceSuccess.com, 336
MyISPFinder, 346
Mystery Meat Navigation, 241

N

naming your business, 12-13
navigation, 241
   customizing, 327
   location of, 126
   Mystery Meat Navigation, 241
   optimizing, 251
   store-navigation features. *See* store-navigation features

navigation elements, storyboarding, 42
Neeps, 158, 337
   accounting, 168
   back-end systems, 166
      OrderMotion, 167
   managing multiple websites, 166
   marketing strategies, 171-172
   multiple website niches with same product line, 164-166
   negotiating shipping costs, 171
   product information, 158
   repeat customers, creating, 173
   shipping and packaging, 171
   system and warehouse layout, 168
   website layout, 158-163
negotiating shipping costs, 171
Net, 340
Net advertising, 191-192
Network Solutions, 344
news versus promotion, 232
newsletters, 33, 173, 193
no-hassel return policies, 281
Nolo, 17, 346
NUA Internet Surveys, 345

O

offers, testing, 229
online branding, 183-185
online businesses. *See* virtual businesses
online communities. *See* communities

online press rooms, 267-269
   e-commerce sites, 53-54
online surveys, 201
Open Directory, 205
operations, 9-10
opt-in email, 194
opt-in email lists, 197-199
optimizing navigation, 251
Order Confirmation pages, 276
OrderMotion, 167, 293, 336
organizational selling proposition (OSP), 182
organizational structures, 22
organizing
   financial statements. *See* financial statements
   products, 326
OSP (organizational selling proposition), 182
Outpost.com, 48
outsourcing, 313-314
   customer service, Pacific Pillows, 151
   Pacific Pillows, 151
   public relations, 272
overbidding, 213
overdelivering, 182-183

P

Pacific Pillows, 144-145, 337
   back-end system, 151
   credibility banners, 148-149
   marketing strategies, 152-154
   outsourcing, 151
   packaged deals, 147-148
   product information, 145
   testimonials, 149-150

tips from owner Craig
  Abbey, 155
 website development, 150
 website layout, 145-147
packaged deals, 118
  Pacific Pillows, 147-148
packaging, 171
  products, 295-296
  USP (unique selling
    position), 37
packaging documents, 167
Page Not Found, search
  engine features, 86
page titles, 207
page views, statistics, 259
pagination, dynamic
  pagination, 77-79
paid inclusion, 210
paid placement, 211
PalzzoPaintings.com, 124
PARM (positioning, acquiring, retaining, and monetizing), 178-179
part-time help, 320
partnerships, 15
pass-alongs, 222
passion, 5
pay levels, setting, 319-320
pay-for-performance, 211
pay-per-click (PPC),
  206, 211
pay-per-click
  advertising, 172
pay-per-click marketing,
  153-154
payments
  automated payment processing, 167
  setting up capability to
    accept payments, 326

PayPal, 326
PayPerClickGuru, 212
PC platform file
  formats, 136
PCC (pay-per-click), 211
PDF files, selling, 136
Peachtree, 168
PepperJam Management,
  154, 172
permission marketing,
  195-197
permissions, 197
permits, 14
personal funding
  services, 25
PetCareCentral.com, 165
pictures, multiple product
  image views, 81-83
plans
  business plans
    competition, 20-21
    implementing, 22-23
  formal business plans,
    7-12
  marketing plans, 17-18
plots, storyboarding, 45
plug-ins, 127
PosCheck, 184
positioning
  businesses, 179
    branding. See branding
    underpromising and
      overdelivering, 182-183
    PARM, 178
    USP (unique selling position), 37
positioning, acquiring,
  retaining, and monetizing (PARM), 178-179
PPC (pay-per-click),
  206, 215

PR Newswire, 272, 342
PR. *See* public relations
press release distribution
  services, 342
Press Release
  Writing.com, 270
press releases
  importance of, 266-267
  sending, 272
  writing, 269-271
press rooms, online press
  rooms, 53-54
price, 185
PriceGrabber.com, 153
pricing, USP (unique selling position), 36
print advertising, 171
print marketing, 154
printable pages, 122
privacy policies,
  224-225, 234
  e-commerce sites, 51-52
product catalogs, 173
product descriptions, 17-18
product fundamentals, 18
product guarantees, 243
product income, 35
product info tables, 73-75
product options, setting
  inventory levels, 290-292
product positioning, 121
product reviews, 172, 243
product samples, 173
products
  guarantees, 123
  multiple website niches
    with same product line,
    164-166
  organizing and adding to
    your store, 326
  packaging, 295-296

professional-looking websites, creating, 122
proforma, 10, 298-299
　creating, 299-306
promoting email programs, 222
promotion, 266
　versus news, 232
　USP (unique selling position), 37
promotion. *See* marketing
promotional options. *See* marketing features
promotions, 37
　mining server logs, 251
protecting
　against return abusers, 283
　your business from fraud, 245-248
PRWeb, 342
public relations, 266
　online press room, 267-269
　outsourcing, 272
　press releases, 266-267
　　sending, 272
　　writing, 269-272
publicity, 266
publishing websites, 327
PubSub, 281

Q

quantity boxes, 104-105
quantity pricing layout, 72-74

R

RabbitCentral.com, 166
rack setup, example, 170
radio button options, 106-107
ranking of sites, 180
RBL (Realtime Blackhole List), 195
Real-Time Inventory, 287-289
real-time inventory checking, 167
Realtime Blackhole List (RBL), 195
Recently Viewed Items section, 82, 85
Redesign stage, 62
references, checking before hiring, 317-318
referral income, 35
referrals, 201
referrers
　Learning Fountain, 30-31
　Statistics, 259
registering domain names, 325
registration pages, 223-226
Related Items, 110-113
　displaying, 78, 81
Related Items section, search engine features, 86
relevancy, search engine marketing, 215-217
repeat customer notification, 167
repeat customers, creating, 172
resources
　e-business publications, 339
　email discussion lists, 337
　employment websites, 341
　financial resources, 343
　Internet resources. *See* Appendix C
　mailing list resources, 342
　press release distribution services, 342
　Yahoo! site statistics resources, 252-254
response options, testing, 229-230
responses, 191
Retailer News Digest, 338
retaining customers, 220
　communities, 234-237
　email marketing. *See* email marketing
　email newsletters, 231-234
　　format considerations, 232-233
　　news versus promotions, 232
　house lists, 221-223
　　registration pages, 223-226
　　subscribing and unsubscribing, 226-227
　importance of, 220
retaining PARM, 178
Return Exchange, 283
return on investment (ROI), 189
return policies, 281
returning customers, 121
returns, 282-283
revenue, increasing, 243-244
revenue streams, adding multiple revenue streams, 34-35
RM Carspares, 277
Roberts, Kevin, 182
ROI (return on investment), 189
ROI calculators, 195

Roving, 227
RTML, 63
   customizing your Yahoo! Stores, 67-68
   quantity boxes, 104-105
   Related Items, 110
   sale items, 109-110

S

Safe Shopping Network, 148
sale items, 109-110
Sanfilippo, Scott, 168
SBA (Small Business Association), 25, 347
screening backgrounds, 317-318
search engine features, 86
   breadcrumbs, 86
   categorized site maps, 86-87
   change page name to text, 86
   dynamically generated metatags, 86
   image alt tags, 86
   multiple breadcrumbs, 86
   Page Not Found, 86
   Related Items section, 86
   text-based menus, 86
search engine marketing, 204-205, 210-212
   ensuring relevancy, 215-216
      checklists, 216-217
   getting listed at search engines and directories, 205-206
   link popularity, 209-210
   microsites, 217-218
   search terms, 212-214
   search-engine optimization, 207-208
   spiders, 208-209
   writing titles and descriptions, 214-215
search engine optimization (SEO), 113
Search Engine Watch, 206, 341
search engines, 204
   content, 37
   optimization, 60
   statistics, 259
search-engine optimization, 204, 207-208
search-engine submission, 204
Secure Shopping graphic, 82, 85
security, Pacific Pillows, 148
seller's permit, 14
selling
   cross-selling, 118
   online, benefits of, 144
   PDF files, 136
   up-selling, 118
SEM. *See* search engine marketing
Send This Page to a Friend, 81-82
sending press releases, 272
SEO (search engine optimization), 113, 210
server logs, mining, 250-251
service descriptions, 17-18
service fundamentals, 18
service sales income, 35
shipment status forms, 114-116
shipping, 171
   packaging products, 295-296

UPS Online Tools, 293-295
shipping and return policies, 242
shipping costs, 242
   negotiating, 171
shipping information, 278
   e-commerce sites, 52-53
shipping policy pop-up charts, 73, 76
shopping cart abandonment, 125, 241-243
shopping cart cookie tester, 82
shopping cart pages, customizing, 120-121
Siegel, Paul, 29
signing up
   for a merchant account, 326
   for a Yahoo! Merchant Solutions account, 325
Siposs, Istvan, 94
site logs, 250
site maps
   categorized site maps, search engine features, 86-87
   e-commerce sites, 54-55
Site Statistics, 252-254
   viewing, 254
Sloganalysis, 184
Small Business Admistration (SBA), 25
Small Business Discussion List, 339
Small Business Journal, 340
sole proprietorship, 15
Solid Cactus, 63, 69, 160, 336

Solid Cactus Complete Commerce, 293
Spam, 194
special offers, 120
spiders, 208-209
staff, assigning and understanding duties, 312-313
staging areas, 62
start-up costs, 23-24
statistics
   Statscounter, 257-263
   Store Editor, viewing, 256
   third-party online services for, 257-258
   Web Hosting Site Statistics, 254
Statscounter, 257-262
stocking status, 278
Store Editor, 65, 252
   statistics, viewing, 256
store layout, customizing, 327
Store Manager, 254
Store Tags, 65
store-layout features, 72
   Add to Cart button, 72-73
   Click to Enlarge Image feature, 72-74
   custom contact forms, 73, 77
   custom option displays, 73, 76
   multiple-product Add to Cart, 73-75
   product info table, 73-75
   quantity pricing layout, 72-74
   shipping policy pop-up chart, 73, 76
store-navigation features, 77
   advanced searches, 78-80
   breadcrumbs, 77-78
   dynamic cascading enus, 77, 80
   dynamic pagination, 77-79
   multiple breadcrumbs, 77-79
   related items, 78, 81
storyboarding, 42
   navigation elements, 42
   plots, 45
   web page content, 44
   web page elements, 43
   writing for the web, 45-46
storyboards, 42
Sub Chapter S corporations, 16
subject lines, testing, 228
subscribing to house lists, 226-227
Sunshine Communications, 151
support, live support, 159
surveys
   after sale surveys, 282
   online surveys, 201

T

tables, product info tables, 73-75
taglines, 181-183, 240
tags, image alt tags, 86
target markets, 19
   customer motivations, 19-20
   customer types, 19
targeted mailings, 167
television commercial marketing, 154
Tell a Friend links, 119
templates, head, 113
TermCheck, 184
Testimonials, 82, 243
   Pacific Pillows, 149-150
testing
   effectiveness of design, WriteExpress, 141-140
   "from" lines, 228
   headlines, 228-229
   links, 230
   offers, 229
   response options, 229-230
   subject lines, 228
   text versus HTML, 230
   usability testing, 122
text versus HTML, 230
text page titles, 113-114
text-based menus, search engine features, 86
TheFerretStore.com, 165
third-party online services for statistics, 257-258
time zones32title companies, 189
titles, 113-114
   writing, 214-215
trackable links, creating, 230
tracking inventory, 292
transaction privilege license, 14
trust, 123-124

U

U.S. Web100, 20
underpromising, 182-183
unique selling position (USP), 28, 35-38
United States Small Business Association (SBA), 347
unsubscribing from house lists, 226-227
up-selling, 118
uploading
   digital products, 134-135
   multiple images at once, 91

UPS (United Parcel Service), streamlining the shipping process, 293-295
UPS Online Tools, 293-294
URLwire, 272, 342
usability, Bestseller feature, 101-104
usability testing, 122
USP (unique selling position), 17, 28, 35-38
    branding, 180
    packaging, 37
    positioning, 37
    pricing, 36
    promotion, 37

V

Value, 185
value proposition, improving, 251
variables, adjusting, 63
venture capitalists, 25
Verified Person, 317-318
vfinance.com, 25
viewing
    Store Editor statistics, 256
    Web Hosting Site Statistics, 254
virtual businesses
    branding, 8-9
    capital, 7
    formal business plans, 7-8
    full-time business, 5-6
    hiring employees, 6
    necessities of, 4-5
Visa, 245
visitors, statistics, 258

W

Wanamaker, John, 190
warehouse floor plans, example, 169
warehouses
    employees, 287
    setting up, 168-171, 286-287
watering-hole marketing, 188-189
web, writing for (storyboarding), 45-46
web analysis tools and services, 343-344
Web Commerce Today, 340
Web Hosting, 252
    customizing your Yahoo! Stores, 65-66
    Site Statistics, 252
        viewing, 254
Web Marketing Today, 237
web page content, storyboarding, 44
web page elements, storyboarding, 43
web pages
    on e-commerce sites. *See* e-commerce sites
    Order Confirmation pages, 276
    printable pages, 122
Web Pages That Suck, 241
WebLog Expert, 253
website development
    Pacific Pillows, 150
    versus e-commerce site development, 28-29
websites
    ACOA, 9
    AdSlogans.com, 184
    Amazon.com, 59
    Better Business Bureau, 52
    Building Brands, 182
    Business Owners Idea Café, 24
    Business.com, 21
    checking rankings, 180
    CI Seek, 20
    designing, considering what visitors see, 119
    Direct Marketing Association, 52
    Dun & Bradstreet, 21
    e-commerce sites. *See* e-commerce sites
    employment, 341
    FerretStore.com, 126
    Hoover's Business Links, 20
    InstaLogo, 179
    Learning Fountain, 29
    Logitech, 50
    managing multiple websites, 166
    Mike's Marketing Tools, 180
    multiple website niches with same product line, 164-166
    Nolo, 17
    Outpost.com, 48
    Pacific Pillows. *See* Pacific Pillows
    PalzzoPaintings.com, 124
    PepperJam Management, 154, 172
    PetCareCentral.com, 165
    PriceGrabber.com, 153
    professional-looking websites, creating, 122
    publishing, 327
    RabbitCentral.com, 166
    Solid Cactus, 63, 69, 160
    TheFerretStore.com, 165
    U.S. Web100, 20
    vfinance.com, 25
    Wholesale World, 5
    WriteExpress, 132
    YellowBrix, 31
WebTrends, 344
"What's in it for me?" (WIIFM), 181

Whitaker, Michael, 94
WHOLE-CONTENTS operator, 109
Wholesale World, 5
WIIFM ("What's in it for me?"), 181
Wikipedia, 180
Wilson Web, 345
Word Press, 34
words that sell, 127-128
WordTracker, 213
WriteExpress, 132-133, 337
    content flow, 141
    evolution of design, 137-140
    marketing, 141
    product information, 133
    testing design effectiveness, 140-141
WriteExpression, images, 141
writing
    for the web, storyboarding, 45-46
    press releases, 269-271

Save big on essential small business services from Yahoo!

 **Offer 1!** **Save 25% for three months plus a waived setup fee on new Yahoo! web hosting and e-commerce plans[1].**

Want to build a business web site?

Utilize Yahoo! Web Hosting to get your business in front of millions. You'll get a domain name, access to easy, free web building tools, business email accounts, and 24 hour toll-free customer support!

Want to sell online?

Build an e-commerce site with Yahoo! Merchant Solutions. Choose the package that best fits your needs, and begin ringing up your online sales. This special offer can save you almost $275[2]!

Sign up now at **http://smallbusiness.yahoo.com/SucceedingAtYourYahooBusiness** and receive 25% off web hosting or e-commerce services for 3 months, plus we'll waive the setup fee! Enter code YAHOONOW at signup.

 **Offer 2!** **Drive traffic to your web site. Get a $50 credit[3] on Yahoo!® Sponsored Search.**

Instead of looking for customers, what if they found you? Yahoo!® Sponsored Search lists your site in search results across the Web, so you connect with customers who are looking for what you have to offer.

Get your $50 credit by visiting **http://sponsoredsearch.yahoo.com/smartonline** or for assisted setup service, call 800-313-1392 and mention promo code US1951B.

---

[1] Offer disclaimer: The 25% discount offer is applied to monthly hosting fees or monthly merchant solution fees for a period of 3 months, after which the current monthly fees will be charged. The waived setup fee and monthly discount offers are open to new customers only, and are limited to one per customer on a single account. Offer expires on 06/30/2007 at 11:59 PM and is only available to purchasers of the *Succeeding At Your Yahoo! Business* book. Yahoo! reserves the right to cancel this offer at any time if in Yahoo!'s sole discretion the offer is subject to fraudulent activity. Offers may not be combined with any other offers or discounts, separated, redeemed for cash, or transferred. Other terms and conditions apply; see the Yahoo! Small Business Terms of Service when you sign up.

[2] Calculation of the total savings is based on a 3 month discount plus a waived set-up fee on the Merchant Solutions Professional service.

[3] Offer is only valid for advertisers opening a new U.S. Sponsored Search account. A new advertiser is defined as one who has not advertised with Yahoo! for the past 13 months. Each account a nonrefundable $5 initial deposit. Advertisers signing up for the Fast Track® service will receive $50 off the service charge. For Self Serve sign-ups, a nonrefundable $50 will be deposited into the account and will be applied toward click charges. Limit one offer per customer, and one use per customer on a single account. Offer may not be combined with any other offers or discounts, separated, redeemed for cash, or transferred. There is a minimum bid requirement of $0.10 per click-through. Sellers of certain legally restricted products may require certification at extra cost. Search listings subject to editorial review. Other terms and conditions may apply. See the Advertiser Terms and Conditions when you sign up.

Yahoo! and the Yahoo! logo are registered trademarks of Yahoo! Inc
© 2006 Yahoo! Inc. All rights reserved.